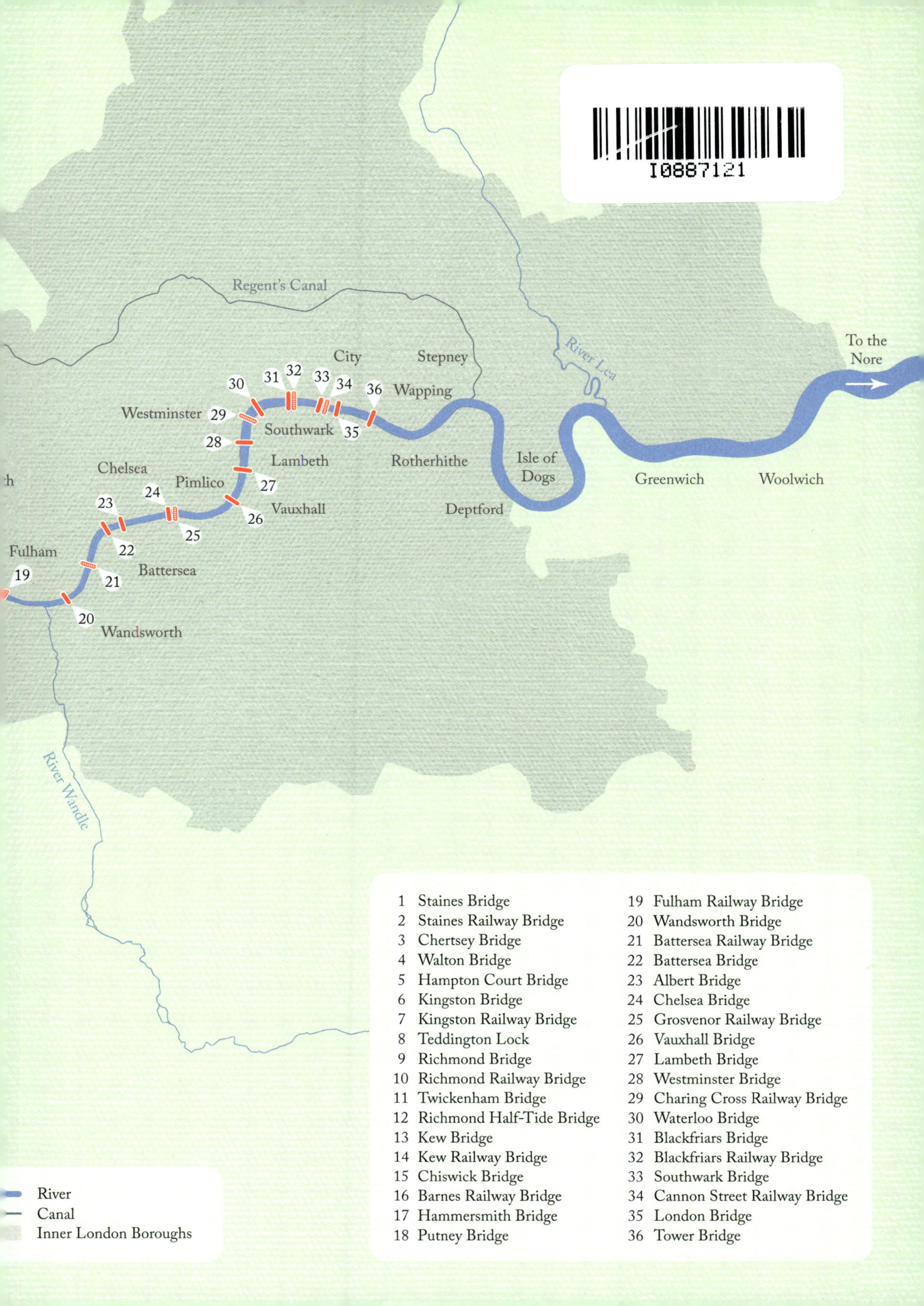
Regent's Canal
River Lea
To the Nore
City
Stepney
Wapping
Westminster
Southwark
Lambeth
Rotherhithe
Isle of Dogs
Greenwich
Woolwich
Chelsea
Pimlico
Vauxhall
Deptford
Fulham
Battersea
Wandsworth
River Wandle
19
20
21
22
23
24
25
26
27
28
29
30
31
32
33
34
35
36
1 Staines Bridge
2 Staines Railway Bridge
3 Chertsey Bridge
4 Walton Bridge
5 Hampton Court Bridge
6 Kingston Bridge
7 Kingston Railway Bridge
8 Teddington Lock
9 Richmond Bridge
10 Richmond Railway Bridge
11 Twickenham Bridge
12 Richmond Half-Tide Bridge
13 Kew Bridge
14 Kew Railway Bridge
15 Chiswick Bridge
16 Barnes Railway Bridge
17 Hammersmith Bridge
18 Putney Bridge
19 Fulham Railway Bridge
20 Wandsworth Bridge
21 Battersea Railway Bridge
22 Battersea Bridge
23 Albert Bridge
24 Chelsea Bridge
25 Grosvenor Railway Bridge
26 Vauxhall Bridge
27 Lambeth Bridge
28 Westminster Bridge
29 Charing Cross Railway Bridge
30 Waterloo Bridge
31 Blackfriars Bridge
32 Blackfriars Railway Bridge
33 Southwark Bridge
34 Cannon Street Railway Bridge
35 London Bridge
36 Tower Bridge
River
Canal
Inner London Boroughs

WATERLOO BRIDGE AND LONDON RIVER

Shot tower and staircase to Waterloo Bridge, a romantic view by Clarkson Stanfield etched by George Cooke, 1832 version

Andrew Saint

WATERLOO BRIDGE AND LONDON RIVER

Investigations and Reflections

LUND HUMPHRIES

First published in 2025 by Lund Humphries

Lund Humphries
Second Home Spitalfields
68–80 Hanbury Street
London
E1 5JL
UK

info@lundhumphries.com
www.lundhumphries.com

ISBN: 978–1–84822–734–7

A Cataloguing-in-Publication record for this book is available from the British Library.

Copy edited by Pamela Bertram
Designed by Jacqui Cornish
Proofread by Patrick Cole
Endpapers by Jennie Anderson
Set in Adobe Caslon Pro
Printed in Bosnia and Herzegovina

Lund Humphries' EU GPSR Authorised Representative is LOGOS EUROPE,
9 rue Nicolas Poussin, 17000, LA ROCHELLE, France.
Contact@logoseurope.eu

FSC www.fsc.org
MIX
Paper | Supporting responsible forestry
FSC® C118234

Contents

Abbreviations

BDCE	*Biographical Dictionary of Civil Engineers*
BM	British Museum
HEA	Historic England Archives
LCC	London County Council
LPA	London Picture Archive
LSWR	London and South Western Railway
MBW	Metropolitan Board of Works
ODNB	*Oxford Dictionary of National Biography*
PLA	Port of London Authority
RIBA	Royal Institute of British Architects
SER	South Eastern Railway

To my beloved daughters
Lily, Catherine and Leonora –
all beyond the Nore

Introduction and Acknowledgements

This will be my last book. That will, I hope, excuse some personal touches and opinions, most pronounced in the final chapter, which carries the main burden of the 'reflections' alluded to in the subtitle. Otherwise what follows is a fairly straightforward exercise in narrative history, spanning from prehistoric times to the Festival of Britain. Waterloo Bridge is its main focus, treated not as an independent structure but in as wide a context as possible, notably that of the tidal Thames – or 'London River', as I have sometimes called it, cribbing a handy term invented by geographers in the 1930s.

The river occupies the whole of the first two chapters. I have dared adding to the countless books about the Thames because I could not find anything which drew together the information I sought on the part that most concerned me – the grand Central London section between Westminster and London Bridge, to which King's Reach and Waterloo Bridge belong. After that come the bridges, Waterloo Bridge above all.

Why devote a substantial book to a single bridge? The original Waterloo Bridge, designed by John Rennie, was one of the noblest structures of British engineering. Its fame was international, and a dogged fight was fought to retain it in the 1920s and 1930s, even after its failings had proved to be all but insuperable. As a landmark of engineering alone, it is worth veneration and full record. But greatly though I admire and have profited from the expertise and precision of modern engineering historians, notably from Ted Ruddock's *Arch Bridges and their Builders* (1979) and Peter Cross-Rudkin's recent full study of Rennie (2022), I never wished to confine myself to structural matters. I have been equally interested in Waterloo Bridge as a means of communication, its impact on the district that grew up to its south, its notoriety as a 'bridge of sighs' and site for suicides, and its allure for artists. I have also tried to elucidate the economics of this and other London bridges, a subject little explored.

London Bridge, Westminster Bridge and Tower Bridge are the only metropolitan bridges that have hitherto earned full monographs. Waterloo Bridge hardly comes behind them in visibility and significance. It is no less fascinating because its history has been troubled; it has always elicited emotions. Accordingly, much of this book is about natural forces and irrational behaviour.

I should like firstly to thank Ida Jager for her unwavering support and enthusiasm, her excellent judgement and her wonderful eye for pictures. Mike Chrimes read the whole of the text and made invaluable comments. Parts were also read and commented on by Roger Bowdler, Simon Bradley, Steven Brindle and John Scott, and by MaryAnne Stevens, to whom I owe a particular debt of gratitude. Special thanks are due to Rebecca Preston, who helped me with pictures during a period of illness. Others who have helped and encouraged me are Richard Buxton, Peter Cross-Rudkin, James Edgar, Mireille Galinou, John Greenacombe, Peter Howell, Carol Morgan of the Institution of Civil Engineers' Archives, Jon Newman, Benny O'Looney, Jessie Petheram of West Cheshire Museums, Robert Thorne and Christine Wall.

For financial support in helping pay for production costs I am deeply grateful to the Alan Baxter Foundation and to my publishers, Lund Humphries. Val Rose at Lund Humphries has been a tower of strength, while copy editing by Pamela Bertram and layouts by Jacqui Cornish have been impeccable, and Sarah Thorowgood has given much assistance. The Paul Mellon Centre made a generous grant to cover the costs of new photography by Chris Redgrave and the end maps by Jennie Anderson; I have greatly enjoyed working with them both and thank them for their skills and dedication. The Marc Fitch Fund has bountifully covered the very substantial picture fees which I incurred. Without such bodies, books of this kind would be impossible. I am grateful to museums and archives for supplying images and hope they are correctly and sufficiently acknowledged in the picture credits.

1 Lord Noel-Buxton in the Thames, 25 March 1952

1

London River

On a chill March morning in 1952, a strange incident took place against the backdrop of the Houses of Parliament. Lord Noel-Buxton, 35 years of age and 6ft 3in tall, wearing just a shirt, pullover, flannel trousers and gymshoes, let himself down into the Thames from the Surrey side at low tide and attempted to *walk* across the river, watched from the banks by a small crowd. He had waded no further than the first pier of Westminster Bridge before the waters closed around him and he was forced to swim. He safely reached the other side and hauled himself out (fig.1), to be greeted by the Commons Speaker, W.S. ('Shakes') Morrison, and wrapped in a towel and blankets. Far from discomfited, Noel-Buxton felt he had proved his point: 'The ford is undoubtedly there', he told the press. 'The water was actually deeper than the chart depth, but I do not think that even when I was swimming I was far off the bottom.'[1] Teeth still chattering, he attended a Labour Party meeting later that morning.

Rufus Noel-Buxton was a man of hobbyhorses. His father, a progressive politician, had been bumped up to the peerage in order to boost Labour representation in the Lords. The son inherited in 1948. He dutifully attended Parliament, speaking now and then on African issues, of which he had some experience. But his wayward mind was always straying to the mysterious origins of Westminster.

Everyone knows that the City of London started out as a Roman foundation and boasted its first and, for sixteen centuries, its only bridge. But Westminster, seat of England's kings and supreme authority, secular and spiritual, not far upriver from the City – how did that begin? That is less certain, though many have speculated about it. A favourite theory is that the riverside nucleus of Westminster, or Thorney Island as it is sometimes called in homage to its marsh-girt ground, developed at the lowest point that the Thames could formerly be forded, on foot or horseback; and that this crossing represents the junction between the two long arms of the age-old route known as Watling Street. To the north-west and south-east of London alike, the line of Watling Street is defined and familiar. The connecting stretch is lost, but simple geometrical projection suggests that it hit the river at or near Westminster, bypassing the site of the City. How old is Watling Street? That too no one really knows. It may have been pre-Roman. Or perhaps it was the original route created by the Roman invaders, who made brief use of the Westminster crossing before a better site was soon identified on gravel further east which could be developed as a port and bridge.

Noel-Buxton plumped for the Roman theory and tried to test it in person. In *Westminster Wader*, the half-crazy little book he composed about his venture (and anything else it occurred to him to say), he proffered this explanation:

> Those old black embankments did him in. The river is narrowed and deepened. In its fury it wouldn't let him across, at what used to be an easy point in the natural conditions.
>
> Also on this March day (if it pleases you) the Thames got in league with a strong east wind; and that east wind checked the ebb in the Estuary, checked it all up the river.
>
> So the river never ebbed out according to tide table.[2]

The Thames, his lordship found, was fickle.

* * *

Indeed, the one thing constant about the Thames is change. Far back in geological time, the environs of London were part of a shallow sea that rested on layers of impermeable clay – the so-called London clay. When the river first emerged from the great alternations in sea levels known to geographers as eustatic changes, the lower Thames may not

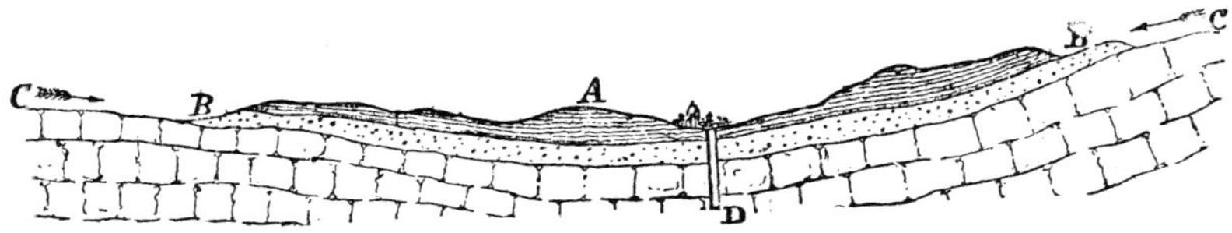

2 Cross-section of the London Basin, from T.H. Huxley, *Physiography*, 1877

have followed its current course. One theory is that it flowed through Hertfordshire and into East Anglia, before advancing ice about half a million years ago forced it into its present course.[3] Another is that the London section of the river ran about two miles further south, before shifting northwards by stages to assume its present position.[4] Quite possibly there was a prehistoric lagoon where London stands.

The Thames basin as it exists today and has done for centuries is at any rate securely understood. It is a shallow saucer or downfold in the chalk structure of the Chilterns and North Downs, lined with alluvial clay brought down by the river and interspersed with strips of sand and gravel, all superimposed upon the deeper London clay and then chalk. Perhaps the most lucid description of it is given in T.H. Huxley's old geological textbook for children, *Physiography,* published as long ago as 1877 (fig.2).[5]

Other factors affect the nature and behaviour of London's river – London River, as it is dubbed in this book, borrowing a handy term used by inter-war geographers.[6] First, its width. Estimates for the width even of today's river vary. Precision is possible only where both shores are embanked – and even there tides and winds cause changes. The standard measure is taken at high water spring tide (HWST). Wikipedia gives 250ft at Teddington, where the writ of the Port of London Authority (PLA) begins, broadening out to 5.5 miles at the Nore, about 68 miles downstream at the limits of the Thames estuary, where the PLA relinquishes its remit. The same article cites the width at London Bridge as about 750ft. But the broadening of the river as it flows downstream is far from consistent. The length of the original Waterloo Bridge, well upstream from London Bridge, was said to be 1,240ft between banks.[7] Another calculation for widths at HWST in 1836, before Victoria Embankment was constructed, offers figures of 1,030ft opposite the Houses of Parliament; 1,450ft at Hungerford

Market, the site of the later Charing Cross Railway Bridge; and 995ft just below Blackfriars Bridge.[8] Such measurements show that round the broad bend in the river known as Hungerford Reach or King's Reach, the Thames was wider than anywhere else in Central London. This 'great embayment',[9] though curtailed by the Victoria Embankment, will be relevant to the story of Waterloo Bridge at the heart of this book.

In the past the Thames was wider. As to how much, we are back in the realms of informed conjecture. The archaeologist Gustav Milne reckons that in Roman times it was about 300m or 1,000ft wide at London Bridge, or broader by about a quarter than it is today, spilling over at high tide onto the south bank by a further 3,000ft or more into muddy creeks and peaty flats.[10] The effect of the river's greater breadth and innumerable, unchecked divagations must have been to slow down its natural current. Or to put it the other way round, every succeeding encroachment onto the waterway or blocking off of its side channels speeded up its flow, with consequences for the riverbed as well as for navigation.

The reductions in width of London River have been almost altogether man's doing. As Samuel Smiles put it, writing just before the Victoria Embankment was made, 'the Thames is an artificial river almost from Richmond to the sea'.[11] A recent and full Wikipedia article, 'Embanking the Tidal Thames', shows how 'a broad, shallow waterway winding through malarious marshlands' was slowly 'transformed into a deep narrow tidal canal flowing between solid artificial walls'.[12] Excavations along the City waterfront suggest that almost half the advances or reclamations of land there took place between AD 100 and 250, as the Romans pushed outwards and switched from beaching boats along the muddy foreshore at low tide to making the rudiments of a dock and wharf system.[13] Sticking to the north side and Central London, the major encroachments upstream came with the Victorian embankments, first from Blackfriars to Westminster, then extending westwards as far as Chelsea. Further down the estuary, the picture is less coherent, but there is evidence aplenty for mediaeval and later land reclamation by means of earth embankments and walls. Along the south side of the river, where the terrain was marshier, these embankments were patchier and had limited effect in reducing flooding; here, little by way of masonry defences was constructed till late in the nineteenth century. Solid embankments were, of course, the foe of the in-and-out sequence of wharves and riverside industries on which London's prosperity for long centuries relied.

The width of any major urban river has a decisive effect on the shape and character of the city which it serves. Paris can have two banks of near-equivalent status because the maximum width of the Seine is about 650ft, much less where it is split by the Île de la Cité. The Tiber at Rome is narrower, at an average of 300ft, and also has islands. In both those cities the two sides grew in parallel; there is a visual relationship between them, and their bridges are closer together, shorter and friendlier. The Danube at Budapest is much wider, averaging about 1,300ft. There the two sides developed as separate cities, linked only by ferry until the famous Széchényi chain bridge opened in 1849. Likewise, it was the taming of the East River, some 2,000ft in width, by the heroic Brooklyn Bridge in 1883 which precipitated the unification of Manhattan with Brooklyn as sister boroughs of New York.

In London, where the width of the Thames sits between the extremes of the Tiber and the East River, the varying nature of the ground on either flank may have done more than the distance between them in destining the two banks to separate development. The north bank, at least in the vicinity of the City, had gentle gravel eminences on which to build, whereas the marshy south bank had none, apart from the spur of firm ground which led to and carried the Southwark end of London Bridge. One must go down river as far as Greenwich and Woolwich before hitting anything like a hill within sight of the water. The soft and tolerably level terrain on both sides had its advantages. Contrast London with Newcastle and Gateshead, where the Tyne, some 500ft in width, drives through between two great rocky slopes, leaving only a narrow strip of level ground in between where the original core of mercantile quays could develop.

Last, but very far from least, the tides. It is a commonplace that London owes its existence to the river. It would be more precise to say that it could never have come into being without the Thames tides. By a miracle, fifty miles west of the open sea, the powerful regular inflow and outflow of water wafted craft of all sizes far up river and back down again twice a day, with little assistance from the wind. Before the era of steam, the whole science of navigation depended on intimate knowledge of the timing and idiosyncrasies of the tides. They have always been perilous as well as beneficial, because of the swiftness of their flow and the big differences in height between high tide and low tide – an average of about 17ft at London Bridge, rising to about 22ft at some spring tides.

Because of the heavy Atlantic seas that chafe at British coasts, the tidal range can be enormous. In the Severn estuary it is even greater than on the Thames. Bristol has a tidal range of almost 40ft, perhaps the greatest for any port city of ancient significance in the western world. London's tides come next in range. Among cities already mentioned, Paris is situated too far inland for the Seine to be tidal. The Mediterranean tides which affect Rome and ports like Marseilles lack the power of those in the North Sea. Yet much has also to do with the shape of the approaches. At Newcastle, closer to the sea than London, the variation in water levels between high and low tides averages about 10ft, while on New York's East River the changes are only about 4–5ft. At Rotterdam, today Europe's leading port city, again not far from the ocean, typical figures are 5–6ft. River tides, then, depend not on direct proximity to the sea, but on the configuration of the estuary, as do the famous 'bores' which seasonally push up the Severn in England and the Garonne in France.

Up river, Teddington is the point where Thames tides cease to make a perceptible impact today (a fake etymology of 'Tide-end-town' has even been constructed for it).[14] Above that starts the peaceable river of locks, weirs, pleasure boats and Jerome K. Jerome. Below Teddington, the open, once-commercial waterway takes over. But there is a question whether tides have always encroached so far west. Lord Noel-Buxton believed, not alone, that Westminster was anciently the lowest ford on the Thames and the site of the first Roman crossing, not just because the water was shallower there, but because it then marked the farthest reach of the tides.

If so, that could have been because sea levels were lower in the Roman period, so that tides did not penetrate so far inland. There is

3 The Thames at Nine Elms, low tide, *c.*2020, looking towards Battersea Power Station, then in the course of redevelopment. The little posts in the foreground are thought by archaeologists to be remnants of a Bronze Age jetty

some evidence for a shallower, more accessible London River above Westminster in prehistoric times, in the shape of the timber remnants of jetties or causeways up river at Vauxhall, observed at very low tides in 1993 (fig.3).[15] Yet, archaeologists, after fruitlessly digging for evidence of a river crossing at Westminster, seem to agree that the Thames was tidal up to there in early Roman times and maybe further upstream. They add that the tidal range may have shifted downstream later on – but not for a very long period.[16]

4 Flaxman Spurrell, family and friends investigating a denehole in Stankey Wood, Bexley, supposedly in 1866. From left to right: Dr Flaxman Spurrell senior; Flaxman Spurrell, geologist and archaeologist; Flaxman junior's brothers, Alfred and Herbert, in the bushes; Captain Matthew James Popplewell in the hole; and Sir John Morillyon Wilson

There are broader theories, based originally on observations made back in the 1880s by Flaxman Spurrell, shy scholar-friend of the Egyptologist Sir Flinders Petrie (fig.4).[17] Spurrell sifted evidence of two main kinds: that the remnants of vegetation in the middle reaches of the estuary pointed to the Thames having once been a narrower and shallower fresh-water river; and that Roman and other artefacts discovered both at the estuary's edges and at Westminster were at a much lower level than might have been expected. As regards the estuary, he argued for a sudden post-Roman irruption of the sea, 'probably in the nature of a catastrophe'.[18] He also suggested that the whole Thames basin had been subsiding for centuries. Many experts since have been inclined to agree with Spurrell's second point. To put it dramatically, the theory is that the whole of south-east England has been slowly tilting downwards into the sea, thus allowing tidewater to penetrate further.[19] A severe flood of January 1928, when many Central London riverside properties were inundated, encouraged the theory, and ushered in a debate which eventually led to the building of the Thames Barrier in 1974–82.[20]

Tidal action up river today is certainly stronger than three centuries ago. Several forces have combined to cause this. One is the narrowing and canalisation of the river; another is the removal of quantities of water by the water companies, reducing the downriver flow; another is dredging. The removal of Old London Bridge in 1832 also allowed freer inward sweep to the river.[21] The extra strength and velocity of the upriver tides are expressed in increased scour along the bed of the Thames. Noel-Buxton was surprised on his walk to find much less mud in the water than he anticipated; he subtitled his book as 'by one who longs for MUDDY WATER'. The shoals that can be seen along London's riverbanks at low tide look very gravelly nowadays. Those who frequent them can hardly be called mudlarks, as once they were. There is plenty of mud in the lower Thames still, but more of it seems to lie out in and around the estuary. Meanwhile, the unrelenting tidal scour of the riverbed has undermined London's historic bridges and been a major factor in condemning them to destruction – about which, more in subsequent chapters.

5 Commuters crossing London Bridge en route to the City, 1965

6 The Pool of London and Tower Bridge seen from London Bridge, 1929

2

Above Bridge

I first lived in London as a teenager, in the early 1960s. My father was the chaplain at Guy's Hospital, just over the Thames from London Bridge; we lived close by. Sometimes I took the dog for a walk across the bridge. In 1964 I wangled a temporary job in the City and joined the host of commuters who poured over the river each morning and back to London Bridge Station each evening – the men in suits and a few still wearing bowler hats (fig.5). We were 'so many', in the celebrated line from *The Waste Land*. A typically morbid adolescent, I already knew the line that comes next: 'I had not thought death had undone so many'.

It must have been the Rennie bridge, not then yet rebuilt, which I crossed, but I did not notice it. What did attract my attention was the frequent presence of a sizeable cargo ship moored on the City side in proximity to the bridge, under the lee of stylish Adelaide House. There were two of them, Spanish ships of the Naviera Aznar line, and they alternated; one was the SS *Monte Urquiola*, I recall. My memory is that they brought bananas from the Canary Islands, scooped out from their holds by old-style cranes and hauled down to dock level.

Those were the last good years of the Port of London, at least of that fraction of it which had a visible connection with the city. Soon enough the quays that lined the upper portion of the Pool of London – the former 'Legal Quays' – fell idle, and the hungry dockers who bought great slabs of meat from the butchers of Tooley Street disappeared. The enclosed docks, too, started to close, one by one, until London lost part of its reality – tired and shabby though that reality had become.

The *Monte Urquiola* and its sister ship could pass the uplifted bascules of Tower Bridge, but there was no way they could have pushed up river beyond London Bridge. The bridge had been a barrier

7 The Pool of London looking upstream towards London Bridge. Print by Thomas Bowles III, 1751 version. Note the tidal wash below the bridge

to most ocean-going vessels for centuries, both in its venerable old form, bedecked with houses, and as rebuilt by the Rennies in the 1830s. Big ships had been confined to the zone 'below bridge', first to the Legal Quays between London Bridge and the Tower of London, then also to the so-called Sufferance Wharves down river beyond the Tower (figs 6 and 7). After the nineteenth-century Port of London exploded in scale, they backed up in motley array along the 'Lower Pool' down to Limehouse, past the intricate network of enclosed docks, and so eventually to distant Tilbury beyond London's official limits.

There have been countless descriptions and illustrations, commercial and romantic, of that elongated stretch of the river once occupied by the Port of London. Many date from the beginnings of its decline. One such is Hilaire Belloc's *The River of London* (1912). It is not one of Belloc's top performances, but it has the merit of looking forward and outward, comparing the Thames with other great European trading rivers.[1] Another is Basil Cracknell's *Portrait of London River* (1968). Considering its date, this book contains few forebodings of collapse. But the author does permit himself to speculate that once the Thames Barrier – then just a glint in the political eye – has been constructed, the port trade will be confined to the lower river and estuary; higher up, hovercraft will ply and it will be 'the rule, not the exception, to fish, swim, sail and water-ski'.[2]

Many such accounts, like Belloc's and Cracknell's, cover the full gamut of the river from Teddington to the sea, or most of it. In *London to the Nore Painted and Described* (1905), for instance, William and Marian Wyllie embark on a rollicking family boat trip down river from Westminster Pier, sketching in words and drawings as they go (fig.8). A different kind of record is that of Dick Fagan, a working lighterman, who describes decades of laborious struggle conveying recalcitrant boats and cargoes from Woolwich to Battersea and beyond.[3] But since the inner docks closed, there has been a tendency to configure the port as starting at the Pool, and to turn London Bridge into an absolute barrier, rather than the relative one which it certainly always was.[4] The *Monte Urquiola* and its sister ship, it has been said, could get no further.

* * *

8 *London to the Nore*, by William and Marian Wyllie, 1905

This chapter is concerned with the comparatively neglected subject of London's port and industries 'above bridge'. Originally, London Bridge had been no sort of obstacle to trade. Today's archaeologists tell us that during Roman times there were as many as three consecutive versions of the bridge, made mostly of timber. After a long gap when there may have been no bridge ('London Bridge is falling/broken down' has many interpretations), the Saxons rebuilt it. That effort in turn was replaced by the renowned stone bridge of *c.*1176–1209, attributed to Peter of Colechurch, which lasted in various guises until 1832.[5] None of the early London Bridges can have been especially hard to negotiate in the small craft of those times, while even on the Colechurch bridge, before houses invested its whole superstructure, there were always drawbridges for taller boats. Navigational difficulties accrued later.

'Lundenwic', as the archaeologists have dubbed the short-lived nucleus of Saxon London, before King Alfred restored the ruinous City to its old primacy from about AD 890, was sited further up river, near the present north end of Waterloo Bridge. It probably grew up during the years when there was no functioning London Bridge. But there were other significant early upriver quays as well. Queenhithe, for instance, just under the site of St Paul's Cathedral and so well 'above bridge', was an important Saxon landing place and may have been a Roman one too. Even after Colechurch's bridge had been constructed, Queenhithe went on pulling its weight. It is shown as the deepest of the City's many dock inlets and quays above bridge on the pre-Great Fire London panoramas by Visscher and Hollar. When the Legal Quays were defined in 1559, they stretched from Queenhithe to the Tower of London. Only after the Great Fire of 1666 were they redefined so as to embrace only the frontage between London Bridge and the Tower.[6] Even so, Queenhithe still counted in the post-Great Fire City (fig.9), while the mouth of the reconstructed Fleet River (where Farringdon Street now runs) took over as the leading upriver site for docking and trade (fig.10).

Meanwhile London Bridge was becoming more obstructive, filtering out the largest boats and negotiable for lighter ones at their peril. Its close-set piers had always limited river traffic. But over time the bridge was widened, the finger-like starlings guarding the piers upstream and

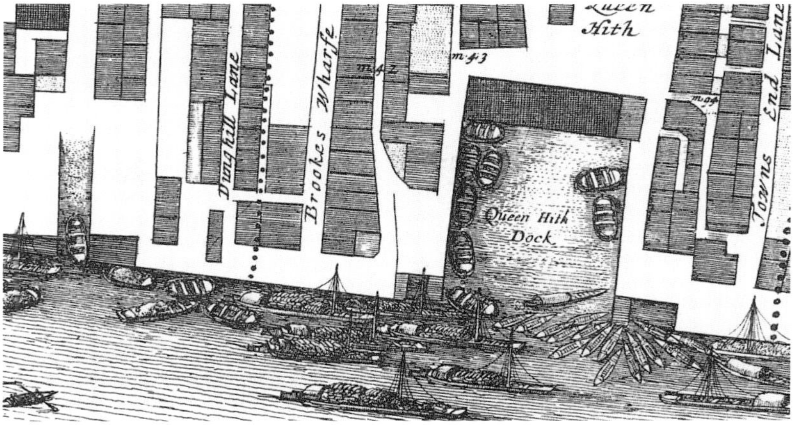

9 Queenhithe Dock, from J. Ogilby and W. Morgan's map of the City of London, 1677

downstream grew longer and thicker, while waterwheels and their cumbrous apparatus blocked some of the side arches. All this created a weir-effect, frequent with multi-piered bridges but exacerbated on ebb tides, when water had to force its flow between all the obstructions (figs 7 and 11). To pass the bridge down river when tide and wind coincided could be highly dangerous, with boats dropping sharply and turbulently through the arches by as much as 5ft. Overturnings and deaths were common; a famous example was the poet Anne Killigrew's aunt, commemorated in verse by her niece after she 'Drown'd under London-Bridge, in the Queen's Bardge, Anno 1641'. The bridge is said to have cost the lives of about fifty bargees and watermen every year in the mid-eighteenth century.[7] Prudent passengers often landed above bridge and re-embarked on the downstream side, while merchant vessels waited hours for the weir-effect to subside.

The problem was not solved after London Bridge was cleared of houses and the two central arches were made into one in 1759. The velocity of the current only increased, while the stronger scour on the riverbed below undermined the central piers. These were the conditions which led, after many delays, to the rebuilding of the bridge in 1832.[8]

By the time the Rennies' London Bridge came into service, a chain of enclosed downriver docks had been constructed, for reasons of

10 *Entrance to the Fleet River*, London, *c.*1750. In a painting formerly attributed to Samuel Scott, various types of river craft are depicted, including spritsail barges

11 E.W. Cooke, etching of Old London Bridge, 'as it stood since the repair of 1760, until its dissolution in 1831–2'. The wash below the bridge is again clearly shown

security and space as much as navigation. There was now little call for ocean-going merchant ships, ever increasing in bulk, to penetrate above the Pool. The new bridge did allow sizeable vessels, including some of the early steamships, to get above bridge. But as long as there was industrial activity on the margins of this upper section of London River, it continued to be dominated by the smaller, more manoeuvrable craft able to ply there and moor at minor quays and inlets, rest midstream or just lie idle by the riverside. A large part of their tasks was lighterage – ferrying cargo to and fro between ships either in the enclosed docks or just lying out in the river and the hundreds of points of manufacture and distribution which made up the port above bridge.

* * *

How and when did this upriver port develop? As London thrust westwards, its growth and commerce were overwhelmingly serviced by river. Before the Civil War, much of the waterfront between the City and Westminster was hogged by the enclaves of the aristocratic elite, with their rival mansions packed side by side, and their walled gardens dropping down to private water gates and jetties for embarkation. The sequence began with the so-called Strand Palaces of bishops and nobles, and culminated up river in the royal palaces of Whitehall and Westminster. But by the eighteenth century these mansions had retracted. Many were supplanted by terraced housing, while wharves and manufactories battened on the river frontage. As Pierre-Jean Grosley remarked in 1770, 'the spacious canal formed by the Thames might present us with as noble and striking an object as the great Canal of Venice, lined with palaces of the most sumptuous magnificence and the most pleasing variety . . . but the banks of the Thames are occupied by tanners, dyers, and other manufacturers, who there have an opportunity of supplying themselves with water.'[9]

Even so, the northern foreshore offered limited frontage. Opposite, on the lowlier south bank, conditions were different. The terrain, though mostly poor and marshy, was good enough to support the makeshift structures customary for early wharfage, storage, boat-building and even manufacturing.

It is seldom appreciated today how far up river the south-bank waterfront had already been built up by the late seventeenth century. Morgan's map of 1682 shows piecemeal development all the way from the original core of Southwark till roughly the site of Waterloo Bridge. Beyond that came copious woodyards. Lambeth 'village', next to the one great south-bank mansion of Lambeth Palace, was already a boat-building centre, and later became so industrialised as to lose all visible identity (fig.12).[10] Further upstream, industrial development was patchier. But there was a riverside sugar house at Battersea in the 1670s, which refined 'very grate quantities yearly' of molasses from Barbados.[11] Beyond that, Wandsworth, astride a navigable Thames tributary, the Wandle, boasted mediaeval mills which from the seventeenth century had been adapted for working iron, copper or leather, making gunpowder or pressing oil; textile workshops also featured.[12] Between these outcrops of waterfront activity came market gardens prone to flood and even the occasional villa.

Over time the isolated industrial sites along the south bank linked up into a tawdry necklace. Most of the beads to this necklace were functional, unedifying and polluting places producing items like cement, bleaching agents, vitriol and other chemicals, all feeding London's growth. But a few were exceptional and inventive, like the Albion flour

12 The Lambeth waterfront, *c*.1865. One of a series of photographs taken by William Strudwick before the Albert Embankment was built. Doulton's potteries are at the left-hand end, followed by various potteries, then Lambeth Rice Mills and James Stiff's drainpipe manufactory

13 *Queen of the Vale*, one of the smaller boats built by John Thornycroft at Church Wharf, Chiswick, 1885. The figures in the boat are probably Thornycroft and his father Thomas Thornycroft, the sculptor. The yard also built torpedo boats and other naval craft

mills beside Blackfriars Bridge, scene of John Rennie's first London performances; Eleanor Coade's artificial stone manufactory and Henry Maudslay's marine engine workshops, both on the future site of County Hall; or Marc Brunel's sawmills and boot factory by Battersea Bridge. The south bank was also popular among major building contractors, whose messy wharves and sheds sprawled along the frontages.

Boat-building was a natural constituent in this upriver industry. As on every major river, boats have always been built and repaired along the full length of the Thames. What has captured the imagination is the construction of great ships down river where there was space to build and depth to float them, like the gargantuan Great Eastern at Millwall or the warships built by the Thames Ironworks Company at Bow. That is to forget the yards of pioneers like Searles next to Westminster Bridge, the younger Rennies besides Blackfriars Bridge, or the Maudslays, whose engines made London's early steamboats practicable.

One outlier far up river dates from a time when boat-building on the Thames is often dismissed as moribund. That was Thornycroft's torpedo-boat works at Chiswick. Thomas Thornycroft the sculptor had his studio at Chiswick and bought land nearby where his ingenious son John could build his first designs (fig.13). Thornycroft junior sold his slim torpedo boats around the world before moving up a scale into destroyers in the 1890s. Their draft was shallow enough for them to be devised and constructed at Chiswick, but they had to have their superstructures removed to ease them under Hammersmith Bridge, to be refitted much further down river. H.G. Wells added a coda to his zestful novel *Tono-Bungay* in homage to the progress of one of Thornycroft's boats, steered by the book's hero: 'X2 went ripping through the dirty oily water as scissors rip through canvas, and the front of my mind was all intent with getting her through under the bridges and in and out among the steam-boats and barges and rowing-boats and piers.' But the Chiswick yard was a flash in the pan, closing in 1904.[13]

The Thames embankments, started in the 1860s and in due course extended along both sides of the river, brought great improvements to the environment of Central London, in sewage disposal, traffic management and appearance alike.[14] They paid homage to the ideal of how a major European city and its river should relate – cleanly and neatly, with the border between land and water defined and fringed by a parade of boulevards and buildings. Though often called for, that was far harder to achieve for a port city like London than for an upriver capital like Paris. Previous embanking schemes for the Thames had envisaged some compromise with the needs of wharfingers and dock-owners for inlets and level access to the water. But the aim of the Metropolitan Board of Works' improvement projects, led by Joseph Bazalgette, was to expel downstream all riparian noxious activities that might have contributed to the 'Great Stink of 1858', sounding the death-knell of industrial activity above bridge.

Things did not work out so simply. On the north bank, the wharfingers lost their hard-fought battle to maintain a presence along the great curve between Westminster and Blackfriars, where the Victoria Embankment runs. But downstream of Blackfriars Bridge the embankment could not pass, in face of commercial interests and the powerful City Corporation. Warehouses persisted on the river front below St Paul's Cathedral, to the shame and embarrassment of aesthetes. They have now been replaced by offices of even lower architectural calibre. The dream of a continuously beautiful waterfront for London has never had more than sporadic support.

Over on the unsung south side, there was more embanking than is often remembered. The Crown took a big surviving chunk of flood-prone fields and market gardens out of circulation when, in the 1840s and 1850s, it painstakingly created Battersea Park, to which pleasure boats were a major means of access in the early years. The Board of Works went on to embank the Thames between Westminster and Vauxhall Bridges. On the Albert Embankment section of this improvement (Lambeth Bridge to Vauxhall Bridge) some concessions were made to the needs of local industry and commerce which relied on a connection with the river. Another chunk of working waterfront was removed in the early twentieth century when County Hall was built next to Westminster Bridge behind a further run of embankment, later extended downstream.

Despite these planned pushbacks against upriver manufactures, the final climax of south-bank industrialisation came as late as the mid-twentieth century. That took the form of the giant Battersea and

14 Industrial pollution and fog in the Thames persisted as late as 1952, when this aerial view was taken looking upstream from Battersea Bridge

Bankside Power Stations, whose detoxified and repurposed hulks today memorialise a long and painful record of subordination to the city across the water. Bankside, slap across from St Paul's, was commissioned by Emmanuel Shinwell, Minister of Fuel and Power, as late as 1947, when Britain was shivering in post-war cold. It replaced a many-chimneyed, highly polluting predecessor on the same site. On walks with the dog, I recall seeing the second half of the great edifice going up in the early 1960s, before it was condemned as environmentally anomalous. Both power stations were supplied by water. Bankside was oil-fired and serviced by flat-bottomed tankers ('flatties'), whereas Battersea, also completed after the Second World War, was coal-fired and required constant servicing by Tyneside colliers to feed its colossal bunkers. Less filthy and corrosive though these giant installations may have been than older power stations, they could not but add to the forgotten levels of pollution that London suffered well up river, especially during winter fogs (fig.14), until the Clean Air Act of 1956 conferred relief.

* * *

15 Monument at Staines marking the western limit of the City of London's jurisdiction over the Thames. Staines Bridge in the background. Engraving by W.B. Cooke after a painting by George Arnald, 1821. A later obelisk was erected just downstream of Teddington Lock

It would be wrong to think of cargoes on London River as passing just between the city and the sea. Both above and below bridge, the port and its industries served and were serviced from either direction. Grain and other agricultural produce were being hauled down to London from as far away as Oxford in the thirteenth century. Defoe's *Tour of Great Britain* mentions long and thin vessels of shallow draught bringing up malt and meal to Queenhithe from Abingdon in the 1720s.[15] By the mid-century 'at least 100,000 tons left the London wharves for the upper Thames', writes Alec Skempton, 'and similar tonnages came back down the river'.[16] Efforts to expedite the route over the years faced the obstructions of millers and landowners. Pound locks began at last to replace the cruder flash locks only from the 1770s, allowing for wider barges and safer and faster transit.[17]

Then came the canals. Coupled with improvements to the rivers which fed them, they caused a revolution in inland navigation. Feeders for the Thames included the Thames and Severn Canal, which debouched at Lechlade in 1789; the Oxford Canal, linking with the Midlands waterways and opened in 1790; and the Kennet and Avon

Canal, engineered by Rennie and joining the river at Reading from 1810. (It was via the Kennet and Avon that Bath stone first came into frequent use in London.) To cope with the mounting traffic, a Thames (West of London Bridge) Navigation Act, also of 1810, authorised the City of London to build a series of locks on the semi-tidal stretch below Staines, where a pillar marked the upper limit of the City Corporation's jurisdiction over the river (fig.15). The lowest of these locks opened at Teddington in 1811. It defined the boundary between the freshwater upriver and tidal downriver sections of the Thames as recognised today.[18]

But the new waterway that made most impact on London's port activities fell into the Thames at Brentford, some way below Teddington. This was the Grand Junction (later Grand Union) Canal, which opened in 1800. Larger in conception and scale than its predecessors, the Grand Junction enjoyed better connections with its hinterland and the Midlands beyond. Coal, pig iron, stone, slate, bricks, timber, lime, grain and agricultural produce were all soon wending their way to locks and moorings at Brentford, thence into the lock-free lower Thames, and so to London's manifold quays and industries. Freight flowed in the other direction too, and not just by way of finished manufactures. There was competition, for instance, between sea coal coming in via the Thames estuary, and Midlands coal travelling in the reverse direction. The Grand Junction also attracted industry along its fringes, notably brickmaking in West Middlesex.[19]

Anticipating this trade, the Grand Junction company built its own sizeable docks and warehouses near Blackfriars Bridge in 1794–6. But it soon realised that it would do better to have its own direct connection with the Port of London below bridge, where the big ships and the new enclosed docks lay. Hence the celebrated Regent's Canal, planned as early as 1802, authorised after a survey by Rennie in 1812 and completed from Paddington over the north side of London to Limehouse in 1820. This allowed canal traffic to bypass the central section of the Thames with its crowded traffic and obstructive bridges. Like all canals, the Grand Junction soon lost its early glamour to the railways. But it upheld its role as a carrier of heavy freight well into the twentieth century.[20]

* * *

Canaletto's Thames paintings present an image of the river above bridge as a tranquil lake, disturbed only by ripples and peopled by neatly dressed gentlefolk and placid working boatpeople. Persons of quality are ferried across to the pleasure gardens of the South Bank, while sporting rowers and the occasional ceremonial barge occupy centre-stage (fig.18). There were certainly such scenes. In 1717, for instance, when to the serene strains of Handel's *Water Music* George I voyaged from Whitehall to Chelsea amidst an entourage of boats, we are told that 'the Barges drove with the Tide without Rowing'.[21] Music parties on the water were naturally best without oars.

Everyday reality was rougher and messier. Giordano Bruno's satiric novella *La Cena delle Ceneri*, based on the renegade priest and philosopher's English visit of 1583–5, graphically evokes the mud of the London riverside and the rudeness of the watermen as he bargains for a short river trip after dark.

Before London Bridge was rebuilt, upriver boat people consisted mainly of watermen, lightermen and sailors of spritsail barges. Watermen were only permitted to carry passengers in their skiffs (otherwise wherries), lightermen freight alone. They belonged to a single body, latterly the Amalgamated Society of Watermen and Lightermen. Watermen have a romantic image, as lightermen do not. They were the opinionated taxi-drivers of the upriver world. By the nineteenth century they were in decline, as the Thames bridges multiplied and foot passengers preferred paying a small toll to unpredictable service and soiling their feet. In the same period, steamboats replaced most of the old ferries. Henry Mayhew, who wrote eloquently about the river trades, described the plight of the watermen. One said: 'people may talk as they like about what's been the ruin of us – it's nothing but new London Bridge. When my old father heard that the old bridge was to come down, "Bill," says he, "it'll be up with the watermen in no time."' Relying on the 1841 Census, Mayhew estimated Thames watermen as 1,654 and lightermen as 1,500. Thereafter the collapse of watermen was precipitate.[22]

'A thing apart among ships', the lighter was a clumsy and ugly craft. The eponymous hero in Captain Marryat's charming *Jacob Faithful*, who was born in a lighter, called it 'a floating sort of a box'.[23] It was flat-bottomed so that it could cram in more cargo and lie easily on the mud at low tide. In old photographs, lighters and punts can be seen littered about the river edges, charged with timber, coals, hay or refuse. The descendants of these vessels have always been moored randomly all along and in the middle of the river, lowering the tone above and below bridge (fig.16).

The lighter was usually fronted with a squared-off, so-called swimhead bow to increase its stability in choppy waters. Having no sail, it was originally propelled by the tide alone, and steered from the back by a man with a massive oar, often the sole crew member. A lighterman could get from Woolwich as far as Nine Elms on a single tide, if he kept to the centre of the river and used his oar well. Manoeuvring the craft through the sequence of upriver bridges required great skill, especially when it was empty and therefore more subject to capricious eddies and changes of wind. The oarsman had to know his bridges. One lighterman reckoned Westminster Bridge (the Victorian version) as the most dangerous: 'it's a beast . . . Look at the piers . . . Cutwaters like knives. Would sink anything.'[24] Another feared Waterloo: 'the old bridge, with its numerous arches coupled with its position on a bend of the river was just about the biggest nightmare to navigation of the lot'.[25] Harry Gosling, born into a Lambeth lighterman's family, was forced by poor health to abandon active work on the river in favour of trade unionism, becoming secretary to the Amalgamated Society, then a London County Council member, and eventually the first Labour Minister of Transport. His memoirs recall manoeuvring massive unwieldy rafts of timber through the upriver bridges alone as a teenager, tide-dependent and secured precariously to his lighter. Gosling also describes a new LCC fire-chief, cocksure because of his experience as a naval commander, smashing a brand-new fireboat into Waterloo Bridge because he misconstrued river navigation.[26]

The spritsail barge (pronounced 'sprits'l') was the other main working boat in the upriver port, surviving well into the days of steam and even diesel. There were still 125 sailing barges on the Thames in 1949. More picturesque than the lighter by virtue of its four-edged sail rigged to a conspicuous diagonal spar called a sprit, its lifting outline appears in many paintings (fig.10). These boats, which seem to go back

to Restoration times, developed to a state of perfect fitness for purpose during the nineteenth century. The smaller versions, operating within the estuary and up river without topmasts and topsails, were worked by just two men and known in Thames jargon as 'stumpies'. They needed to drop their sails and masts to get under the bridges, so they depended on tides and oars as well as winds.

Lighters and stumpies shared the task of ferrying upriver cargoes to and from the seagoing boats moored in mid-Thames below bridge or in the enclosed docks, to which they had free access by law. That was what lighterage was mainly about. Lighters could carry cargoes of great weight; for instance, the engines and boilers constructed by Maudslays of Lambeth for Brunel's *Great Western*, which was built at Bristol but fitted out on the Thames, were conveyed down river by lighterage. But the lighter could not get far beyond Woolwich, whereas

16 Looking upstream from Waterloo Bridge, coloured lithograph by Thomas Shotter Boys, 1842. Moored lighters in the foreground, second shot tower and Lion Brewery to the left, Westminster Bridge and Abbey in the distance

the spritsail barge was as familiar on the Medway as on the Thames. In later coasting versions, equipped with complex and powerful rigs and a larger crew, it could reach the Nore to unload from colliers and other vessels, saving them time, and even venture as far as East Anglian destinations, hugging the coast.[27]

The advent of steam power for water-borne vessels in the years after Waterloo presaged the slow decline of the independent Thames barge and lighter. Small or large, steamships were the first boats that could withstand or actually oppose the tides. They took two main forms, tugs and passenger boats, both initially driven by paddle wheels. Steam tugs were a feature of London River from the 1830s. At first they could not go far down river or haul heavy boats, but soon they were venturing out to sea and seeking out inbound sailing ships in order to bring them efficiently into the estuary and port. In the docklands and up river, convoys of barges could now be hauled along midstream by tugs, as they continue occasionally to be. Until at least the Second World War, each barge had to be manned by a lighterman, who on occasions might still be required to deliver his craft and cargo on his own, propelled by tide and oar-muscle alone.[28]

Up stream, steamers for passengers – the precursors of today's tourist boats – were introduced on the Thames from around 1815. The earliest steamer known to have been built in London was the *Regent* of 112 tons, designed by Marc Brunel with engines by Henry Maudslay. On its maiden voyage in 1816 it reportedly ran from Blackfriars Bridge to Battersea Bridge in thirty minutes and then 'back through London Bridge [this was still the old bridge] in fifty-two minutes'.[29] According to Philip Banbury, 'by 1820 the Thames was building river steamers by the dozen'.[30] At first they were fickle and even dangerous – the hulls were built of perilous wood. But from the 1840s iron versions began to supersede them. Boilers could also blow up, as on the *Cricket* beside Adelphi Pier in 1847, killing about 30 people (fig.17).[31]

Steamboats were often sneered at. But when skilfully piloted, they were more manoeuvrable than sailing boats. They could cross the crowded river, dock neatly and cope with adverse current. They could also advertise regular, tide-flouting timetables. Carrying excursion

17 Rescuing victims from the explosion of the steamboat *Cricket* in front of the Adelphi, 1847

passengers, they were soon plying far up river under the guise of steam-launches, to the fury of smaller craft and anglers, and as far down the estuary as popular Margate. To cope with the bridges, they had hinged or retractable funnels. Well before the Victoria Embankment was built, there were several passenger piers for steamboats along the river front below the Strand. For West Enders, it was much more convenient to embark from a pier here or attached to one of the bridges, than to take a sailing boat down river and change at Gravesend, as earlier generations of travellers had done. There were some commuter steamboat lines, but then, as more recently on the Thames, they did not do well. A traffic survey of 1855 estimated that the steamboats were carrying 30,000 passengers per day.[32]

Commercial steam vessels became common up river rather later than passenger steamers, but they too eventually became well-established and superseded much of the work done by lighters. Steam colliers, for instance, serviced Battersea Power Station when it was first built, to be replaced by funnel-less diesel-boats only in the post-war years. Diesel-fuelled tugs represented the ultimate shape of functional craft plying on the upper reaches of London River.

3

Three Bridges

First there was London Bridge which, in its sturdy mediaeval form, lasted more than six centuries. Next within the tidal range of the Thames came Putney Bridge (opened 1729), then Westminster Bridge (1750), Kew Bridge (1759, replaced 1794), Blackfriars Bridge (1769), Battersea Bridge (1772) and Richmond Bridge, which alone survives (1777). A spate of bridges followed in the Regency years: Vauxhall (1816), Waterloo (1817) and Southwark (1819). Started in time of war and built simultaneously, these three bridges are the main subject of this chapter. All have gone.[1]

Most of the river crossings listed above, though not quite all, began as toll bridges. Like roads and also waterways, bridges have to be paid for and maintained; the infrastructure of travel can never be free. Tolls are as old as roads; and a bridge is a natural point at which to control travellers and exact payment, as the surviving arches, once gated, atop many ancient bridges attest. In Georgian England tolls became the normal way to defray the cost of major new bridges, as of major roads. This was the heyday of the turnpike system, whereby trustees took on the improvement of roads and travellers paid fees at tollgates. Such tollgates and booths commonly stood at the end of bridges. Much resented, they were often the focus of disagreements, cheating, robberies and violence; it was a hazardous job to be a toll-keeper.

Toll bridges in London survived the demise of the turnpike system, to be abolished by the Metropolitan Board of Works in the 1870s. There are still a few toll bridges here and there in England. But the usual assumption today is that bridges, like most roads, should be free at the point of use, and their upkeep paid for out of general taxation. Perhaps that is curious: nobody expects that ferries or locks on rivers and canals should not charge fees. But the advocates of road-charging are still a minority.

The toll system for major Thames bridges followed from the fact that they were mostly private initiatives. In loosely administered Britain, unlike France, national governments saw no reason why they should plan for infrastructure or pay for it directly. In theory, county justices were still responsible for bridges, but where a bridge spanned between two counties, as on the Thames, they were reluctant to run to the cost and complexity of co-operating on a river crossing. Instead it was left to trustees or private companies to take the risk, if they calculated there would be enough demand to recoup the expense of a multi-arched bridge out of toll income fairly soon. Often, as it turned out with the London toll bridges, their expectations were disappointed.

The body with the biggest stake in river crossings on the lower Thames was the City Corporation, which owned London Bridge and claimed ancient rights and fees in the bed and foreshore of the lower river all the way from Staines to the Nore until 1856, when the Thames Conservancy was created. These rights were murky and sometimes successfully questioned, but they bore down on every proposed new river crossing.[2]

The City was inveterately hostile to bridge projects promoted by others, since it feared that alternative crossings would divert travellers from London Bridge and detract from its trade. In 1670–71 a City MP opposed an early suggestion for a bridge between Fulham and Putney 'in an almost hysterical flood of verbiage'.[3] When Westminster Bridge, the first new truly metropolitan bridge, came forward, the City and its allies the watermen (who stood to lose income) hampered it and dragged their feet as long as they could. The same pattern of jealousy and obstruction manifested itself with the Regency trio of bridges, though by then the City was not quite so powerful.

The City was not wrong to view Westminster Bridge as a threat, because alone among the enterprises listed above, it turned out not to be a toll bridge. The City Corporation had never been averse to charging tolls on London Bridge itself.[4] Along with the rents from the houses on top and from property owned by the City in Southwark, these had

provided the basis of the revenue for the City's Bridge House Trust. But when Westminster Bridge opened in 1750 it was free to use for vehicles, equestrians and foot passengers alike – 'unhampered by tolls or pontage'.[5]

This was despite the fact that its construction had been extremely costly. In its early stages there had been schemes to build the bridge economically from timber, like Putney Bridge and its toll-financed upriver successors at Kew and Battersea, or at least with a timber superstructure on stone piers. But when the Swiss-born engineer Charles Labelye finally took over at Westminster from his rivals, it was resolved that the whole bridge, piers, fifteen arches and all, would be constructed of Portland stone. As the biggest modern bridge yet built over a tidal river, it attracted international notice (fig.18). Some sense of its size and cost is conveyed by Labelye's claim that there was twice the amount of stone in his bridge as in St Paul's Cathedral.[6]

How was this feat achieved? Though Westminster Bridge had been started without a clear plan of how it was to be paid for, it was supported

18 Canaletto's most famous view of Westminster Bridge, painted three years before the bridge opened and showing Lord Mayor's Day, 1746, with the artist's typical embellishments. The sculptural group of Thames and Isis in the centre is a fantasy. The artist gives priority to processional barges and watermen's boats

by an influential body of commissioners, including peers, MPs and prominent residents of Westminster. The steadiest and shrewdest of these was the 9th Earl of Pembroke, who played a part in designing the bridge. The first idea was to pay for it by lottery – a common device for Georgian ventures needing capital, but contentious, inefficient and increasingly frowned upon for moral reasons. After two lotteries, much more money was still needed. The commissioners now resorted to applying directly to Parliament for yearly subsidies to complete the bridge. These were voted with surprising ease, in financially good and bad years alike. A half-finished scheme will often attract funds which a new one would never obtain; and besides, Westminster Bridge was within sight of the Parliament House. One lesson from this hand-to-mouth saga was that lotteries were unreliable means for funding big capital projects. For later Thames bridges, as we shall see, they were superseded by the device of the joint-stock company.

Westminster Bridge was a game-changer. The challenge of free passage at Westminster came about just when rebuilding London Bridge was for the first time in serious contemplation. As yet, the City Corporation lacked the courage or would not stomach the cost of going the whole hog. In the half-reconstruction of 1758–62, the old houses were removed, the central arches widened into one larger opening, and the bridge was given a slight incline to the centre to allow taller shipping to pass (fig.11). All this was paid for in the first instance by raising the bridge tolls and even trying to impose charges on boats passing beneath. Retrospectively the City Corporation managed to get a subsidy from Parliament to pay for most of the work.[7] After all, if Westminster Bridge had been supported by Government, why not London Bridge too?

The City had a second string to its bow in response to the threat from Westminster Bridge, which was to build a rival bridge of its own. Blackfriars Bridge was partly meant to relieve London Bridge. But there was more to it than that. While the north end of this new bridge abutted on City territory, on its south side the projected Blackfriars Road led to City-owned land which the Corporation's subsidiary, the Bridge House Estates, planned to develop. The money to build the bridge came largely from the Coal and Wine Duties, chiefly a tax on

coal coming into London, which accrued to the City every year. We shall meet these controversial taxes again later. The Corporation prided itself that Blackfriars Bridge, designed by the young architect-engineer Robert Mylne, was built faster and more cheaply than Westminster Bridge. Even so, the second half of its construction was delayed for financial reasons, so that the bridge opened only in 1769, nine years after its commencement (fig.19).

19 Blackfriars Bridge, an anonymous drawing of *c.*1800, showing the awkwardness of the double columns applied by Robert Mylne over the piers of a sloping bridge

At that point, with typical caution, the City imposed tolls on its new bridge. They were supposed to be temporary, until the costs had been paid off, after which both London and Blackfriars Bridges were to be made free under an Act of 1767. The tolls infuriated the City community, which saw, or thought it saw, travellers and trade going instead to Westminster. The Blackfriars toll houses were destroyed in the Gordon Riots of 1780. Even so, they were rebuilt and the charges reinstated, increasing the sense of aggravation. Foreshadowing future complaints, a campaign was mounted to abolish them at least for foot passengers as 'not only a great grievance to the industrious mechanics and labouring poor, but a great disgrace to the first commercial city in Europe'. Another objection was that the tolls had wrecked development plans for the south side: 'a new Town is started up in the Vicinity of Vauxhall, to the Inrichment of Westminster, when St. George's-fields are all Swamp and Ruins'.[8] The Blackfriars Bridge tolls were abolished in 1785 – except on Sundays. London Bridge had been finally freed from tolls three years earlier.

So, from the mid-1780s, travellers could choose between three free bridges – 'three stupendous bridges', Smollett called them in *Humphry Clinker* – to cross the river: London, Blackfriars and Westminster. For more than a generation no further bridges were seriously proposed. But London continued to inflate, the south bank was accumulating industry, houses and population, and there were still long gaps, on the north side especially, between these three bridges across a wide and difficult river, inconveniencing everyone except the watermen.

The one major initiative affecting London River during these years turned out to have no immediate outcome in terms of bridges. In 1799–1800 a Parliamentary Select Committee on the Port of London reviewed schemes to reduce the downriver chaos of ships backing up insecurely beyond the Legal Quays by addressing the blockage at London Bridge and building enclosed docks. Now that it was toll-free, London Bridge had to take more traffic than ever. But it was still in a makeshift state despite the works of 1758–62; its replacement was long overdue. Two famous projects were presented for rebuilding it and opening the river above it up to Blackfriars for ocean-going vessels. Thomas Telford and James Douglass suggested a single revolutionary cast-iron arch which would cross the river at high level in a single span, while George Dance junior proposed double bridges whose central arches would open and close to shipping alternately, so that the road traffic was never interrupted (figs 20 and 21). Both schemes were non-starters because they entailed intolerably heavy incursions by the bridge approaches into the fabric of the City. Nor was the City Corporation yet ready to move on rebuilding London Bridge. So the first of the enclosed docks below bridge, the London Docks, went ahead from 1801 under the auspices of a private company, while the bridge had to await reconstruction for a further thirty years.

* * *

20 Thomas Telford and James Douglass, design of 1800 for a single arch in cast iron for London Bridge, so as to allow large boats to penetrate beyond the Pool

21 Aquatint of 1802 by William Daniell showing George Dance the younger's fantasy design for a double bridge at London Bridge, another means of allowing access to the Thames above the Pool without impeding traffic. This view looks downstream

The next crop of bridges originated largely from the supply side. That is to say, they began not with Londoners north or south of the Thames clamouring for new crossings but with 'projectors', to use the language of the day, who planned on harnessing the money slushing round the British economy during the Napoleonic Wars to advance what they hoped would be profitable construction schemes via the vehicle of joint-stock companies.

Joint-stock companies typically combined subscribers for shares, otherwise proprietors, who took most of the risk, and holders of loan stock who invested for a fixed return. They were far from new. But the South Sea Bubble debacle of the 1720s had turned public opinion against them. For the next seventy years or so, most major transport initiatives like turnpike roads were promoted by trusts combining public and private finance. Then, from the 1790s, joint-stock companies stormed back into favour. They helped sustain the canal-building mania of that decade, for instance. Not that they could be formed so easily. Every such company had to be approved by Parliament. There was much opposition to their proliferation, and to the powers of compulsory purchase and the monopolies which they often entailed. Yet, eagerly promoted by City-based investors, they overran such different domains as insurance and transport infrastructure.[9]

The climax of these promotions came in 1807–8, 'a period of almost universal excitement, leading as usual to hazardous adventure', wrote Thomas Tooke. During this frenzy, complained a writer to the *Morning Chronicle*, joint-stock companies arose daily 'with so little pretension to public countenance and were established with such facility that it was only necessary to insert an advertisement in the newspapers to procure a subscription of a million for any project whatsoever'.[10] A fresh craze for canal-building financed in this manner smote south-east England in 1807–11. It was a joint-stock company that promoted the London Docks, against official opposition from the City Corporation. Another enduring promotion from these years was the powerful Gas, Light and Coke Company, incorporated in 1812, whose accumulating wharves and works were to make a grisly impact up and down the river.

The three new proposed Thames bridges conformed to this pattern. They were authorised in the first place by Acts of Parliament passed in

1809 (Vauxhall and Waterloo Bridges) and 1811 (Southwark Bridge). These Acts were not the start of the story. Previous Bills for a Vauxhall Bridge had been floated before Parliament in 1806–8. The Waterloo Bridge project, whose background is traced in detail in the next chapter, went back to the 1760s; shares were being traded in the proposed company in 1807.[11]

Vauxhall Bridge was the most plausible of the three. Its outlying position promised to bypass Westminster and link the elongating West End and prospective Pimlico-Belgravia with the main routes south from the City and the nascent suburbs beyond. Among the Vauxhall Bridge Company's early proprietors, alongside industrialists with premises on the southern shore, were the brothers Henry and Samuel Thornton, MPs, bankers, abolitionists and possessors of eligible villas at Clapham. But the prime movers behind both the Vauxhall Bridge and Waterloo Bridge Acts of 1809 were the Dodd family: Ralph Dodd and his two sons, George and Barrodall Robert Dodd. Two further obscure Dodds are named among the 1809 proprietors of the Vauxhall company.[12]

Pity the Dodds. An architect can make and retain a reputation on the strength of a handsome project without hope of realisation. Such, for instance, were the various fanciful designs for a 'bridge of magnificence' next to Somerset House (pp 65–9). But civil engineers, as Ralph Dodd and his sons claimed to be, have little chance of being taken seriously unless they can show that they can carry a scheme through to construction and completion.

That was what the Dodds failed to do. Ralph Dodd in particular habitually promoted engineering schemes that turned out to be flights of fancy.[13] He was the brother of Robert Dodd, a minor marine artist who painted several views of the lower Thames. After an early career as a painter himself, Ralph was sucked into the mania of the 1790s for canal and harbour projects. None of his early promotions came off. A plethora of schemes around London followed. They included an ambitious Thames tunnel from Gravesend to Tilbury, started but then abandoned; a cast-iron bridge not unlike Telford's to replace London Bridge; and a ream of canal and waterworks projects. Dodd also acquired an interest in the South London Waterworks Company, which had been authorised in 1805 to draw water from the Thames near the site of Vauxhall Bridge.

In 1809 Ralph's son George Dodd produced the outline scheme which allowed the first Strand (later Waterloo) Bridge Act to pass through the legislature. But the Dodds were about to be rumbled. Some sort of scuffle involving George Dodd, which may or may not have been about Vauxhall Bridge, got into the papers during the summer of 1809.[14] That autumn, a scathing article on 'Modern Projectors' appeared in a magazine called *The Satirist*. It exposed 'RALPH DODD, Esquire, and the two *Squires*, his sons' as among a class of men 'who appear to be possessed of such an utter insensibility to shame, that the most perfect detection of their infamy, the most marked contempt and aversion of all honorable men, do not in the least affect or move them'. After reciting some of Ralph Dodd's earlier failures and deceptions, the writer homed in on the Vauxhall Bridge Company, which he claimed Dodd had defrauded to the tune of £5,490 on the strength of a few drawings for a masonry bridge.[15] Possibly *The Satirist* was too harsh. The Dodds survived to float further promotions, including some plausible schemes for steamboats, due mainly to George Dodd. But after the father's death, in an aside to the chequered progress of the Thames Tunnel, the *Mechanics' Magazine* had no compunction in pronouncing Ralph Dodd 'a man neither of common-place understanding, nor of experience, but a very ingenious schemer, without any practical talent whatever'.[16]

At Vauxhall Bridge, the upshot was that by January 1810 the Dodds had been supplanted by John Rennie.

* * *

If the Dodds were pygmies in British engineering history, Rennie (figs 22 and 23) was a giant. His industry was prodigious, his range of competences remarkable, his probity unquestioned. When he died in 1821, to be laid to honoured rest in St Paul's Cathedral, James Perry supplied this encomium:

> His loss cannot be adequately supplied by any living Artist, for, though we have many able engineers, we know of none who so eminently possessed solidity of judgement with profound knowledge,

22 John Rennie as a young engineer by Martin Archer Shee, *c.*1794. In the background is the Lune Aqueduct near Lancaster, part of Rennie's Lancaster Canal of 1793–7

23 John Rennie, a posthumous engraving by Edward Scriven after a portrait supposedly by S. Kirven

24 Rennie's Dundas Aqueduct of 1796–9 taking the Kennet and Avon Canal over the Avon near Monkton Combe, Somerset, photographed in 2021

> and the happy tact of applying to every situation, where he was called upon to exert his faculties, the precise form of remedy that was wanting to the existing evil. Whether it was to stem the torrent and violence of the most boisterous sea – to make new harbours, or to render those safe which were before dangerous or inaccessible – to redeem districts of fruitful land from encroachment by the ocean, or to deliver them from the pestilence of stagnant marsh – to level hills, or to tie them together by aqueducts of arches, or by embankment to raise the valley between them – to make bridges that for beauty surpass all others, and for strength seem destined to endure to the latest posterity, Mr. Rennie has no rival. Every part of the United Kingdom possesses monuments to his glory, and they are as stupendous as they are useful.[17]

There is little exaggeration here. But though Rennie has always been admired, he has never earned the affection and worship lavished on his contemporary Thomas Telford or on the two Brunels, subjects of pioneering biographies by Tom Rolt and many later panegyrics. Rennie's austere Scottish-Presbyterian personality may partly be responsible for this. With that went a streak of caution alongside his undoubted courage, a certain aversion to extreme engineering gestures. There is

25 Rennie's unexecuted design for Vauxhall Bridge, aquatint by William Daniell, 1810, looking downstream. Millbank and Westminster Abbey are to the left, Westminster Bridge in the centre, with St Paul's Cathedral in the far distance to the right

no Menai or Clifton Bridge in his oeuvre, no Paddington Station or Great Eastern. A Rennie structure is always ingenious and trustworthy, often elegant but never heroic. The Lune Aqueduct and the Plymouth Breakwater are noble and handsome works, but they do not seize the imagination or linger in the memory.

Rennie has also been unlucky in respect of his metropolitan works. By adoption he was a Londoner. He arrived from East Lothian in 1784 as a skilled mechanic to install revolutionary Boulton and Watt steam engines in the Albion Mills, on the south-east side of the new Blackfriars Bridge. He never left the district. Rennie created his home, workshop and offices near the mills just west of the bridge, while on part of the site of Albion Mills, which had burnt down in 1791, he built a factory in 1810 to handle his sizeable mechanical engineering portfolio in the way of millwork, minting machinery, cranes, diving bells and much else. After his death, under his sons this became the premises of J. & G. Rennie, successful ship and marine-engine builders.

But it was as a tireless consultant civil engineer that Rennie rose to fame. The schemes he undertook were seldom cheap and often overran, but they worked, and they usually paid their investors. The Kennet and Avon (1794–1813) was the longest of the many canals he laid out (fig.24); it was probably on that account that he was hired to advise the City Corporation on the Thames navigation above Teddington. In the metropolis proper, he became a key figure in the mammoth operation of building enclosed docks during the French wars. He was chief engineer to the London Docks, assisted Ralph Walker at the East India Docks, and built extensions and some remarkable sheds at the West India Docks. For the Admiralty, Rennie made wartime improvements to the Thames naval bases, including a superb steam-powered smithy at Woolwich and a new dockyard at Sheerness. This formidable range of projects was crowned by the new Waterloo and Southwark Bridges and the original design for rebuilding London Bridge, eventually carried out by his sons. Yet of all this, nothing survives except for a few fragments in the Docklands. No wonder that Rennie has slipped from popular esteem.

Vauxhall Bridge was the project that got away. That was because of expense. The design made by Rennie in 1810 was for a seven-arched

26 Vauxhall Bridge, as built in 1813–16 to designs by James Walker. Engraving by T.H. Shepherd for Elmes's *Metropolitan Improvements*, 1828

bridge faced in blue Dundee sandstone,[18] 'a straight bridge like those of antiquity', reported one paper,[19] the arches of varying width, the total length 920ft (fig.25). It was to follow a different line from the Dodd design, which had been planned askew to the river, whereas Rennie insisted that the bridge must be 'square to the flow'.[20] That meant buying extra land. The contractors were to be Adam and Robertson, in other words William Adam, last of the celebrated brothers Adam, together with Alexander and Daniel Robertson. Despite the rain, 2,000 were said to have attended the laying of the foundation stone by Lord Dundas in May 1811, when the name Regent's Bridge was toted.[21] Then the work stopped; the reconstructed Vauxhall Bridge Company could not come up with the money. In due course the equipment on site, including Boulton and Watt engines and Rennie-designed cranes, was sold.[22]

It took a new Act of Parliament, a smaller committee and a passing flirtation with a design by Samuel Bentham of the Navy Board before a fourth engineer, James Walker, got Vauxhall Bridge on track again in 1813.[23] Walker's competent design, using iron arches for economy, was rapidly built by the experienced contractors Jolliffe and Banks (William Adam and the Robertsons having failed by then). Despite its troubled history, when it opened in August 1816 Vauxhall Bridge was the first of the trio of Regency toll bridges over the Thames to be completed (fig.26). An article in the *Morning Chronicle* made some interesting points:

> This Bridge consists of nine arches of equal span, formed of cast iron and raised upon stone piers. The span of each arch is about 80 feet, and the width of each pier about 14 . . . The length of the Bridge is about 800 feet; its width, exclusive of ample foot-ways, affords sufficient room for four carriages to pass abreast . . . The roads are so judiciously constructed, that the ascent to the Bridge is scarcely perceptible, although originally elevated so much above the level of the ground on each side of the river, while the slope of the Bridge itself is so gentle as to form a very striking contrast indeed to the precipitate acclivity which so materially derogates from the Bridges of Westminster and Blackfriars, and which renders them so very inconvenient, if not dangerous, to waggons and carriages heavily laden . . . This Bridge presents some resemblance of Bonaparte's celebrated bridge of Austerlitz, but is far its superior in extent and elegance. For although Austerlitz bridge has been so much extolled throughout Europe by the vanity of the French nation, or the habitual gasconade of its founder, it is not so extensive by one-third as the bridge at Vauxhall. Yet Austerlitz bridge was built under the patronage of the Imperial Government by the famous Gauthey, and was seven years in constructing, while Vauxhall Bridge, which had no other patronage than that of private individuals, has been erected by an engineer to fame unknown, within the short space of three years.[24]

The vexed theme of bridge approaches and levels, and the itch of commentators looking over their shoulders to see how bridges in Paris were made and paid for, will recur when we come to Waterloo Bridge.

Financially, Vauxhall Bridge did quite well in its early years. There were tussles in the 1820s with watermen, who undercut the tolls by plying for hire at the bridge foot on either side until they were stopped by legislation.[25] The coming of the South Western Railway to a terminus at Nine Elms in 1838 boosted toll receipts, but when the line was extended to Waterloo, most of that revenue was lost. Like its fellow bridges, Vauxhall became a target for reprobation as a burden on the working classes until the tolls were abolished in 1879.

* * *

27 Rennie's Southwark Bridge, an anonymous aquatint dating from about the time of its opening in 1819

Southwark Bridge (fig.27) is the odd one out of our trio. It started out as the brainchild of one altruistic individual, with the sole intention of relieving London Bridge, which it seemed the foot-dragging City Corporation would never get round to rebuilding. There was even some fear at the time that it would collapse.

The individual in question was John Wyatt (1752–1818). A member of the famous Wyatt dynasty, he was no sort of promoter of the Dodd genre. He started out in London as the trusted agent and friend of the great Matthew Boulton. In 1794 he went freelance and established *The Repertory of Arts and Manufactures*, an Enlightenment-style compendium of useful knowledge encompassing new discoveries, designs and patents. Around 1809 Wyatt and his son Walter Henry Wyatt sold the *Repertory* to devote themselves to their bridge project.[26]

The proprietors they gathered in order to form a company and obtain an Act of Parliament had a slightly different flavour from those who subscribed to the other two bridges. City merchants were naturally to the fore, led by John Jackson, MP, a naval supplier and wartime crony of Admiral Elphinstone, later Lord Keith. Among other early proprietors was the eminent septuagenarian mathematician Charles Hutton.

Hutton, 'pit boy turned professor' and a somewhat prickly character, had long been interested in bridges. From time to time he was brought in to offer calculations on iron bridge designs. He had been among those called upon to comment upon the great 600ft iron arch proposed by Telford in 1800 as a replacement for London Bridge. Hutton and Rennie concurred in thinking that, though it was feasible, it was poorly suited to navigation, and in favouring a three-arch iron bridge instead – exactly what was to be built at Southwark. Hutton went on to write some notes on the history of iron bridges and to make some criticisms of the pier designs at Southwark, which Rennie did not follow.[27] His calculations were checked instead by the equally distinguished Thomas Young.[28] But Rennie had respect for Hutton; among the last acts of his life was to write from his bed subscribing to a bust to 'that most eminent man' and asking for a cast of it when it was ready.[29]

Rennie's appointment as engineer for Southwark Bridge is unlikely to have had to do with Hutton. His experience made him the obvious man for the job – a source of assurance for proprietors and parliamentarians. The Southwark Bridge Act passed in June 1811.[30] Rennie completed his design later that year and it was soon published by Ackermann. It was the boldest of his Thames bridges, consisting of just three wide cast-iron arches, the side ones of 210ft sloping upwards to a level arch of 240ft in the centre. This strategy, which probably followed from Rennie's earlier thoughts about the rebuilding of London Bridge, paid heed to the fact that the river was actually narrower at this point than at Vauxhall or Waterloo, but a good deal deeper, making it wise to reduce the granite piers in midstream to just two. The minimal piers and broad spans were also devised to appease the City Corporation, which as usual had objected to the bridge, this time on grounds of obstructions to navigation.

The granite for the piers included pieces of between fifteen and twenty tons from Peterhead near Aberdeen. The task of requisitioning and transporting these huge stones by boat to London fell to John Rennie junior, later Sir John Rennie, for whom Southwark Bridge marked a debut as his father's trusted lieutenant; his epic efforts at Peterhead are proudly recounted in the early pages of his autobiography.[31] As to the looks of this first major iron bridge in the heart of the metropolis, great efforts were made to harmonise the bridge pylons with the ironwork. 'Like most of Rennie's architectural essays, the theme of the design was Dorian', wrote a later commentator.[32] Details included fine severe lamp standards.

Jolliffe and Banks were the main contractors for the bridge, but Walkers of Rotherham, who had made the ironwork for the pioneering 1793–6 single-span iron bridge at Sunderland, were crucial subcontractors. Some piling took place in 1814, but the main work began only after the foundation stone had been laid in May 1815 by Lord Keith. Its text struck a triumphal note: 'The funds for building the Bridge were raised by subscription of private persons, incorporated by Act of Parliament, and the work was commenced at the glorious termination of the longest and most expensive war in which the nation has ever been engaged.'[33]

Work dragged on until 1819, probably because W.H. Wyatt, the company secretary, found it hard to extract the needed funds from subscribers. The opening, in March 1819, three months after John Wyatt's death, was a subdued affair, probably because of cost overruns, though one paper claimed the bridge was completed within the contract price.[34]

Southwark Bridge was the last of the three Regency toll bridges to open. Though a remarkable structure and the most important of Rennie's several iron bridges – 'nothing in which I have ever been concerned has proved more satisfactory than this bridge', he wrote[35] – it was never a success. It cost more than twice as much as Vauxhall Bridge and took a good deal longer to build. Potential users jibbed at the tolls, and only two years after it opened the City Corporation at last commissioned the rebuilding of London Bridge – from none other than Rennie. Built to his designs after his death under his sons John junior and George, the new London Bridge opened in 1832, toll-free like its predecessor. At that point Southwark Bridge lost its main purpose. As one newspaper commented in 1853, over and above its tolls, the narrowness and steepness of the approach roads were a deterrent. 'So far from being any real use as a London bridge, that of Southwark might just as well have been left standing in the green field at Rotherham, where it was first put together.'[36]

And so to the last and greatest of our Regency trio of toll bridges: Waterloo.

28 The first proposal for a Strand Bridge, to be called St George's Bridge, extract from map in John Gwynn's *London and Westminster Improved*, 1766. The scheme predates the rebuilding of Somerset House

29 The Savoy and its surroundings: an excerpt from Samuel and Nathaniel Buck's panorama of the Thames, published in 1749. Old Somerset House appears at the right-hand end of the view

4

Strand Bridge

The story of Waterloo Bridge begins with the architect John Gwynn. In his *London and Westminster Improved* (1766), Gwynn threw out dozens of suggestions for improving and beautifying the streets of the metropolis. Few were practicable, many were pie in the sky, but the best of them persisted in the public memory as harbingers of the joined-up planning absent from the London of Gwynn's time. A few were eventually implemented.

One such idea was for a bridge across the Thames from the Savoy (fig.28). To justify the proposal, Gwynn argued that the Savoy was equidistant between Blackfriars Bridge (then building) and Westminster Bridge, and that his bridge would ease communication across the river. New roads on the South Bank, he suggested, would link up with lines of communication from the existing bridges. Gwynn was more interested in building embankments all along between the bridges on the north bank and setting the houses back – an idea not yet feasible given the interests of trade. But his point of departure was plausible. The remnants of the former Savoy Palace (fig.29), once occupied by John of Gaunt, had sunk by the mid-eighteenth century into a ramshackle warren of barracks, a military prison and a Lutheran church.[1] As elsewhere in his book, Gwynn made no detailed suggestion as to how the whole scheme might be implemented. Nor, so far as is known, did he make any design for the bridge.

This was not the first time Gwynn had grappled with the challenge of Thames bridges. When Blackfriars Bridge had been put out to competition in 1759, he was among several architects who sent in elaborate designs in the fond hope that the public mood would stretch to sanctioning a costly bridge bedecked with sculpture commemorating

British victories in the Seven Years' War and honouring William Pitt the elder. With the City Corporation as paymaster, that was never going to happen. Despite support from his friend Samuel Johnson, Gwynn's Blackfriars design was subjected to withering criticism and set aside. All the same, in the years after *London and Westminster Improved*, Gwynn successfully built four solid bridges over the River Severn, two of them at his native Shrewsbury.[2]

Some background for the fanciful architect-designed bridges proposed for Blackfriars should be given, since they were to influence future schemes for the Savoy site and indeed the eventual Waterloo Bridge. A vogue for monumental or 'triumphal' bridges had been set by Piranesi and a group of budding architects who gathered around him at Rome in the 1750s. Inspired by surviving Roman bridges plus bridge designs by Palladio, they were usually depicted as laden with grandiose superstructures, so that the roadway had to be level (fig.30). The Blackfriars competition was the first British outing for these ideas. Gwynn was not alone in exploring them; they featured also in designs sent in by William Chambers and by Robert Mylne, both of whom had been recently in Rome. Eventually Mylne won the day, but with a drastically simplified scheme and a road that was not level (fig.19).

30 This famous Piranesi design for a 'ponte magnifico', published in 1756, was to be the inspiration for a succession of English bridge fantasies. The coupled columns on the piers were taken up in many executed bridges

Newspaper snippets of 1768 and 1770 show that something like Gwynn's proposal was not dead. The first claimed that 'an ingenious gentleman' had proposed a live cattle market in St George's Fields, to be reached by a bridge from the Savoy. The other referred to a bridge 'Intended soon to be built opposite Southampton-street, Covent-garden'. That would have placed it rather to the west of the Savoy, linking it with the Duke of Bedford's properties.[3]

Then came the rebuilding of Somerset House from 1776 onwards. This noblest of public projects in Georgian London was the masterpiece of Sir William Chambers, a former competitor for Blackfriars Bridge. The new Somerset House transformed the looks and psychology of this reach of the river. Its main block and great Thames front were essentially finished by 1790 (fig.31). The western range remained unbuilt until the 1850s, so that a Savoy Bridge could not yet be its immediate neighbour. All the same, a context of monumental grandeur had been set. This gave the cue for the notion of a triumphal bridge over the Thames to take a second outing.

The Royal Academy, of which Chambers was the senior architect-member, had been promised a home in Somerset House. It cannot be coincidental that the Academy set a 'bridge of magnificence' or triumphal bridge as the subject for its Gold Medal competition in architecture for 1776, the year in which construction on Somerset House began. Nor can it be doubted that the initiator and main judge would have been Chambers himself, recollecting his Blackfriars effort. The winner was the young John Soane. His entry had been prepared in collaboration with his master, George Dance, and its success gave Soane the chance to travel to Rome. Recast and fancifully illustrated over the years, as became Soane's habit, it is today the most famous of triumphal bridge designs.[4] There are various versions, ranging between five and seven arches wide, always depicted as level, broad and bearing elaborate superstructures. It was essentially an ideal conceit, though one late variant worked up by Soane's perspectivist, J.M. Gandy, shows an upriver Thames context, about where Lambeth Bridge now stands. In a more finished view, Soane's design stands self-contained in a dream landscape, leading from nowhere to nowhere (figs 32 and 33).

31 William Daniell's aquatint showing the rebuilt Somerset House from across the river, 1804, from the artist's *Six Views of the Metropolis of the British Empire*. Both ends are shown in their unfinished state. The Savoy, partially destroyed by the line of the future Strand Bridge, is shown to the left

32 J.M. Gandy, 'Design for a triumphal bridge', 1799, perspective of John Soane's suggested bridge of magnificence, originally drawn for the Royal Academy's 1776 Gold Medal competition, in an imaginary context

33 Unfinished drawing by J.M. Gandy, *c.*1826, showing Soane's bridge of magnificence on approximately the site of the future Lambeth Bridge at a time when a bridge there was being proposed. The viewpoint is downstream with Westminster Abbey and Westminster Bridge behind

There must have been other competitors for the 1776 Gold Medal. There is one strong and, in the context of the future Strand Bridge, intriguing candidate: Thomas Harrison, a young architect of promise, back that year from Rome. It is known that Harrison made a design for a triumphal bridge in 1776–8, supposedly for the site of Waterloo Bridge, though that conjecture comes from his Victorian biographer and could be misleading. The drawings seem to be lost, and the only description we have of it is also from a later source, which calls the design 'remarkable for the profusion and richness of its ornaments: superb Ionic columns rise from . . . the cutwaters up to the top of balustrade and terminate in pedestals which are to receive statues of victorious admirals'.[5] Harrison soon left London for his native Yorkshire and became, like Gwynn, a major masonry bridge-builder, but more distinguished. His surviving bridges at Lancaster and Chester are much admired. The Skerton Bridge at Lancaster was Harrison's first major commission, won in competition in 1782, not so long after his triumphal bridge design (fig.46). As we shall see, he comes back into the Strand Bridge saga at a later date.

Hard on Soane's and Harrison's heels came Thomas Sandby. In 1780 the Royal Academy moved into Somerset House. As its first professor of architecture, Sandby gave annual courses of lectures, so that may have been when his scheme for a level bridge of magnificence was added to his lecture illustrations. Surviving drawings (fig.34) show that his bridge, enriched like Soane's with colonnades and two-storey structures with domes at the ends, was definitely intended for the Thames. The site seems to have been conceived as running west of Somerset House from the Strand. In other words, it rose over the Savoy, which like most of the so-called 'Strand Palaces' dropped by stages down to the water. Beside it Sandby depicted another monumental block in Somerset House style, while below it came an embankment and regular quay fronts of the type suggested by Gwynn.[6]

Scattered press references between 1777 and 1791 show that the Savoy Bridge idea was far from dead. Some may have been speculative, others seem to allude to a genuine scheme or schemes. One mentions Perronet's Pont de Neuilly, recently completed though not yet published (fig.35), and trusts that the new bridge will likewise be built with arches of

equal width and start from a high level, unlike the sloped Westminster and Blackfriars Bridges – 'foreigners reprobate such fatal parsimony'.[7] Another hints that the Savoy Bridge, like the completion of Somerset House and the rebuilding of London Bridge and Newgate, has been delayed by the latest French war.[8] Yet another (of 1784) cites Mr Wyatt, presumably James Wyatt, as the chosen author of the bridge.[9] A fresh flurry of items, in 1788–91, calls for coffer dams instead of caissons for the piers, and deprecates landing places at the bridge foot, suggesting that the high-level version was still in play.[10] 'Fame speaks highly of the designs intended for the Savoy Bridge, but they must be super-excellent indeed, if they surpass those of Mr. Dance for the rebuilding of London Bridge', reports one paper.[11] Yet nothing happened.[12]

34 Thomas Sandby's Thames bridge of magnificence, perspective of *c.*1780. The view seems to position the bridge where the future Strand Bridge was to go. A block in similar style to Somerset House is suggested upstream for the site of the Savoy

* * *

The next step, after an interval, introduced a new title and the hustling methods of the joint-stock bubble. Its first token was a 'Plan of the new intended Strand Bridge and New Road, together with those parts of London and the Environs that will be particularly accommodated. As proposed and surveyed by George Dodd, Engineer, 1807'. The Dodds, whom we have met at Vauxhall Bridge, had then yet to become utterly suspect. Among their multifarious projects had been a Grand Surrey Canal through districts south of the Thames, which got some way before Ralph Dodd was dismissed for neglecting the work and overpaying himself.[13] So the Dodds had nodding acquaintance with South London. The 'New Road' of son George's plan was presumably

35 Two arches of the Pont de Neuilly, Paris, a plate from Jean-Rodolphe Perronet's great bridge book of 1782–3. The surface of the bridge is shown as level, while the arches end in so-called *cornes de vache* to ease the passage of water during flood tides, a feature seldom copied by British bridge-builders

36 George Dodd's nine-arched design for Strand Bridge, closely based on the Pont de Neuilly and published in 1808. The view looks upstream, with the earlier of the South Bank shot towers shown opposite Somerset House

the 'Kent and Surrey New Great Avenue' which he was promoting a year later, claiming support from some of 'the principal inhabitants of Southwark'. It promised to bypass Kent Street, the 'deplorable' existing road south of Borough High Street, on the route to and from London Bridge.[14] There must also have been a plan to connect this with the new bridge. Here at least was the germ of an idea as to where it might lead.

Dodd junior's Strand Bridge in the first instance was to be of timber, with the prospect held out for its replacement by a masonry one once enough money from tolls had accrued. But in the process of getting together a Strand Bridge Company and pushing the scheme through Parliament, after one failed attempt, that idea fell away in favour of a level masonry bridge, such as had been proposed in the past, following the French lines of Perronet's Neuilly bridge and having nine broad 130ft arches (fig.36). George Dodd, no expert draughtsman, let alone an architect, can hardly have made this design himself. Two 'ghosts' were later hinted at: William Capon and John Linnell Bond. Both were competent in their own spheres, but neither knew anything about bridging a tidal river.[15] Yet this nine-arch design was to become the starting point for the ultimate form of Waterloo Bridge.

On paper the direction of the Strand Bridge Company looked strong, with three MPs and several bankers on the board. These were enough to withstand the usual objections to the bridge, chiefly from the City. It was supported by the shopkeepers of the Strand, where the company's office was installed, and also by south bank wharfingers around the proposed bridge foot at Cuper's Gardens, Lambeth, a former pleasure garden looking across to Somerset House. Property transactions were taking place hereabouts in 1809–10, in anticipation. Some of this land belonged to the Duchy of Cornwall, which acquired a special Act in the Prince of Wales's name permitting development there.[16]

The monumental bridge was exhibited under George Dodd's name at the Royal Academy in 1810. But by then he had lost control of the project, the Dodds' reputation having plummeted. Even before the company's formal establishment, as early as February 1809, the design had been shown to Rennie and William Jessop who, in a firm if moderately worded report, commented adversely.[17] They were not alone, however. This is where Thomas Harrison, by then of Chester and

37 An arch design for a masonry bridge by Thomas Harrison, believed to be his suggestion for Waterloo Bridge, 1809. Coupled columns are shown on the piers

a bridge-builder of repute, comes back into the story. An obituary of Harrison says that he was consulted over the bridge, 'for which purpose he came up to London'.[18] Canon G.C. Blomfield, who wrote a memoir of Harrison in 1863, embellishes this:

> When the building of the present bridge was in agitation, finding that a plan had been adopted by the committee which appeared to him to be a mere copy of the bridge over the Seine at Neuilly, he addressed a remonstrance to them with such effect, that they renounced the plan, removed the engineer, and employed Rennie to build the bridge which is now the ornament of the river.[19]

Three surviving drawings of single arches by Harrison go some way to support this. One shows what appears to be the Neuilly design, while the other two present alternatives of 110ft width: one has an elliptical arch and single columns on the cutwaters; the other has a segmental arch and double Doric columns on the cutwaters (fig.37), not unlike Rennie's Kelso Bridge.[20]

Whatever happened exactly, Rennie supplanted the Dodds at Vauxhall by January 1810, and the same soon happened at the Strand Bridge. There was some lobbying in favour of Soane or another architect, on the usual grounds that the bridge should be ornamental and a source of pride for posterity.[21] But on 21 June the General Assembly of the Strand Bridge Company elected John Rennie as its engineer 'by a very great majority'. In a face-saving gesture, George Dodd was appointed resident engineer; he soon disappeared.[22]

* * *

The next six months were spent in preparation. The first step was for Rennie to procure from his assistant Francis Giles, later a canal and railway surveyor in his own right, a new and accurate survey of London River at this, its widest point in Central London.[23] Meanwhile Rennie made his revisions to the Dodd design with particular reference to Somerset House, thought through his techniques for the all-important pier foundations, and established a site office on the south bank at Cuper's Gardens, not far from his home and office in Stamford Street. Here materials began to be assembled. Until a contractor was appointed, the expenses must have been borne directly by the Strand Bridge Company.

The company itself had teething troubles. A banker of eminence, Abraham Goldsmid, headed the original list of directors but got into trouble over a Government loan, resigned from the company and shot himself in September 1810. There was also an embarrassment with the treasurer, Edward Boldero, whose bank failed early in 1812, though the company claimed to have been unaffected.

The man who kept the enterprise afloat through many ups and downs was Henry Swann, MP, chairman from about 1810 right through until he was dismissed in 1819. Swann is a shadowy figure. Coming from a modest gentry background, he trained as a barrister and married a Jamaica plantation heiress, allowing him to enter politics. He fought the Cornish constituency of Penryn in 1802 but lost. Returning to the fray in 1806, he won, representing Penryn on and off until his death in 1824. In Parliament Swann usually supported the Administration, but a tendency to duck and weave, plus episodes of maverick behaviour earned him the nickname 'Swim-Swann'. He was not much trusted, and never won office.[24]

Penryn was a notoriously corrupt constituency. Potential representatives had to bribe electors and offer local incentives. Following his re-election in 1818, Swann was prosecuted for bribery, ejected from Parliament and lost his connection with the bridge. But there was another side to these activities. Penryn was a granite-quarrying town and a rival port to neighbouring Falmouth. Swann cultivated and boosted the local granite industry. Conceivably he got onto the board of the Strand Bridge Company in the first place so as to lobby for the use of Penryn granite on the bridge.

Granite's hardness and endurance made it an excellent choice for bridges. It had so been used since antiquity, despite the difficulties involved in splitting and cutting it and in transporting large blocks. Cutting and dressing techniques for granite masonry advanced rapidly throughout the British Isles after 1750; there is a world of difference between, for instance, the rough blocks employed in the so-called General Wade bridges in Scotland, built after the '45 Rebellion, and the sleek, dressed-granite faces of nineteenth-century bridges.[25] An important step in the application of Cornish granite for engineering works had been its use in precisely cut blocks for Smeaton's Eddystone Lighthouse (1759).

But granite was not a metropolitan material. All building stone for London had to be imported by sea and river. In the eighteenth century, Portland stone had been favoured for architecture, York stone for paving. Scottish granite began to make inroads for London's street-paving from the 1760s, as did Dartmoor granite a little later. Neither was yet used in standing structures. But the shortcomings of the Portland stone employed on Westminster and Blackfriars Bridges were becoming manifest; blocks were spalling, and some had to be completely replaced. In the circumstances, the thoughts of a Scotsman like Rennie turned to granite. He had hoped to use Aberdeen granite in 1805 when working with Robert Stevenson on the famous Bell Rock Lighthouse off the Scottish coast, though in the end Craigleith sandstone was employed there.[26]

Swann, then, must have persuaded Rennie to select Penryn granite for the Strand Bridge. The choice proved far from problem-free. The Cornish granite industry was less developed than its Scottish counterpart. As yet it was largely confined to the splitting and extraction by 'scapplers' of outcropping boulders and the dispatch of unfinished blocks to the local port, which at Penryn was at no great distance. The loading of the blocks onto stout boats and their carriage up the Channel and unloading in London must have been costly operations. The finishing of the blocks was mostly performed at Cuper's Gardens by Scottish masons.[27]

Penryn granite was also dispatched in large quantities to Chatham Dockyard at this time. But for difficulties of procurement more than performance, it was not deemed an overall success. Rennie turned to Aberdeen granite for the piers of Southwark Bridge, as for the balustrades of the Strand Bridge. For the infill at the Strand Bridge he again used Craigleith stone from Scotland. At London Bridge his sons chose Devon granite from Dartmoor. The Dartmoor quarries had the drawback of lying inland. They were more consistently exploited after the building of Dartmoor Prison at Princetown began in 1806. Some Dartmoor granite was used in Plymouth Breakwater, one of Rennie's most famous achievements, which was constructed in parallel with his metropolitan bridges. The stonework for London Bridge came from the Devon Haytor Granite Company, set up in 1825, which took advantage of a railway built from Princetown to Plymouth.[28]

* * *

The contractors for the Strand Bridge were Jolliffe and Banks. They must have been appointed by the time that Swann, escorted by some gentlemen and 'several elegant females', laid the foundation stone on 11 October 1811.[29] The contract marked this exceptional firm's London debut, unless it was narrowly preceded by their rebuilding of an entrance lock at the West India Docks, also under Rennie. There, Rennie described Jolliffe and Banks as having 'much experience in the building of Bridges'.[30] They went on to construct no less than five Thames bridges and became regular collaborators, partners almost, with the Rennies.[31]

In histories of British construction, much has been made of the great building firms and railway contractors of the 1820s onwards, like Thomas Cubitt or Samuel Morton Peto. In comparison, the canal builders have been undervalued. Yet in terms of scale and organisation, they, along with the public works contractors who built barracks and defences during the Napoleonic years, foreshadowed the railway moguls. The canal mania of the 1790s saw figures like John Pinkerton and Hugh McIntosh tackle jobs of unprecedented size which transformed them into major contractors.[32]

Edward Banks (1770–1835) fits that picture exactly (fig.38).[33] He is first heard of carrying out dyking and draining works in his native Yorkshire. In 1791 he contracted for part of the Leeds and Liverpool Canal, followed by the Ulverstone Canal, an offshoot of Rennie's Lancaster Canal. He must then have been illiterate, as he and his wife Nancy both signed their marriage certificate in 1793 with crosses. But though uneducated and, as it seems, shy of the limelight, Banks could never have risen as high as he did without business abilities and personality.

By 1800 he had worked under both William Jessop and Rennie, and had developed a second line in the canal carrying trade. His tie-up with the Jolliffes, a gentry family with an entrepreneurial streak, came about after Banks was drawn into extending Jessop's Surrey Iron Railway from Croydon to Merstham, where the Jolliffes had their main seat and part-owned profitable lime works. The original contractor for the extension seems to have been Jessop's friend and ally Benjamin Outram, with whom Banks had been working in Derbyshire; he may have come in after Outram died suddenly in 1805.[34] Later he maintained a connection with the Butterley Company, Outram's successors in supplying ironwork.

In the next step Colonel Hylton Jolliffe, who had recently returned from Army service and inherited the family estate, brought Banks into the Merstham Limework Company. Soon after that the Colonel's younger brother, the Revd William Jolliffe, abandoned his clerical duties and went into the contracting business with Banks. Their first known job was the Croydon Court House (1807). Extensions of 1809–10 at Dartmoor Prison may have introduced Banks to building in granite. By the time Jolliffe and Banks took on John Rennie's Howth harbour in Dublin Bay in 1810, they were on course to becoming the great engineer's favourite contractors. They were also building a lighthouse on far-flung Heligoland under the architect-engineer Daniel Alexander.

left

38 Edward Banks the builder, miniature by William Patten junior. A fuller version of the portrait is in the National Portrait Gallery and tentatively ascribed to 1822, when Banks was knighted

below

39 Monument to Sir Edward Banks, *c.*1835, Chipstead Church, Surrey. Proudly shown are the three metropolitan bridges which Banks constructed for the Rennies: Waterloo, Southwark and London Bridge

40 Basin at Sheerness Naval Dockyard constructed for the Rennies by Jolliffe and Banks. Coloured print by T. Garner after a drawing by T.M. Baynes, 1830

In all these contracts the Jolliffes seem to have been largely sleeping partners, supplying capital when needed, while Banks's men did the work on the ground. Jolliffe and Banks soon acquired a high reputation for efficiency, ingenuity and workmanship.

To prolong the story beyond the London bridges, Jolliffe and Banks continued unsurpassed until 1833, though Rennie complained that the firm became less reliable as it expanded.[35] If one feat were to be singled out, it would have to be Sheerness Naval Dockyard on the Isle of Sheppey (fig.40). The expansion of Sheerness, started in 1813 while the war against Napoleon was at its height, was one of Rennie's major undertakings and continued under his sons at a slower pace until about 1830. The Jolliffe and Banks contracts there amounted to about one and a half million pounds. At the ceremonial opening of the first phase in 1823, the works at Sheerness, constructed on a quagmire and with a superstructure entirely of granite, were hailed as 'a stupendous monument of the genius of the late Mr Rennie'.[36] Banks took a personal lead in developing the town of Sheerness, laid out what was briefly known as Banks Town and sought to establish his family as squires of a kind on Sheppey. His son Delamark Banks settled there, laid out a racetrack and rebuilt the church of Warden; it later eroded into the sea – like so much of Sheppey.[37]

Banks cultivated Tory court circles around George IV. No doubt that was how he came to be knighted in 1822, the first British builder to be so honoured. He then gave a Sheerness address, but in later life he lived mainly at Chipstead, Surrey, near the Jolliffes at Merstham, having married as his second wife William Jolliffe's sister-in-law, while one of his daughters married a son of Jolliffe's. So this former illiterate was drawn into the Jolliffe family. Banks and his partner both died in 1835. His monument in Chipstead Church, crowned with his bust, memorably depicts Waterloo, Southwark and London Bridges in relief – his three proudest achievements (fig.39).

Jolliffe and Banks's main London base was at Beaufort Wharf, Strand, created for the Strand Bridge works but retained after the bridge was finished. From here a subsidiary company ran an early steamboat service to Sheerness and beyond from 1824, using boats built by the firm. In practice Beaufort Wharf and the Cuper's Gardens site opposite must have been shared for landing and storing materials, equipment, fabricating centres and preparing stonework. As the bridge was built from south to north, the workforce naturally gathered on the south bank. Here the labourers were paid at a 'pay-table' attached to the Feathers pub.[38]

Rennie and Banks were both natural collaborators – which may partly be why they are less than household names today. Throughout the making of the Strand Bridge, James Hollinsworth was Rennie's experienced site engineer. He had started off as a mason working on canal contracts, not least bridges, but after 1800, apart from one long break, he was employed practically full-time by the Rennies. As an expert on bridge foundations, Hollinsworth also played a crucial role in preparing for London Bridge, but died before it was finished. John Rennie junior was initiated into the harsh realities of engineering works on the Strand Bridge under Hollinsworth. He remembered that 'during the inclement winter of 1813–14, when the frost lasted about two months, and the Thames above London Bridge was frozen for several weeks, I was obliged to attend the piling of the foundations of the first and second piers on the Surrey side of the river night and day for three days each week, which severely tried my constitution.'[39]

Banks's leading lieutenant on the Strand Bridge was Henry Outram Henfrey, whose middle name suggests a connection with Benjamin

Outram. Most or all of this little-known engineer's career was spent with Jolliffe and Banks, who eventually took him into partnership. Henfrey married James Hollinsworth's daughter Mary in 1812, and when a child of theirs was baptised in 1816 he gave his address as Waterloo Bridge. After Mary died, he promptly married her sister Harriet – in other words he married his deceased wife's sister, often a taboo in those days.[40] When the foundation stone of the new London Bridge was laid in 1825, Henfrey's name led the list of skilled 'operatives' who took part in the ceremony; neither Jolliffe nor Banks seems to have been present.[41] In 1827 they put in the trusted Henfrey, known as an expert on granite, to sort out the badly managed Devon Haytor Granite Company, as they were then buying up that company's stone for London Bridge. But he died before he could achieve anything.[42] An obituary stated that he had worked on Waterloo, Southwark and the impending London Bridge. Henfrey was living in some style in Great Surrey Street (Blackfriars Road) at the time of his death. In his will he claimed a one-sixth share in the Jolliffe and Banks business.[43]

The Strand Bridge also marked the debut of Banks's young nephew John Plews, who worked on four of the five Jolliffe and Banks Thames bridges, helped manage the Merstham lime works, and sat on the board of the Waterloo Bridge Company into the 1840s while pursuing his own career as a contractor. Another close member of the Banks entourage was his confidential clerk William Mason Harvey, whose address was Beaufort Wharf at the time of his death in 1825.[44]

* * *

When Swann laid the Strand Bridge's foundation stone in 1811, the works were already 'in considerable forwardness', said *The Globe*, which invoked (in the original Latin) the simile used by Virgil to liken the building of Carthage as witnessed by Aeneas to the ceaseless activity of bees. Two coffer dams had already been excavated, while piles for a third had been driven; water was being pumped out by an eight-horsepower steam engine. The workforce, added the paper, consisted mainly of 'natives of the sister island', in other words Irish.[45] That tallies with labour practices on the canals, where the most tractable navigators or navvies, so called long before the railways, had been Irish.[46] Physical strength was paramount. Take Peter Ward, an Irishman convicted of knocking down two watchmen. Ward, it was said, 'found ample employment for his strength' driving piles for the Strand Bridge, which 'compelled him to keep late hours, and caused him to regale himself sometimes with beer, to the great concern of his wife' – this at a time when night shifts were being used to push the bridge ahead. The magistrate let him off.[47]

The Strand Bridge's nine semi-elliptical arches of 120ft (reduced by the prudent Rennie from George Dodd's vaunted 130ft) were built up in order from south to north. Excavation, centring and masonry work proceeded simultaneously in sequence on different sections of the bridge. The essential ring of each arch was completed in turn, leaving the final superstructure and roadway to be added at a late stage, along with the approaches at either end.[48]

First came the coffer dams and piling for the piers. Coffer dams were customary practice for bridges and other forms of marine construction. The selected area of water was walled off by driving rows of interlocking timber piles into the sea bed or river bed and then pumped clear of water. At least two rows of these piles, thoroughly caulked with an infill packed in between them, would be needed in order to get a good enough seal against the inrush of water. At the Strand Bridge the early coffer dams nearest the south side, where the water was fairly low, were composed of just two rows of piling, but for the piers in deeper water where water pressure made drainage harder, Rennie added a third. In plan these coffer dams started out as rectangular but eventually changed to elliptical, and this became the standard shape of the coffer dams successfully used by Rennie's sons at London Bridge. Within the rows of piling came an infill of brickwork interspersed with 'puddle', a mixture of clay and sand, plus gravel. With help from a hydrostatic ram, the piles were driven 16ft into the riverbed by titans like Peter Ward. The days of steam-hammered piling had yet to come. But a small steam engine, perched atop a platform at the edge of the piling, was used to pump the water out.

Within the pit of each coffer dam, once it had been pumped clear, an area corresponding to the width of the pier foundations was then

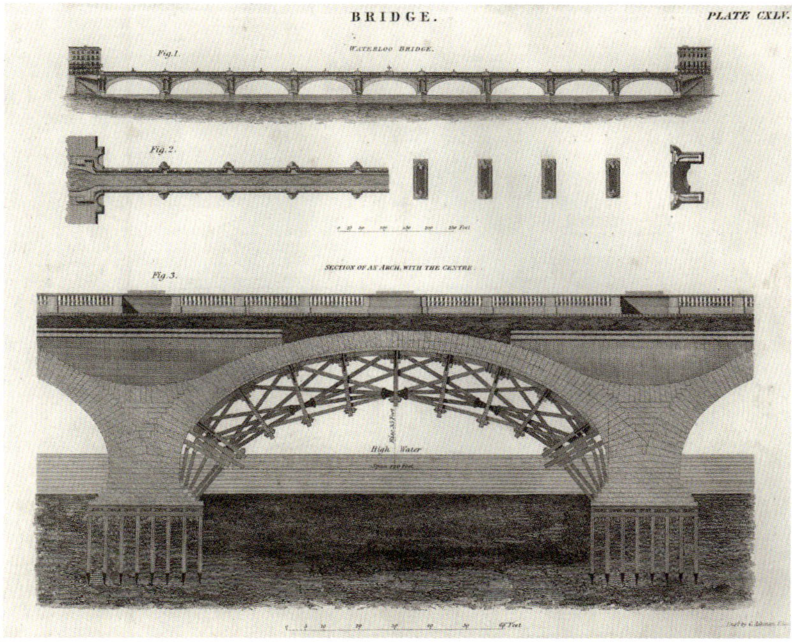

41 Waterloo Bridge, piles, piers, centering, arch and roadway showing construction, from the 8th edition of *Encyclopaedia Britannica*, 1860

excavated down below riverbed level by some 9–10ft. Then further stout piles were driven down by about 14ft to supply a foundation for the granite piers. These (fig.41) were the crucial piles, whose distortion, fracture and possibly insufficient depth were to be diagnosed in later years as the proximate cause for the bridge's failure. Baulks of timber were set horizontally over the top of the piles to receive the first courses of the granite piers, which stepped upwards in four stages from a width of 32ft at the base to 20ft above water. When the piers had been built up high enough, the surrounding walls of piling would be removed and the river would rush in.

This dismantling of the coffer dam walls, for reuse in connection with other piers, must have been as tricky and time-consuming as their original assembly, but they had to be removed completely in order to allow space for safe navigation. At Westminster Bridge the ingenious Labelye had invented another system for founding piers, the caisson, which was built on shore, floated out to the site of the intended pier,

42 Construction of the first arch of Waterloo Bridge beside the Lambeth bank, drawn by Edward Blore and engraved by George Cooke, 1817

and then sunk on top of the prepared area of piling by means of building the first courses of masonry within the caisson, the outer sections of which could then be released and towed back to shore. Labelye's system of caissons was used again, with modifications, at Mylne's Blackfriars Bridge, and by James Walker at Vauxhall Bridge. Rennie considered using them at the Strand Bridge but decided against it, probably on grounds of the greater accuracy obtainable with coffer dams; and indeed caissons were seldom used thereafter.

If Rennie's coffer dams were conservative, the assemblage by Jolliffe and Banks of the carpentry centres for the 120ft arches was something new (fig.42). Each centre was composed of eight parallel trussed ribs, 40 tons in weight, shaped to the elliptical arch profile of the bridge. Each rib in turn was built horizontally on shore, then raised vertically by crane onto three barges lashed together, floated out and raised with the help of the tide to reach its exact position on the rising piers, to which they were attached with wedges. A lateral framework connected the eight ribs and provided the surface on which the arch masonry was laid. As with the piling, when the masonry arch atop the centres had been completed, they could be 'eased', in other words dropped, by knocking out the wedges, floated off by barge again and reused for another arch.

The quantity of timber used for the piling and centring must have been prodigious, though not a stick of it would be visible in the completed bridge. The wharves next to the south side of the bridge rose high with timber during the early stages of construction, while in July 1814 it was reported that a team of six horses pulling down an oak tree from a park in Wimbledon for use at the bridge strayed into a pond and almost all drowned.[49]

The granite superstructure, absolutely new in London, gave the bridge its sober magnificence. It was composed of great stones dressed into shape by Jolliffe and Banks's Scottish masons from the raw blocks that arrived from Penryn. Very important in Rennie's eyes were the voussoirs of the arches, which increased in size as they dropped downwards towards the piers (figs 43 and 44). This arrangement, satisfactory though it looked on the outer surfaces, ran right through the depth of the bridge, so it was not just an aesthetic trick. It derived from what in masonry bridges was called the theory of equilibration. The phrase has several interpretations, but in Rennie's mind it implied that the forces in each arch should be self-contained and not passed on asymmetrically to neighbouring arches, with possible consequences of disturbance. The shaping of the voussoirs allowed each arch to pass on its thrust in an even and controlled manner to the piers.

These piers were equipped front and back with cutwaters, as was usual in masonry bridges to ease the flow of water and divert pressure off the bulk of the piers. The loading of these cutwaters was another fundamental aspect of Rennie's conception. As Jessop and he put it in their preliminary report on George Dodd's design (the report may have been Rennie's alone), loaded cutwaters had 'the treble purposes of giving an equality of weight as far as may be on the foundation, strength to the spandril walls, and ornament to the bridge'.[50] In other words, the double Doric columns which became so striking a feature of the bridge piers went well beyond mere decoration.

The success of Rennie's structural dispositions was confirmed by the fact that when the centring was removed, very little deflection or dropping of the crown of the masonry arches took place, as might have

43 Northernmost arch of Waterloo Bridge in its completed state, before the Victoria Embankment was built. Drawing by G.F. Robson published by J. Britton, 1827

44 The steamboat *Citizen* framed by the second arch on the north side of Waterloo Bridge in 1878. The Victoria Embankment to the left now covers the northernmost arch

been expected in spans of this dimension: a maximum of 1⅝ inches was reported, often much less, whereas at the Pont de Neuilly the deflection had been far greater. In terms of the superstructure, the construction was as perfect as could be hoped.

* * *

What about the bridge's appearance? Its most striking feature, repeatedly remarked upon, was that it crossed the river on a level, the first Thames bridge to do so. Earlier ones had all risen incrementally to the centre, so as not to obstruct navigation. They were obliged to do so because their abutments began at or near the shore, not much above high water level. Elsewhere, a level bridge suitable for navigation would have entailed approaches reaching far back into the city, too costly to contemplate; that had been one of the great issues attending the contemplated rebuilding of London Bridge.

But from the time of the earliest 'Savoy' schemes, a feature of the Strand Bridge was that it departed from the road of that name, next to Somerset House, high above the river. Such a level bridge from the north side had always been contemplated; it did not originate with Rennie. On the south side, however, the bridge approaches had to incline sharply from the point of landfall, since there was no high ground on that side. The same feature is repeated by the present Waterloo Bridge, which drops away very perceptibly for several hundred feet. It was possible to take up so much space because land was not expensive on the south side.

There had been no dearth of level bridges before the Strand Bridge. They were feasible wherever the flanking banks were high enough, or a river did not have to accommodate headroom for large vessels. The Romans built some level bridges, but more level aqueducts. The French began to interest themselves in creating level bridges in the mid-eighteenth century. There is an instructive difference between two great multi-arched bridges, fortunately both extant, over the Loire, comparable at some 900ft in width to the Thames; while the noble bridge at Blois (1717–24) ramps up to the centre, lower down the river the Pont Cessart at Saumur (1756–70) is flat. The craze for triumphal

45 Kelso Bridge, built to Rennie's design in 1802–4, in a tinted Edwardian photograph. The level surface and coupled three-quarter columns on the piers make it an obvious precedent for Waterloo Bridge

bridge designs, with semi-circular arches and enrichments over a level superstructure, belongs to the same period, as we have seen.

Not everyone was enamoured of level bridges. Telford, for instance, was among their critics. They were no help to navigation. Rennie was not rigidly wedded to making major road bridges level – his later design for London Bridge, for instance, had a slight inclination up to the centre. But he was certainly attracted to the sweep and grandeur characteristic of the type, and its aptitude for enrichment. He had also built several 'aqueducts' before the Strand Bridge – not lengthy viaducts in the Roman sense, but canal bridges crossing rivers. The outstanding example was his Lune Aqueduct outside Lancaster (1794–7). He was proud enough of this early achievement to inscribe his name on it; it also features in the portrait of the young Rennie by Martin Archer Shee (fig.22). Both the Lune Aqueduct and its successor, the Dundas Aqueduct on the Kennet and Avon Canal (fig.24), were enriched with Doric features such as projecting entablatures, friezes and, at the Dundas, the bonus of doubled pilasters flanking the central arch. The device recurs, now in the form of three-quarter columns, on Rennie's level five-arch bridge at Kelso (1802–4), often regarded as the Strand Bridge's precursor (fig.45).

46 Thomas Harrison's Skerton Bridge, Lancaster, 1783–7, with open aedicules on the piers

Though impressive, Kelso Bridge lacks the Strand Bridge's majesty, which derives in part from its crowning balustrades. Westminster Bridge also had balustrading, the first major bridge to do so; but Rennie is more likely to have borrowed the feature from a bridge he is known to have admired, Thomas Harrison's Skerton Bridge, Lancaster (1783–7). Skerton (fig.46) combines elliptical arches with classical enrichments on the piers, strictly a solecism, and this too recurs on the Thames bridge. In view of Harrison's intervention in 1809, it is possible that he and Rennie were in friendly touch during the early development of the Strand design. Skerton comes early in Harrison's oeuvre. Its pier enrichments are just pretty aedicules, lifted from the Roman bridge at Rimini (or Palladio's later cribbing of the motif), and can have had no impact on the structure. But Rennie, as we have seen from the 1809 report, argued that his pairs of three-quarter columns were functional as well as ornamental, by helping to load the cutwaters. In this respect, his ideas about construction and architecture alike develop from the early aqueducts via Kelso to the Strand Bridge, perhaps after discussion with Harrison.

Rennie had strong aesthetic instincts, and a lively and personal grasp of the classical orders. Though he may have taken advice from Harrison, the architecture of the Strand Bridge was surely his alone. He could never, for instance, have committed Robert Mylne's solecism at Blackfriars Bridge of slapping the Roman orders, including Piranesi-type pilasters on the piers, onto a rising bridge elevation, with painful results; the Strand Bridge corrected its eastern neighbour in materials and looks alike. Rennie's first affection was for the Doric order, which he believed right for major bridges. Among the most memorable features at the Strand Bridge were the stairs down to shore level on both banks, enclosed at the bottom by an arch flanked by primitive-type baseless Doric columns on a curved plan. They cost almost £20,000 extra, an astonishing amount for the proprietors to fork out at this late stage.[51] It is much to be regretted that these were not spared when the bridge was destroyed. Even the four toll houses, two at either end, were 'appropriate Doric structures'.[52]

To conclude this chapter, it may help to compare Rennie with Perronet, the pre-eminent masonry bridge-builders of their times. One must say times in the plural, because Perronet's most famous bridge, the level Pont de Neuilly, had been built back in 1768–74 and published in 1782, long before the Strand Bridge (fig.35). But it continued to fascinate British bridge-builders. Perronet was a better experimenter and teacher than constructor. He took risks; for instance, unlike most leading British engineers he saw his arches as structurally interdependent. All the centrings for the Neuilly arches were erected simultaneously, and when they were removed the crowns which they supported dropped substantially. Rennie took pains to avoid that at the Strand Bridge. Perronet also pioneered so-called *cornes de vache*, in other words the streamlined chamfering away of the lower courses of arches to expedite the flow of water. Telford tried this once (at Over Bridge on the Severn), Rennie never. Evidently, he preferred the clear-cut rectangular profile to arches which belonged to classical construction. When Perronet used the classical orders, it was to infer structural clarity, as the ponderous use of monumental piers in some of his bridges betrays. It was a kind of theoretical gesture. Rennie never taught – in the British engineering culture of his day there was nowhere to do so – nor did he theorise much, though his mathematics were more than adequate. Essentially he was a first-rate constructor, up to date in technique, conservative in his aesthetic preferences.

5

Waterloo Bridge

The Battle of Waterloo took place on Sunday, 18 June 1815. Famously, it took until the Wednesday evening for reliable news of this greatest of British victories to reach London. A recent book by Brian Cathcart has quashed many myths of how the news arrived, not least the story that carrier pigeons brought the first tidings to Nathan Rothschild, who for a few crucial hours was able to manipulate the stock market. In reality it took relentless driving, sailing and even rowing by Major Henry Percy for Wellington's official dispatch to get to the Government, scotching feverish and contradictory rumours about the outcome.[1]

War is always nasty. But the climax of the final campaign against Napoleon was especially so – 'simply brutal', says Cathcart, as thousands of soldiers pounded one another at close quarters and fell in hideous quantities.[2] Translated into triumphal language, which Wellington strictly eschewed in his dispatch, the name of the little Belgian hamlet of Waterloo soon rang and re-echoed throughout Britain, coming to eventual rest on the Strand Bridge.

In the long run, not everyone felt comfortable with the title. The architect Hector Horeau called for it to be changed, feeling that it was 'derogatory to any nation, claiming the front rank in the march of civilisation, to perpetuate the remembrance of human slaughter'.[3] And Robert Louis Stevenson told an anecdote about 'the *Frenchman* who, travelling by way of *Southampton*, was put down in *Waterloo* Station, and had to drive across *Waterloo* Bridge. He had a mind to go home again, it seems.'[4] That was pot calling kettle black. The Greeks and Romans never named public streets and monuments after military victories. The pioneer in such official provocations was Napoleon. Among much else, new Paris bridges had been named after Austerlitz and Iena. In London a few minor West End streets had informally recorded battles (Blenheim Street; Quebec Street), while suburban Maida Vale took its name from a pub, the Hero of Maida, otherwise Sir John Stuart, who had worsted the French in a minor engagement of 1806. Waterloo Bridge now took the fashion to fresh heights of patriotic self-congratulation, preceding Trafalgar Square by some twenty years.

How did the mantle of commemoration fall on the Strand Bridge? The story is not an edifying one.

Before June was out, Castlereagh, the Foreign Secretary, was backing an address from Parliament to the Prince Regent calling for a memorial to the fallen at Waterloo, a pillar or triumphal arch, 'in short, a grand architectural monument'. *The Times* was confident that it would go in St James's Park. Silence followed, apart from a letter in the same paper urging the appointment of a committee with advice from the Royal Academy.[5]

The trouble was that Parliament, and Government, had no proper mechanism for initiating such art-projects, though they might be persuaded to subsidise them. The rash of patriotic monuments erected in St Paul's Cathedral from 1795 onwards had been paid for – controversially – from the public purse. Fed by the emotions of war and a sense that Britain should be emulating the art-achievements of foreign powers, especially France, a taste for commemoration and architectural monumentality began to make itself felt during these years, with some impressive results, especially in the 1820s. But it was always a patchy business and seldom commanded lasting political commitment. Most British monumental buildings and urban improvements of the day originated outside the legislature, sometimes in the circle of the art-loving Regent, sometimes through individuals.

So it was that the earliest Waterloo monuments rose outside London as private landmarks – in the form of hilltop towers, obelisks or cairns (fig.47), built on aristocratic or collective initiative.[6] Countless plantations, woods, copses, streets, crescents, villas and cottages adopted the Waterloo name. So inevitably did pubs: the usual title was the Hero of Waterloo, in Wellington's honour. One such pub lent its name to the settlement of Waterlooville in Hampshire. The Liverpool suburb of Waterloo was likewise called after a Royal Waterloo Hotel. In London,

47 The Waterloo Cairn, Kinrara, Inverness-shire, erected in August 1815 by the Marquess of Huntly in memory of two officers from Highland regiments who fell at the Battle of Waterloo

48 Waterloo Bridge, Betws-y-Coed, Conway, built to designs by Thomas Telford, 1815–16

a Waterloo Place slipped into Nash's revised plan for Regent Street, while Waterloo Bridge itself bequeathed its name to a tatty district and hence to a railway terminus, of which more in later chapters. There were even other Waterloo Bridges: a three-span bridge at Christchurch, Hampshire; a pretty iron single span at Betws-y-Coed by Telford, carrying commemorative inscriptions (fig.48); and a minor masonry one by Rennie himself outside Leeds, though its name soon changed to Wellington Bridge.[7]

Not that the plans for an official commemoration died out. In January 1816 the Treasury authorised prizes for designs or models for a Waterloo Monument and advertised for entries in the press.[8] The following month Castlereagh was back before the Commons, calling now for two monuments – a naval one for Trafalgar and a military one for Waterloo. In debate, the members sowed their usual confusion.[9] As the artists too were at odds, the Royal Academy agreed to 'do nothing' and leave things to Government.[10]

A 'Committee of Taste' chaired by Charles Long, MP, the usual Regency fixer liaising between Government and Court on matters artistic, now ground into action.[11] In May its members 'had not yet had a plan submitted to them which they can wholly approve'. The first suggested site, St James's Market, elicited no enthusiasm.[12] Over a year later the Committee reached its final decisions and dissolved itself. It recommended models for a Waterloo Monument by William Wilkins (assisted by J.P. Gandy), promising a four-storey tower surrounded by a colonnade, and for a Trafalgar Monument by Robert Smirke, to cost half as much, in the form of a naval trophy on an eight-sided base.[13] Where were these to go? St James's Park soon supplanted the approach to Regent's Park as the favoured site for the Waterloo Monument. Both projects would go straight ahead, asserted the press, providing work for the growing host of post-war unemployed. But the *National Register* urged caution. Only part of the expense would be voted this parliamentary session, it warned; experience suggested that the Waterloo Monument, which comprised much sculpture, would take at least ten years to complete.[14]

Despite long delays and changes in form, authorship and location, the official Trafalgar memorial survived, to become Nelson's Column in Trafalgar Square. But the Waterloo Monument disappeared, because time had been taken by the forelock. In June 1817, the very month that Long's committee made up its mind, Waterloo Bridge was ceremoniously inaugurated by the Duke of Wellington and the Prince Regent. Their presence conferred semi-official status to the project and let the Government off the hook.

* * *

What had happened to catapult the Strand Bridge into the picture? At the time of the battle it was far from completion. That month there occurred the worst accident to beset its construction when, after the centring for the fifth arch from the south side had been struck, four ribs collapsed into the river, taking several workmen with them. No one was drowned.[15] But the mishap was a reminder of how much work remained. By the end of the year the keystone of the last arch had been set, workmen could now cross, and the approaches were being tackled. Completion in 1816 looked assured.

The first rumour of a new name, 'the Bridge of Waterloo', was recorded in July 1815, six weeks after the battle. It probably emanated from the hard-pressed proprietors.[16] That Christmas one 'Pontifex' wrote to the *London Courier*, arguing that since it was 'not only the largest and finest bridge in the world, but the most durable', it was 'worthy of so distinguished a title . . . as a monument to our great Captain and his victorious army'. Pontifex added: 'Some ornamental additions may be made by the Government, and a monument to perpetuate that great achievement formed at no very considerable charge to the country.'[17]

In February 1816 John Nash, always quick to see where the wind was blowing, wrote to Rennie suggesting a triumphal arch for the bridge. He got an answer 'in the negative'.[18] But the proprietors were serious at least about the change of name. They now applied for a new Act of Parliament which, as often for projects of this magnitude, modified existing provisions or added new ones. It was passed in June 1816. The core was clause 22.

> And whereas the said Bridge when completed will be a Work of great Stability and Magnificence; and such Works are adapted

> to transmit to Posterity the Remembrance of great and glorious Achievements: And whereas the said Company are desirous that a Designation be given to the said Bridge which shall be a lasting Record of the brilliant and decisive Victory achieved by His Majesty's Forces, in conjunction with those of His Allies, on the Eighteenth Day of June One thousand eight hundred and fifteen; be it therefore enacted, That from and after the passing of this Act, the said Bridge shall be called and denominated *The Waterloo Bridge*, and shall cease to be called by the Name of *The Strand Bridge*.[19]

Naturally the name of the Strand Bridge Company changed too.

If the company calculated that the Waterloo name would prompt the Government to dig them out of their severe financial plight, as Westminster and London Bridges had been helped in the previous century, they were sorely disappointed. Not a penny of public money was spent on the bridge itself, nor were the calls to embellish it with sculptures, arches or even inscriptions heeded. To the contrary, the 1816 Act saved the Government hundreds of thousands of pounds and thrust the deliberations of Long's committee into irrelevance. On the other hand, it added a final pre-eminence and gravitas to the conspicuous achievement of Rennie – as well as Edward Banks and his intrepid workforce.

Meanwhile, the politicians had found a let-out for themselves. For some time a body of churchmen had been badgering Lord Liverpool's Government to vote a large sum of money – a million pounds, far more than any Waterloo monument could have cost – to build new churches, sorely needed in Britain's rampant cities and industrial districts. When the measure came to Parliament early in 1818, it commanded cross-party support and, with some amendments, sailed through. It was the Whig opposition leader in the Commons, George Tierney, hitherto a vocal supporter of the Waterloo Monument, who suggested that the money pledged should be appropriated to the sacred end of church-building. In due course the churches erected under this legislation and successor Acts became known informally as 'Waterloo churches'. One of them, originally the only Waterloo Church, was to be built immediately south of the bridge (fig.59).[20]

There seems to have been little resentment about this shift in policy. Even William Wilkins, winner of the Waterloo Monument competition (if such it can be called), pronounced himself content:

> A strong expression in favor of a Church, as an appropriate and useful building for the commemoration of the battle of Waterloo, having been manifested then in the Session of the last Parliament, it seemed highly probable that my design for a commemorative monument . . . would undergo revision; and that a building more called for by the exigencies of the period would be ultimately substituted for it.[21]

The exigencies of the period? Or just shabby parsimony? The whole procedure was certainly very British.

Some commentators took pride, ironic or otherwise, in the fact that the greatest masonry bridge in the world had been built without a penny of public money. One paper wrote:

> It is well known that in France and other foreign countries, all the public buildings are erected by the order, and at the expence of the Government. Some foreigners were therefore surprised to hear that the Waterloo bridge was built by a company of private adventurers. 'And has the present Government left no monument of its magnificence?' 'Yes,' said a bye-stander, 'the Wooden Pagoda Bridge in the Park was raised under their direction.'[22]

The *Commercial Chronicle* waxed truculent:

> Not only has this great ornament been added to the metropolis without increasing the public burthens; but above a million of money has been raised by public-spirited individuals, out of which many thousand pounds have been paid to Government for duty upon the stone of which the bridge is built; so that the public has already been considerable benefited by the undertaking.[23]

* * *

The dedication, on the second anniversary of the Battle of Waterloo, was a great occasion. There had actually been a dress rehearsal. Three years before, when the Allies believed they had beaten Napoleon for ever, the King of Prussia and Emperor of Russia converged on London to confer with the Prince Regent and his ministers, in uneasy preparations for the Congress of Vienna. Blucher was there too, but not Wellington. The monarchs and their retinues processed in barges from Whitehall Stairs to Greenwich, sailing through one of the bridge's completed arches, to be greeted by huzzahs from a crowd perched perilously on top. 'Never was the Thames more honoured – never had London more reason to triumph – or the inhabitants of the British Empire more reason to be proud. It is indeed a rare, a dignified, a glorious spectacle', crowed one paper.[24]

Since then, there had been sharp swings in the public mood. First came Napoleon's resurrection, then the euphoria after his final defeat, then the post-war collapse of employment and trust in the Government. Earlier in 1817 mass protests took place at Spa Fields, and just a week before the bridge opened the Pentrich uprising of stockingers in Derbyshire. Now, for a day, all that was forgotten in favour of a Thames carnival.

This time Wellington was in London, on leave from his role as commander of the occupation forces in Paris and guarantor of the second French Restoration. He was staying with his brother William Wellesley-Pole in Richmond Terrace, not far from the bridge, which he visited informally beforehand.[25] Wellesley-Pole liaised with the Waterloo Bridge Company over details of the ceremony. A rumour ran about that the Duke would ride across the bridge on his chestnut charger Copenhagen, which was being brought over specially from France, with four or five thousand troops behind him.[26] That was not Wellington's style. Meanwhile the Royal Circus and Surrey Theatre got up a 'Burletta Divertissement' called *Waterloo Bridge*, 'introducing an extensive representation of that superb edifice, with carriages and figures in motion, and a grand Panorama of the Battle of Waterloo'.[27]

On 18 June 'the sun shone all day'.[28] The Thames was packed from Blackfriars to Westminster with hundreds of thousands of spectators, many standing on barges.[29] 'Elegantly dressed females' jostled with 'sable waggoners' who took money from those eager to watch from the coal wharves. Scaffolds for viewers stretched even along the Strand, whence hardly a glimpse of the river was possible. On the Surrey side, the scruffy fields beyond the bridge were strewn with booths, shows, roundabouts and refreshment tents. 'One would suppose that all the people of London had gone to pass a festive night upon a spot, which hitherto was in some manner an inaccessible swamp.' Opposite, in a fenced-off area around the north end of the bridge, the company provided paying seats for 1,500. Waterloo veterans took possession of the bridge itself that morning and set out copious cannon – allegedly 202, supposed to be the number taken at the battlefield – together with captured eagles and other standards to be raised in the bridge's four recesses at the moment of climax. Between these, several bands stood ready to play competing music.

At 3 pm the Prince Regent, the Duke of Wellington and Prime Minister Lord Liverpool embarked from the private jetty at the back of Fife House, Liverpool's Whitehall residence. The moment is depicted in the foreground of Constable's great painting of the event, which also shows the first distant puff of cannon discharging from the centre of the bridge (fig.49). Twelve other barges carrying royal princes and princesses, aristocrats, ministers and sundry potentates completed the party.[30] One was the Lord Mayor's, asserting the City's traditional rights to the river – it is said to have got in the way at one stage. The flotilla passed through the bridge and some little way beyond downstream, turned majestically, and deposited its passengers on the Surrey side. They climbed the steps, paid the pedestrians' toll – a gracious gesture – crossed and then descended on the Middlesex side where the boats had come over to meet them. All this amid a deafening chaos of cannon shots, music and cheering (fig.50). Once re-embarked, the boats of the invitees processed back to Fife House for a dinner. Everything was over by 7 pm. At that point the populace flooded onto the bridge, crossing back and forth and milling about until one in the morning. Just that once, they were allowed to pass without payment.

In the aftermath there was still much to do. The handsome gas lights, for instance (it was still early days for gas lighting), had still to be put up,[31] while the road leading south from the bridge awaited completion.

49 John Constable, *The Opening of Waterloo Bridge ('Whitehall Stairs, June 18th, 1817')*, exhibited in 1832. This is the version in the Tate Gallery; another is at Anglesey Abbey. An earlier sketch is shown at fig.96

The Prince Regent had ordered that a medal be struck to honour the directors and proprietors for 'the great national work'.[32] They must have found it a hollow honour. Before they recouped a penny, the tolls had to raise £200 a day just to pay the annuitants, who had priority. No one expected the bridge would ever make a profit; indeed how its completion had been financed is a mystery.

50 *The Opening of Waterloo Bridge*, the anonymous version of the event published by R. Ackermann, 1817

Henry Swann, still the company's chairman, insisted that once the road had been completed, income from the tolls would treble. That was pie in the sky. The best that could be extracted from Government was the promise of a mortgage on the tolls which would go towards finishing the southern road.[33] Though their bridge had been lauded to the skies, the proprietors, as one piece of doggerel put it, were

> . . . not dispos'd to praise it much;
> Because their hundreds they have seen,
> Brought down in worth to pounds fifteen.
> They mourn that their imprudent zeal,
> Has harmed them for the public weal;
> And hold kind sympathy their due,
> *As sufferers of Waterloo*.[34]

No wonder that keen attention was paid to the factory-style turnstiles attached to the tollgates, contrived to prevent fraud. Only one passenger or rider could pass at a time, the turning mechanism communicating with a clock in the adjacent tollhouse which recorded the numbers.[35] That did not deter frequent attempts to avoid the penny toll for foot passengers, not to mention occasional assaults on the toll-keepers and robberies of the proceeds.

It was to little avail. Almost a decade after the bridge opened, the return on the million pounds or more spent on its construction was reported as less than £14,000 per annum. 'Even of this sum, the original adventurers get, we believe, nothing, as it is swallowed up by the interest on money borrowed. The Government does not seem to have given the Company anything for the liberty of calling it *Waterloo* Bridge, so that a national monument has been got on very easy terms.'[36] All this naturally presaged skimped future maintenance.

For some, the bridge's completion reignited indignation that the Government had not done enough to commemorate the heroes and victims of Waterloo. The remedy, argued a correspondent in *The Sun*, was for the authorities to take on the bridge, free it from tolls, and thus make it a genuine public monument to the battle. 'At present, it is only a public name given to a private work; a kind of national swindling, giving credit to the Public for an edifice in which it has no interest, but, on the contrary, is paying a daily and perpetual tax for its use.'[37] William Cobbett likewise lashed the parliamentary 'Boroughmongers' with his best rhetoric:

> What are become of your intended *Pillars* and *Triumphal Arches*? Early in 1816 you talked very big on this subject. You voted millions? Mr TIERNEY, "his eye in a fine fit of pious phrenzy rolling," proposed to build a brace or two of "solemn temples" with "cloud-capp'd towers." In sober sadness, tho', are all these really sunk down into a "Waterloo-Bridge", built by private speculators? Your folly marks you out for the contempt of mankind: your injustice and cruelty for its hatred.[38]

All in all, though, public opinion took pride in Waterloo Bridge. Superlatives and comparisons abounded. Praise from foreigners earned

51 Waterloo Bridge, a view of the whole bridge in a drawing made by Edward Blore long before completion and published by W.B. Cooke, 1814

special remark, betraying how chauvinist pronouncements alternated with the common English failure of nerve when it came to judgements about art. A literary gentleman 'from the French academy' was supposed to have hailed the bridge as 'by far the finest erection of the kind in Europe'. But why, he asked, was Somerset House left still unfinished?[39]

The most celebrated compliment came from the great Italian sculptor Antonio Canova who, it is claimed, called Waterloo Bridge the noblest in the world, and alone worth the journey to London. There is some mystery about this. Canova came to Britain only once, late in 1815, as the Pope's representative in discussions about repatriating artworks looted by Napoleon. His courtesy and sensibility made a deep impression on his hosts. Since he was keen to see all the public monuments and artworks he could, his tour naturally took in the Elgin Marbles, which he was recorded as saying alone were worth his trip.[40] Did he also take much notice of Waterloo Bridge? In the copious reports of his visit there seems to be no record of it. Its superstructure was then incomplete, though the last arch had just been struck, so it hardly yet looked like an art-monument. Can he have seen drawings or prints? The only plausible image of the bridge dating from before the opening was a perspective by the young Edward Blore, engraved by the Cooke family and published in 1814 (fig.51).

52 An early photograph of Waterloo Bridge by Roger Fenton, *c.*1857. The view is from the north bank looking downstream, before the Victoria Embankment was built

53 Waterloo Bridge seen from the Victoria Embankment soon after its completion. Photograph by Frederick York, probably of the 1860s

The earliest allusion to Canova's praise seems to be a passing reference in a newspaper article of August 1816 where the sculptor is stated to have called it 'the finest bridge in Europe'. Just before the opening, another paper went on to claim that on his return to Rome, Canova declared 'that the sight of this Bridge alone would have well repaid the trouble of his journey to England'.[41] These in essence are the two statements that have been repeated from that day to this. Early photographs of the bridge suggest that we can take them at face value (figs 52 and 53). They were corroborated by good critics of later generations. To cite just one, the great architect-educator Beresford Pite found in London's two Rennie bridges 'a purity of taste, refinement of architectural knowledge and power of constructive skill, an achievement to which England had not heretofore attained'.[42]

6

Troubled Township

Building a bridge is very well, but it has to have a use, must lead helpfully from one place to another. In that respect Waterloo Bridge, not alone among London bridges, proved problematic. This chapter is mainly about the early struggles associated with the place that grew into being to its immediate south. That place became known, after the bridge, as Waterloo. The name has stuck.

* * *

The approaches must come first. In order of construction they followed the bridge. But the land they occupied had to be purchased at an early stage, or at least requisitioned under the Strand Bridge Acts. On the north bank the approach road took up valuable commercial property fronting and running back from the Strand, as well as a big chunk of the old Savoy Palace, owned by the Duchy of Lancaster, which proved hard to destroy.[1] The toughest battle was with Durs Egg, a gunsmith of repute. Though Egg's Strand business and workshops were in decline after the Napoleonic Wars, he refused to accept the compensation figure agreed. So the Bridge Company took possession by force, resulting in a costly action for damages over and above the legal award.[2]

The northern approach road sloped up from the Strand to bridge level by a hardly perceptible 2ft. It was constructed on arched foundations which are still, residually, there today, despite the excavation of a subway under the Strand in the 1960s. Originally known as Somerset Place, it became Lancaster Street in 1818, while the wider space before the bridge and tollgates where vehicles gathered was christened Lancaster Place.[3] Here on the western side Robert Smirke built the Duchy of Lancaster

54 Lancaster Place (then part of Wellington Street), looking north towards the Strand in 1896. Left, corner of the Duchy of Lancaster Office and the terrace called Lancaster Place; right, James Pennethorne's western extension to Somerset House

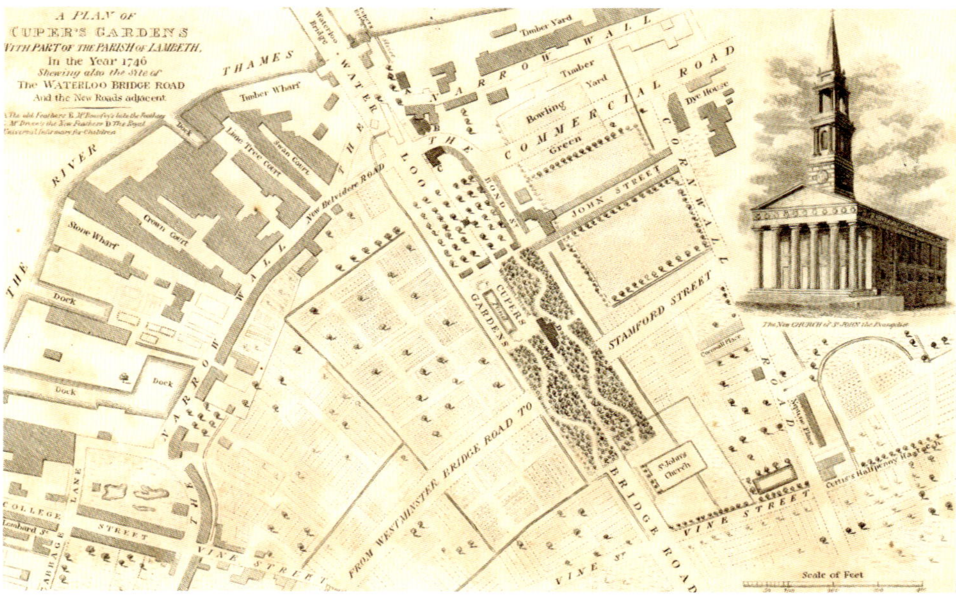

55 'A Plan of Cuper's Gardens', made for Robert Wilkinson's *Londina Illustrata*, 1825, with the course of Waterloo Bridge and Waterloo Road overlaid on earlier buildings and gardens. To the right, a vignette of St John's, Waterloo Road

office in a suitable, stone-fronted classical style, with a terrace of good houses behind it. In the 1830s the title of the approach road, though not the terrace, changed to Wellington Street, after the street which still carries that name was laid out northwards from the Strand towards Bow Street and Long Acre. The bridge company contributed to the new street's construction, as it helped improve the poor northern access to the bridge, which had hitherto stopped short at a bald T-junction with the Strand.[4] It must also have eased access to the lucrative trade of Covent Garden Market. Despite hope that this route would extend much further northwards and become a main north–south artery for London, so aiding the bridge proprietors, that was not to be.[5]

Opposite the Duchy office and Lancaster Place, the eastern flank of the approach road was filled in 1851–6 by the long-missing western wing of Somerset House, designed by James Pennethorne. The dignity which they jointly conferred on this side of the bridge (fig.54) was upheld when the Duchy of Lancaster building and terrace gave way to the bulkier Brettenham House in 1931–2. But by then the old bridge was doomed. It was in the throes of rebuilding when this stub of Wellington Street was renamed Lancaster Place in 1939, perpetuating the former terrace's title.

The southern approach was a different kettle of fish. It sloped down sharply from the bridge, oversailing riverside wharves and works. This long decline followed from the choice of a level bridge; as H.H. Statham put it, 'when a cabhorse strained up with one from Waterloo station to the top of the hill, he was doing that because Rennie wanted a horizontal bridge'.[6] The length of the approach accentuated the variation of levels which have haunted this whole area of the South Bank ever since. It was constructed on arches because the ground was bad, and has since been completely replaced. One of the arches was left open for a new service road laid out by the company behind the riverside properties, to replace the inadequate former 'Narrow Wall': this became the present Belvedere Road and Upper Ground. The main acquisition in the waterfront region was Beaufoy's Vinegar Factory, which occupied much of the old Cuper's Gardens pleasure grounds (fig.55); the owners extracted £36,000 from the Bridge Company, allowing Beaufoy's to erect new premises at Vauxhall.[7]

* * *

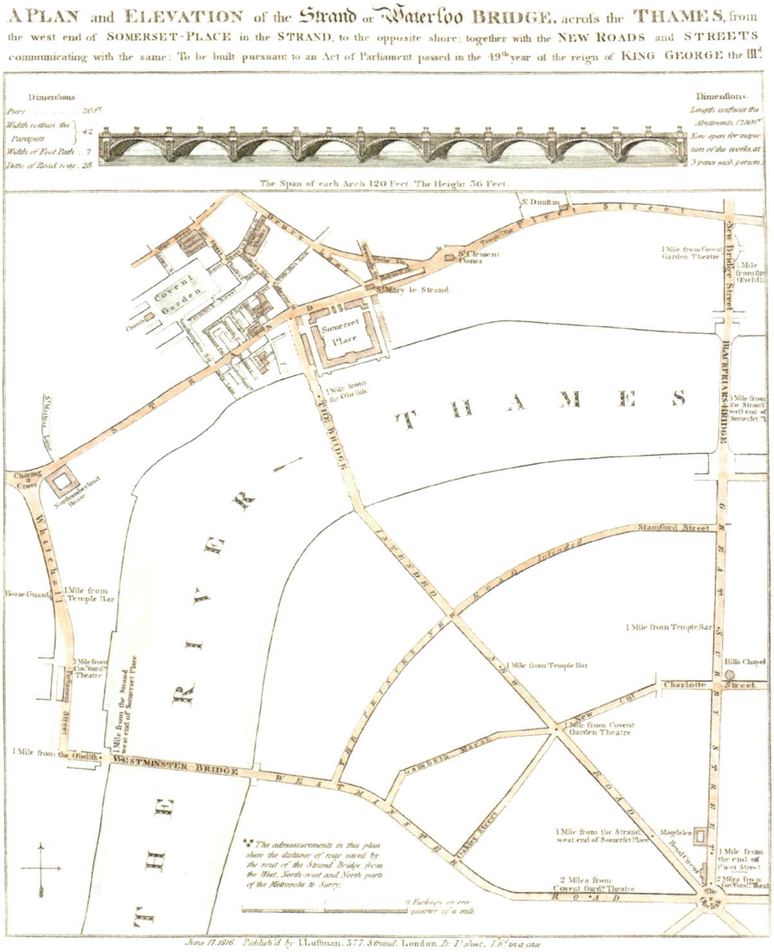

56 Plan published by I. Luffman, 1816, before Waterloo Bridge was finished, showing road layouts proposed south of the river and their co-ordination with routes from Westminster and Blackfriars Bridges

The bridge approach counted as part of Waterloo Bridge Road – or Waterloo Road, as it became. Where it made landfall, new roads were promised under the company's acts. One ran eastward to connect with the existing stub of Stamford Street west of Blackfriars Bridge, where the Rennies had their base. The westward equivalent linked up with the industrial district at the foot of Westminster Bridge (fig.56). This wholly new line, known as York Road, was only cut through in 1824. South of the junction with Stamford Street and York Road, Waterloo Road stretched straight as a die in a south-south-easterly direction to a point next to the obelisk at St George's Circus, three-quarters of a mile away. All these roads had to be made at the bridge company's expense. Under an Act of 1818, only once they were completed, fenced and lighted could they be handed over to the Trustees of the Surrey New Roads, the body responsible for thoroughfares in these marshy and scrappy tracts of South London.[8]

Were these new roads, and hence Waterloo Bridge, intended mainly for long-distance or for local traffic? Taking the long-distance issue first, it must be remembered that the Thames runs from south to north at Westminster, then turns in a majestic arc till it resumes its true west–east course at Blackfriars. That imposed a specific destiny on the portion of South London within the arc, which is crisscrossed by roads at varying angles. By and large, their lines are dictated by river crossings. Protracting the direction of the bridges on the south side of the river along the arc, they largely intersect around the neighbourhood of unloved Elephant and Castle, as it is today. The road system actually achieved was never quite rationally geometric. But all the projectors of roads south of the Thames tried to make connections with one another and with the main routes south out of London.

The roads leading to and from Westminster Bridge were the pioneers. This bridge was poorly positioned in relation to existing routes in and out of London. But soon after its completion, a new line of roads made it possible to take a shortcut by land from Westminster to the City – essentially a chord cutting off the bend in the river. George II is said to have inaugurated this route in 1752, and shortcutting travellers have followed suit ever since.[9] Connections to the old main roads out to Kent and mid-Surrey followed on shortly.

The route from and to the new Blackfriars Bridge linked into this system of turnpike roads in 1769. The obelisk at St George's Circus was duly erected to mark where Blackfriars Road (originally Great Surrey Street) joined the roads leading to and from Westminster Bridge. It was to this network, much of it laid over waterlogged ground, that the Waterloo Bridge Company now sought access by protracting their road to a point next to the obelisk. Once that had been achieved in 1819, in theory, long-distance travellers from the south could choose to cross by Waterloo Bridge. But why should they opt to pay the toll there, over and above the turnpike tolls payable on most of these roads, when they could cross free of charge at Blackfriars or Westminster?

The advantage was not obvious, unless they had business at or near Covent Garden Market.

Such considerations must have induced the Waterloo Bridge Company to focus locally, by promoting developments around the line of their new main road. The precedent of Blackfriars Road was encouraging. As Horwood's map shows, its environs had been substantially built up by 1800. Within fifteen years of Blackfriars Bridge's opening, this western division of Southwark parish could boast a parish church, a major dissenting chapel and a theatre. By contrast, little development had taken place west of the parish boundary in neighbouring Lambeth, where Waterloo Road and its offshoots were to run. Could the company repeat the trick? In the short term it did, as the second edition of Horwood's map shows (fig.57). Waterloo Road soon attracted a church, a hospital and a theatre. But as regards housing, the company failed to control the development of Waterloo,

57 Excerpt from Faden's version of Horwood's map, published in 1819, showing development south of Waterloo Bridge at that date

58 The Coburg Theatre (later the Old Vic), as illustrated by Robert Schnebbelie for the second volume of Robert Wilkinson's *Londina Illustrata*, 1825. The play shown is William Barrymore's *Trial by Battle*

as the City Corporation better could around Blackfriars Road because it owned much of the land.[10]

* * *

The theatre came first. Its story goes back to the Royal Circus and Surrey Theatre. This pioneering enterprise, founded by the actor-composer Charles Dibdin in 1782, occupied the bottom of Blackfriars Road next to St George's Circus. It enjoyed a fitful history, surviving changes of management and two fires. Here was held the spectacle to celebrate the opening of Waterloo Bridge. But by then the Surrey Theatre was back in trouble. In debt and facing a high rent rise, its lessee, James Jones, absconded with allies plus the scenery and props to build afresh on a site beside the future Waterloo Road. Their architect was Rudolph Cabanel, who had overseen the latest reconstruction of the Surrey Theatre.

This brave new venture briefly attracted the patronage of Princess Charlotte and her husband, Prince Leopold of Coburg. Hence its original name, the Royal Coburg (or Cobourg) Theatre, later the Victoria Theatre, today the Old Vic. Its foundation stone was laid nine months before the bridge opened, on an isolated site where the unfinished Waterloo Road intersected with an existing lane, broadened into the 'New Cut'. A modicum of housing may just have been emerging out of the ground nearby.

Overcoming a building strike, the Royal Coburg opened in May 1818 (fig.58). A celebrated clown, Richard Usher, put on a set of displays to lure punters across the river. One antic was to harness four tom cats to a contrivance which drew him down the Waterloo Road to the theatre in less than three minutes. This Usher supplemented by squatting in a tub attached to four geese (Gabble, Gibble, Gobble and Garble) who were to convey him by river from Waterloo Bridge to Battersea. Predictably, these performances did not always work. 'The geese tended to get tangled up', reported the *Morning Advertiser* of one foray, while 'The cats ran rather resty, but having them tight reined, he made as good driving as could be expected. Usher declared he felt more pleasure in driving geese than he could enjoy from driving any other animals. The geese, said he, once drove me off the stage, and now I have the satisfaction of driving them.'[11]

'The Old Vic owes its existence to Waterloo Bridge', begins Terry Coleman's book on the theatre.[12] The relationship went beyond location. The Waterloo Bridge Company owned a stake in the Royal Coburg and exempted early theatregoers from tolls. In the pioneering days, the bridge's carriage gates were thrown open after performances, allowing not less than 700–800 patrons to drive through, it was claimed.[13] For pedestrians the journey was hazardous. The company was asked to expedite the lighting along the bridge and the road, and also to better fence the footpath 'against the accidents of persons in the dark falling into the marshes'.[14]

Princess Charlotte having died before the Royal Coburg opened, it was sustained in its earliest years by the stage-struck Joseph Glossop, son of a wealthy Soho tallow chandler, but when he fled the country with a leading lady it fell back on a diet of 'Pantomimes, Melodramas and Shrieking Tragedies'. Hazlitt, visiting in 1820, felt himself 'in a bridewell or a brothel, amidst Jew-boys, pickpockets, prostitutes and mountebanks'.[15]

The decline of the Royal Coburg had much to do with the reascent of the rival Surrey Theatre's star. Soon, tolls for theatregoers on Waterloo Bridge were reimposed, whereas those for the Surrey could cross without paying at Blackfriars. Audiences from across the river therefore fell off in favour of rowdy local ones.[16] The change of name to the Victoria, together with the development of the New Cut district with poor housing, hardly helped. In 1840 the critic F.G. Tomlins thought it situated in one of the worst neighbourhoods and its audiences 'of the lowest kind', but flattered their appreciation of 'genuine pathos, and even genuine wit and poetry'. Later, he was harsher: 'The Victoria lives by reflecting back the violent taste and manner of its audience; a great proportion of which consists of youths.'[17] It took years of changing names and uses, including a spell as a reforming coffee tavern, before the venue threw off its seediness and earned secure fame as the Old Vic.

Six full years after the Royal Coburg opened, Waterloo Road at last gained other facilities. St John's Church and the Royal Infirmary for Children were both inaugurated in 1824 on the east side close to Stamford Street. Meanwhile, one puffing article claimed that housing would soon stretch all the way from the bridge to the obelisk.[18] Fitful development certainly took place, extending to a pair of nonconformist chapels and a short-lived private swimming bath. Pubs near the bridge included a new version of the Feathers, replacing the venue where the bridge workers had been paid, and an inevitable Hero of Waterloo at the corner of the future York Road.

The church was the obvious guarantor of local respectability (fig.59). In a vote of confidence, Lambeth Vestry chose to allocate to the infant township one of the four Commissioners' Churches built in the parish under the 1818 'Waterloo' Church-Building Act.[19] Stone-fronted, porticoed and stack-towered in the best neoclassical style by its architect, Francis Bedford, it was also at some £18,000 the costliest of the four. Much of the money must have been absorbed by the ample burial crypt which, on John Rennie junior's advice, was piled to a depth of 35ft, as the swampy site featured a pond described as the resort 'of a

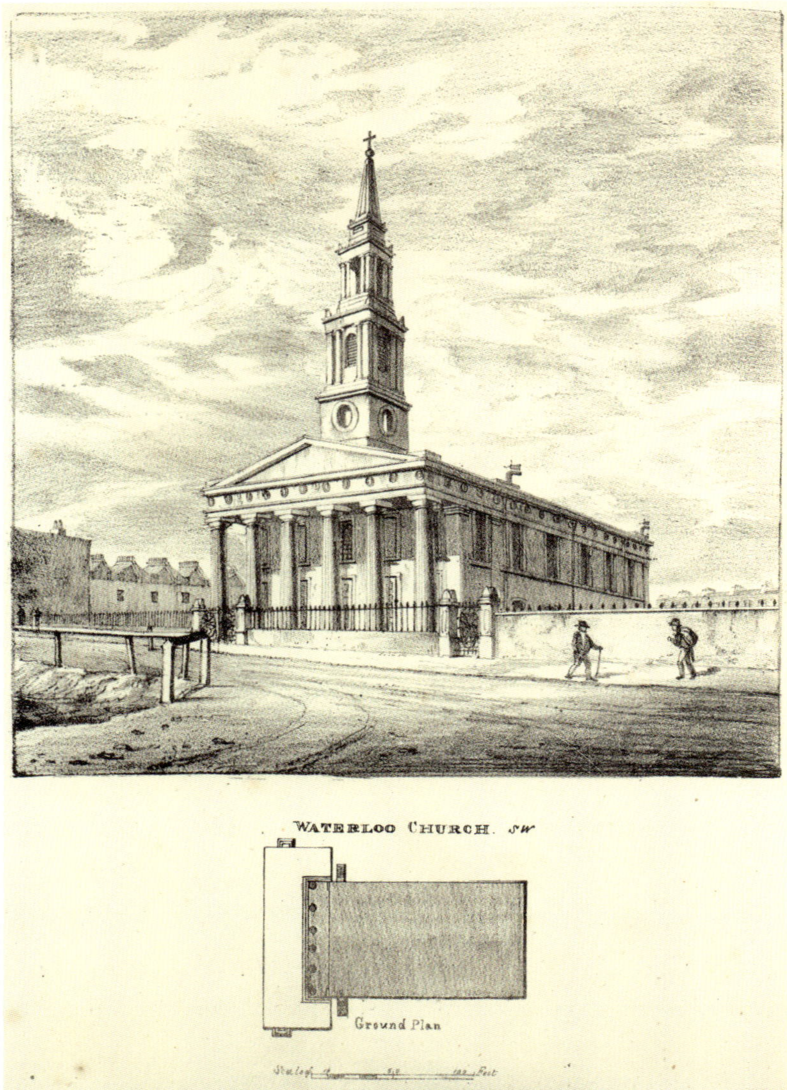

59 St John's Church, Waterloo Road, in early context, lithograph from C.T. Cracklow's *Views of the Churches and Chapels of Ease in the County of Surry*, 1827

numerous flock of geese and ducks'.[20] Here, customarily, were laid out the muddy corpses so often washed up from London River. St John's remains the one building of real merit on Waterloo Road, a welcome landmark in this marginalised neighbourhood. Its first churchwardens were prosperous timber merchants with wharves along the river. A parochial school behind offered lessons for local youth.

* * *

So far, so good, perhaps. But as exemplified by the experience of Lewis Cottingham, social progress in Waterloo proved elusive. Cottingham was an architect and designer of integrity and antiquarian bent. His personal house-museum was second only to that of John Soane, while his pioneering cathedral restorations at Hereford, Rochester and St Albans earned even the hypercritical Pugin's respect.

That this fastidious character, hitherto resident in Great Queen Street, St Giles in the Fields, should have been sucked into development at Waterloo is puzzling. Perhaps he hoped it would underwrite his other activities. At any rate, Cottingham was engaged by a wax chandler, John Field, who had taken a long lease of a block of property just below the bridgehead. The layout, started around 1826, consisted of four substantial houses facing the west side of Waterloo Road, eight round the corner in York Road, and a run of nineteen smaller cottages at the back. Though plain, the Waterloo Road terrace was discriminatingly detailed. The corner house was reserved for the York Hotel, while Cottingham kept the southernmost one for himself, over a shop (fig.60).[21]

This was the kind of housing that Waterloo needed. That Cottingham had trouble with the foundations is no surprise, given the nature of the ground. Yet 'the buildings have not cracked or given way', stated Field in a testimonial for his architect, 'but on the contrary are greatly admired both for the design and the substantial manner in which they are constructed'.[22] Less steady was the local community. At a meeting held in July 1826, Waterloo residents rued the prevalence of unruliness and criminality. St John's urgently needed high churchyard walls to protect the dead and living alike from depredation and 'gross profanation of the Sabbath'. Cottingham himself

> drew an alarming and frightful sketch of the vices of the youths of both sexes, who are found nightly in the vaults of empty houses, all huddled up together. Their occupation was robbing by day, and prostitution at night. Having no legal check on them, owing to the want of a place of confinement, they dared everything, and were the disgrace and terror of society.[23]

60 Elevation of Bazing Place, a terrace of houses designed by L.N. Cottingham, Waterloo Road, 1826. Cottingham's own house was the last on the left, behind and over a shop; at the right-hand end was the York Hotel

61 A Gothic fragment remaining in the basement of L.N. Cottingham's house at 86 Waterloo Road, recorded in 1961 not long before its destruction

The meeting called for the remedy of a watchhouse. One was promptly supplied in a corner of the churchyard, but it proved of limited use. In 1829 an unnamed local developer (possibly Cottingham again) prosecuted a thief for stealing lead from the roof of a Waterloo Road house. Hardly a night elapsed without some sort of organised attack, he claimed. He had heard burglars using a crowbar at the back door 'whilst the watchman was amusing himself with a rattle in the front'. He and his neighbours all had firearms, and on one occasion seven shots had been fired before a watchman put in a sleepy appearance. The root of the trouble was that the local magistrates had only eight of the new policemen to cover a large area of Southwark and Lambeth.[24]

It is a tribute to Cottingham that he stuck it out, augmenting his 'Museum of English Antiquities' and admitting visitors until his death in 1847. Afterwards his collections were dispersed, but built-in features of his house survived until it was destroyed when the present Waterloo Bridge roundabout was formed in the 1960s. Fortunately, they were recorded by London County Council photographers (fig.61).[25]

The disorders of the 1820s proved to be more than teething troubles, especially as regards prostitution. Reports of brothels in Waterloo piled up, while in 1839 a Commons Committee deliberating on bridge tolls heard about the 'debased and infamous state of the immediate neighbourhoods of the bridges, and the profligate scenes which nightly occur on some of them'.[26] The bitterest indictment came from Flora Tristan. This half-Peruvian, half-French radical feminist published her excoriating impressions in *Promenades dans Londres* (1840). Accompanied by 'two men armed with canes', she made an evening excursion to Waterloo Road to record the spectacle of vice.

> This district is populated almost entirely by prostitutes and people who live off prostitution. It would be extremely dangerous to walk there alone in the evening. It was a very warm evening: the women were looking out of windows or seated at their doorsteps, laughing and jesting with their pimps. They were half-dressed; several were bare to the waist. They were revolting, disgusting, and the cynical and criminal expressions on the faces of their pimps were frightening.

> The pimps were in general very good looking, young, tall and strong; but from their coarse and common look one had the impression that they were animals with no other instinct than their appetites . . .
>
> We walked about all the streets near Waterloo Road and sat down on the bridge to watch another spectacle. Around eight or nine o'clock, the Waterloo Road women pass by in groups on their way to the West End. They carry on their trade during the night and come back around eight or nine in the morning.[27]

Allowing for prudish exaggeration, Flora Tristan's picture is grim. When she visited, the railway had yet to arrive in Waterloo. Districts surrounding railway termini are notoriously blighted, but patently the blight at Waterloo was there from before.

Not everything was that bad. There were some good houses in Stamford Street, as well as some tolerable working-class streets behind Waterloo Road, like Roupell, Theed and Whittlesey Streets, where the little cottages now sell for over a million sterling.[28] A towering terrace built along the upstream side of the bridge approach had a certain hulking grandeur, with three storeys on the higher level resting on another three dropping down to the lower road beneath. But even that was a come-down, the inferior levels consisting of 'stories under stories of cellars – the lowest of which no eye may fathom, but which terminate in subterraneous regions, inhabited only by dray-horses, and lumbering wains, and burly coalheavers'.[29]

Waterloo never recovered from its bad press. When Philbrick, the shady Llanabba School butler in Evelyn Waugh's *Decline and Fall* (1928), remarked that 'You've only to say Solly Philbrick, of the "Lamb and Flag", anywhere south of Waterloo Bridge to see what fame is', savvier readers would have known just what to make of him.

* * *

One feature of the early Waterloo district remains to be accounted for: the changes along the river after the bridge was built. Industry intensified along both the upstream and downstream frontages in the 1820s and 1830s. Timber yards and wharves gave way to a diversity of uses and manufactures, upstream especially. The increased density, dirt and smoke prompted resident proprietors to decamp to the suburbs. That reduced the middle-class quotient of the local population and, with it, the solidity of institutions like St John's, Waterloo.

Most conspicuous along the riverside was James Goding's Lion Brewery of 1836–7, one of the few industrial buildings to make an architectural fist of the Thames frontage, topped off by the famous Coade stone lion (fig.16). This alone lived on when the brewery was sacrificed for the Royal Festival Hall. Today it stands in giant defiance at the end of Westminster Bridge.

The other unique structures were the shot towers. Towers for making lead balls and bullets by the curious process of dropping them in their molten state from a great height, so that they form perfect spheres as they descend and cool, were an eighteenth-century invention. They were built in quantity and survive the world over – but none alas on the South Bank, which once boasted at least three.[30]

The earlier of Lambeth's two shot towers (fig.62) was built by Watts, George & Co., a firm started to promote the 1782 patent taken

62 The two South Bank shot towers: left, the square-sided tower of 1789, downstream of Waterloo Bridge; right, the later and taller tower of 1826 upstream of the bridge

out by the Bristol plumber William Watts, usually assumed to be the origin of shot towers. It stood between 1789 and 1937 in a prominent position east of Waterloo Bridge. Square-sided and tapering, it rose to 140ft and was capped with a little pyramidal roof or dome. Samuel Ireland, writing in 1791, opined that 'it cannot be considered an object ornamental to the Thames', but later generations disagreed.[31]

The more celebrated shot tower was sited just west of the bridge. 'Ambitious as the tower of Babel',[32] it was round and tapered in plan like a brick chimney but, at about three times the diameter of the Monument, broader than any chimney, and 163ft high. The first shot tower having been damaged by fire, Thomas Maltby, an erstwhile partner in its management, seized the opportunity to devise this imposing successor, which was supposed to have cost £30,000, in 1826. Its architect was D.R. Roper or, some have said, his assistant Alfred Clayton. Eventually it was taken over by the company that had rebuilt the first tower and revived its fortunes, Walkers, Parker and Co. They continued to make lead shot here until 1949.

The second Waterloo shot tower soon eclipsed the first in fame. One newspaper joked that this 'striking and handsome' object should be dubbed the Trafalgar Column, just as the bridge had been called the Waterloo Bridge, so saving the Government the expense of building the long-delayed Trafalgar monument – but it advised the proprietor to extract better terms than the company had.[33] Clarkson Stanfield executed a dramatic drawing, engraved by George Cooke, showing the tower rearing over the southern bridge stairs with steps dropping to the water and attendant figures, as in some fabled harbour scene, but interrupted by a crazy timber structure which could only have belonged to the Thames foreshore (fig.63). Constable made the venial mistake of including this second tower in his great picture of Waterloo Bridge's inauguration, completed in 1832 (fig.49); in fact, it did not yet exist when the opening took place. Together the downstream and upstream shot towers stood sentinel on either southern flank of the bridge – the industrial equivalent of classical pylons.

There were at least two blithe Victorian essays about the later shot tower and its workings, one in *Household Words* by the Dickens

63 Shot tower and staircase to Waterloo Bridge, a romantic view by Clarkson Stanfield etched by George Cooke, 1832 version

disciple John Hollingshead, the other, anonymous but illustrated with sketches, in the *Strand Magazine*.[34] Both journalists climbed the 327 steps and marvelled at the sheet-stream of lead careering precipitately into a great pot at the base. The tower evoked the sublime. Hollingshead wrote:

64 The western shot tower next to the Royal Festival Hall at the time of the Festival of Britain, 1951, surmounted by a gun carriage and radio antenna. The Dome of Discovery is to the right

> If ever I am to be sent suddenly into the lap of eternity, let it be with my body nicely beplumbed with the smooth, round glossy shot that I have seen manufactured at Lambeth.

Famously, the second tower survived the first Waterloo Bridge and the post-war clearances all around. Gerald Barry witnessed its last days of operation while planning the Festival of Britain. At that stage the idea was to give it 'a hefty whack with a wrecking ball'.[35] Instead it was honourably incorporated into the festival, its top surmounted by a lighthouse-type beam and a large radio antenna borne on an anti-aircraft gun carriage (fig.64). Alas for posterity, this homage to British industry, old and new, vanished when the shot tower was demolished for the Queen Elizabeth Hall. In the brighter Britain of the 1960s, all symbols of South Bank manufacture had to be expunged.

7

Enter the Railways

After Waterloo Bridge came London Bridge (1824–31), rebuilt by the younger Rennies to their father's design and likewise constructed by Jolliffe and Banks. New London Bridge (figs 65–7) was almost as heroic an enterprise as Waterloo Bridge, and even more in the forefront of public attention. Because it had official backing from the City Corporation, it enjoyed secure funding and proved more stable and enduring.

It was also the last traditional masonry road bridge to span London River. By the time of its completion, Hammersmith Bridge had been opened (1827). There followed Hungerford Bridge (1845), Chelsea Bridge (1858), Lambeth Bridge (1862) and Albert Bridge (1873).[1] All these were suspension bridges (in the last case, of hybrid type). They were of light construction, relatively cheap and had the great merit of dipping only two legs in the water in place of the multiple piers of long masonry bridges. At the same time, suspension bridges were fragile and vulnerable to heavy moving loads. The French built none for a century after the Pont de la Basse-Chaîne at Angers collapsed in 1850, plunging 226 soldiers to their death. Only after the Roeblings completed Brooklyn Bridge did Europeans regain confidence that a suspension bridge could last and even carry railways.

The short-lived Hungerford Bridge (fig.68) is the one most pertinent to the Waterloo Bridge story. This Cinderella project of that great engineer, Isambard Kingdom Brunel, though sound from the structural standpoint, lasted a bare fifteen years. It was then destroyed in favour of a harsh iron bridge, after railways smashed across and cut up the whole face of London River.

By a short margin, the plans for Hungerford Bridge preceded the railway's transformation of the Waterloo district. The curious idea of a

65 New London Bridge nearing completion beside the old bridge: a famous view by E.W. Cooke, 1830. The view looks over to the South Bank, with the Tooley Street shot tower next to St Olaf's, and St Mary Overie, later Southwark Cathedral, both visible on the skyline

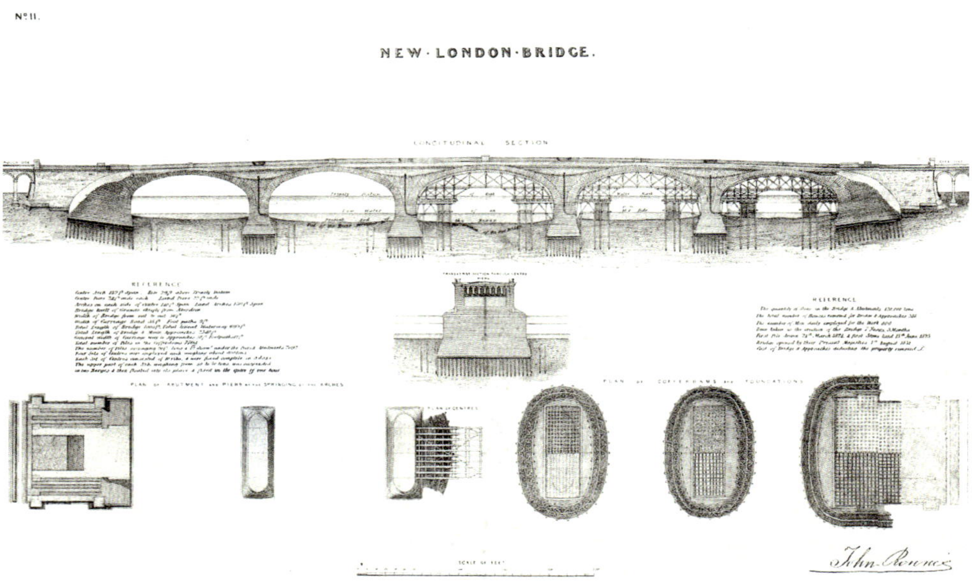

66 Plans and sections of the Rennies' New London Bridge, lithographed by Robert Martin, *c.*1830

67 Northernmost arch of London Bridge, *c.*1895, looking through to the Pool of London and the new and open Tower Bridge behind. A patriotic demonstration seems to be taking place on the bridge

suspension footbridge to link Belvedere Road on the South Bank with the Hungerford Market near Charing Cross seems to have emanated around 1836 from the head of William Hawes. The entrepreneurial Hawes brothers had inherited a large South Bank soap-boiling firm, with a riverside plant just downstream of the Lambeth–Southwark boundary, though the main factory had relocated to New Cross. William's brother Benjamin had married one of Marc Isambard Brunel's daughters, so was Isambard Kingdom Brunel's brother-in-law. Benjamin Hawes ('Mr Soap-Boiler') was an outspoken Radical MP and during the 1850s a Government minister in the War Department: hence Brunel's celebrated plans for a prefabricated hospital during the Crimean War. William Hawes was a businessman with a lively mix of cultural and social interests. The brothers were among the younger Brunel's closest friends.

68 Hungerford Bridge looking towards the South Bank, as depicted in *The Builder*, 12 April 1845

It is usually said that the Hungerford Footbridge was built to rescue the ailing Hungerford Market from insolvency. That was certainly among its aims. The two-level market, created in 1682 on sloping ground beneath the Strand on the site of the Hungerford family's former mansion, had never done well. A new company bought it in 1830 and reconstructed it to clever designs by Charles Fowler, architect of the rival Covent Garden Market, but failed to turn around its fortunes. Connecting the rebuilt market with the South Bank might boost its attractions, or so it was hoped.

But there was more to it than that. For a cost estimated by its promoters at a fraction of the fabulous sums spent on Waterloo Bridge, pedestrian access could be gained to the growing population and industry of Lambeth, and vice versa. No land need be bought on the north side because the high-level bridge would lead straight into the market, while on the south side passengers would just walk up or down a stair close to Belvedere Road. If a tenth of the pedestrians who used Westminster Bridge were to transfer their patronage to the new footbridge, free from the 'annoyance and danger' of horse traffic, a penny toll would collect £7,000 per year. Another lure was the potential steamboat traffic from

Hungerford Pier. This was the business of the London and Westminster Steam-Boat Company, another venture floated by the Hawes brothers. Its vessels were to tie up against the northern pier of the new bridge, accessed by a short pedestrian ramp from the Embankment (fig.69).[2] In 1838 William Hawes and Brunel revised the bridge design, costed now at just over £100,000. Meanwhile, Benjamin pushed through a parliamentary Bill exempting the steamboat company from various restrictions in the Watermen's Acts.[3]

Hungerford Bridge finally went ahead from 1841. Why then? Probably because of the advent of the railway. In the same year as the design was revised, the London and Southampton (soon to be the London and South Western) Railway opened its first leg from Woking up to Nine Elms, just upstream of Vauxhall Bridge. The location had once interested Brunel, wearing his hat as engineer to the Great Western Railway. But as a passenger terminus Nine Elms proved too remote from town. An inward extension of the London and South Western Railway (LSWR) was promptly sought, but only sanctioned in 1844, when Hungerford Bridge was nearing completion. As it took shape in 1846–8, it consisted of a high-level, four-track line on arches, above the marshy South Bank terrain. It ran parallel to the river from Vauxhall and terminated at the first Waterloo Station, built to William Tite's designs just south of York Road.

It may seem odd that the footbridge should have gone ahead just as a railway was being planned to terminate next to its southern foot. Why not take the line on across the river? That was certainly contemplated when Hungerford Bridge opened.[4] Then came the Royal Commission on Metropolitan Railway Termini, set up by Parliament in 1846 during the first 'railway mania'. The Commission's report robustly defended Central London against further encroachment, arguing that passengers had no need of new termini any closer in than Paddington, Euston and King's Cross. But for the South Bank the report was potentially devastating. Land was cheaper there, house property worse and traffic less. The Commissioners suggested developing big termini at London Bridge and Waterloo with linking lines. As the LSWR was already building its extension to Waterloo, it might as well take it on to London Bridge.[5]

69 A steamboat at Hungerford Bridge pier, with Waterloo Bridge and the shot towers behind. Anonymous painting of *c.*1850

How travellers were to get across from the new southern termini to Central London the Commissioners did not address. They wanted no railway bridges across the Thames into the centre, though they did contemplate a circular line linking the different termini with a bridge somewhere west of Vauxhall. Their report had no statutory force and enjoyed only a decade or so of respect. But it probably prevented any Thames railway crossing from being planned at that juncture. There was another consideration. The technology, the confidence and the investment to build a long and heavy railway bridge over the tidal Thames were not yet in place. Only after Robert Stephenson had built his major rails-over-rivers bridges of the late 1840s did the idea gain traction.

All the same, to the Hungerford and Lambeth Suspension Foot-Bridge Company, the prospect of the railway's advent at Waterloo was naturally 'a matter of great importance'. William Hawes and other proprietors of South Bank wharves and works – notably big builders like Thomas Grissell and William Chadwick, the new bridge's main contractor – lobbied to influence the final course of the line and the station site. They hoped to improve the poor connection between the proposed terminus and the southern steps to the bridge. But they did not want the railway carried across the river, said Grissell, as that would bring no benefit to Lambeth people.[6]

Hungerford Bridge was completed in early May 1845, only a year later than predicted. P.P. Baly was the overcommitted Brunel's site engineer. This neglected figure, best-known for promoting and planning London's first public baths and washhouses, spent the last third of his career designing railway and other infrastructural works in Russia. The bridge was a technical success. Remarkably, the tall square piers were not piled at all but consisted of four deep corner stacks of brickwork each, set in cement and connected with inverted arches. They separated spans of 333ft, 670ft 6in (the widest yet in any bridge) and 333ft again. The pathway, only 14ft wide, was stiffened with trusses to mitigate the wind sway that bedevilled early suspension bridges. It cambered upwards by 9ft 6in from the ends to the centre, where its topmost point was 32ft above high water. The great bar chains, supplied by the Cornish firm of Sandys, Carne and Vivian – well known to Brunel – were anchored at

70 The first Waterloo Station, *Illustrated London News*, 1 July 1848

the abutments in tunnels with huge iron girders embedded in brickwork and strengthened with concrete.[7] Famously, these chains were taken down at the end of the bridge's brief life and transferred to the Clifton Suspension Bridge, then languishing unfinished. No scaffolding was used, nor were major accidents reported. Here was a modern way to span London River.

Criticism of the bridge's appearance can be confined to the piers. Brunel was not against enriching the piers of suspension bridges, having designed fancy ones of his own for Clifton. His sketchbooks show him toying with alternatives for Hungerford Bridge, including a version of the great Venice campanile that might have been fun.[8] In the event he plumped for Italianate towers with picturesque pyramidal cappings. Consumed as he was by railway work, Brunel handed over their working-out to the architect J.B. Bunning. They were charming anomalies on London River.

As for the first Waterloo Station, when it opened in 1848 it was just a temporary affair, planned for possible extension eastwards towards London Bridge (fig.70). It replaced 'haystalls and cowyards, dungheaps etc.' between Waterloo and York Roads. Like the present station, it was raised above ground level in response to the high level of the tracks, and reached by a ramp from Waterloo Road.[9] The alighting traveller wishing to cross the river could either descend the ramp and take Waterloo Bridge, or drop down on the other side, muddle through some side streets, cross York and Belvedere Roads and climb more stairs again up to Hungerford Bridge. The curse of levels must have made all this something of a mess. Whichever route was taken, a halfpenny bridge toll had to be paid.

A complicating factor now loomed. In 1846 the South Eastern Railway (SER) announced that it too intended to bring its lines across from London Bridge and points southwards to Waterloo, where it would build 'one great west-end terminus, which will open on the Waterloo-road and will be in immediate communication with both Waterloo and Hungerford bridges'.[10] That ought to have entailed a whole-hearted link with the LSWR and the replanning of Waterloo as a single joint station, as the Commissioners' report had suggested. But in private-enterprise Victorian Britain, such co-operation was too much to hope for. Instead, the South Eastern foresaw some sort of separate station of its own. Hence the absurdity, perpetuated down to the present day, whereby Waterloo acquired two separate high-level stations, Waterloo proper and Waterloo East, divided by the chasm of Waterloo Road.

The SER's idea stalled for a decade, as overstretched railway promoters retrenched. Its appetite returned with a vengeance in 1858 when, after a strong parliamentary hint about overcrowding at their London Bridge Station, the SER determined to cross the river not once but twice, and to build termini both at Charing Cross for the West End and at Cannon Street for the City. The impetus to bust the recommendations of the 1846 Royal Commission came in large measure from the company's secretary. This was none other than Samuel Smiles, who was keen to galvanise the SER in face of competition. The workaholic Smiles was just then gearing up his leisure hours for his path-breaking *Lives of the Engineers*, published in 1861–2. Aspects of the scheme, which was assigned to a technically separate company, echo his relentless prose style.[11] Nor was the SER alone. The London and Brighton and the London, Chatham and Dover railway companies barged across the river at the same time, with bridges leading to new stations at Blackfriars and Victoria. Upstream at Battersea too came a new railway bridge for the West London Extension Company. By the mid 1860s the whole metropolitan Thames landscape had been transformed – or degraded.

Scenically, the most obstructive of these bridges came at Blackfriars and Charing Cross. At Blackfriars, the blocked river prospect suffered further damage when a second railway crossing barged across in the

1880s. But Charing Cross Railway Bridge, at the climax of the noble river bend, was almost more grievously positioned.[12] After toying with Northumberland House as a site for its new terminus, the SER battened upon the hapless Hungerford Market. That spelt destruction for Brunel's Hungerford Bridge which, it was now claimed, had been neither popular nor, in Smiles's canting phrase, 'a paying property'.[13] Worse, it administered the coup de grâce to the 'sight so matching in its majesty' evoked by Wordsworth, as he gazed awestruck downstream from Westminster Bridge.

The SER's engineer for both Charing Cross and Cannon Street Railway Bridges was Sir John Hawkshaw, while the resident engineer at Charing Cross was the young John Wolfe-Barry, later the eminent designer of Tower Bridge (fig.71). Hawkshaw was highly competent, but no aesthete – indeed aesthetics seldom came to the fore in girder railway bridges of that era. Both here and at Cannon Street, elephantine iron cylinders packed with brickwork and concrete ploughed down through the water and deep into the riverbed, interspersed among the reused brick piers from Brunel's footbridge. These at any rate ensured

71 Workmen and engineers completing Charing Cross Station. The top-hatted figure with a beard may be the young John Wolfe-Barry. Photograph by James Bulbeck, probably of 1863

72 Cannon Street Bridge and Station, photograph by Frederick York, probably of the 1860s

the stability against tide and scour which had eluded the old Thames road bridges. The Cannon Street piers (fig.72) enjoyed the enrichment of large-scale fluting, but here too they gave the bridge 'a curious air of standing in the water up to its knees'.[14]

Both bridges led into coarse, round-arched station sheds that loomed over the river like 'Brobdignag poke-bonnets', as one journalist phrased it.[15] These artless sheds have both since been destroyed by modern office developments over the tracks. The Cannon Street replacement has little merit; Embankment Place, the Terry Farrell development over Charing Cross Station, is overbearing but at least attempts to engage with the riverscape.

At Charing Cross Bridge (fig.73), Hawkshaw's ingenious lattice of truss-work enclosing the tracks compounded the indelicacy of the piers. To be fair, the impenetrability of view was not so pronounced at the outset, but it became disastrous as the bridge kept growing in girth (fig.74). The two-track railway first planned quickly gave way as built to four tracks, making the initial crossing 'the widest railway bridge in the world'.[16] It became wider still when further tracks were squeezed along its upstream side in 1882–8. Furthermore, the legislation which sanctioned the cross-river line and Charing Cross terminus in place of

73 Charing Cross Bridge shortly after its completion, looking downstream towards Waterloo Bridge, photograph by James Bulbeck

74 Charing Cross Bridge experienced as a barrier, looking upstream from the South Bank in 1973, before the footbridges were replaced

the Hungerford Bridge and Market included a stipulation that narrow footways (on which a toll was still at first payable) had to be replicated along both sides of the bridge. That added to its girth, making an unprecedented total breadth of 125ft, about three times that of Waterloo Bridge. In 2000–2002 the two footbridges were rebuilt, widened and enlivened with masts. They do little to offset the unsightly and grinding affront still presented by this bridge.

Charing Cross Bridge has generally been hated.[17] William Tite, the experienced railway architect and designer of the first Waterloo Station, abandoned his usual discretion while president of the RIBA in 1862 to inveigh against the new metropolitan railway bridges. At Blackfriars, where the outcry was particularly loud, Tite thought the company had chosen 'the very worst design of the lot', while he condemned Charing Cross Bridge as lacking in sensibility, and altogether 'very ugly'.[18] The Swiss historian Jacob Burckhardt, on a visit to London, called it 'an enormous act of desecration'.[19] Émile Zola likewise labelled it 'hideous' and 'aggravating': 'up stream the view is spoilt'.[20] Its unwelcome intrusiveness became an incentive to a later generation of architects and planners to get it removed altogether, as will be seen.

Why were Charing Cross Bridge and Station built in the first place? Smiles and the SER's general manager, C.W. Eborall, sold it to the authorities as a means of alleviating London's traffic problems. London Bridge Station and consequently the bridge itself were perpetually crowded, as was the road route through the City to the West End. The Cannon Street and Charing Cross branches were expected to relieve the pressure. Smiles claimed that the new terminus and line achieved this: 'a great advantage was thus conferred upon the public'.[21] Charing Cross Station was certainly handy for those unwilling to spend the time and the toll crossing via Waterloo Bridge. Like some more recent railway projects, it most helped people in a hurry. In support of the scheme, Whitehall officials argued that a Charing Cross terminus would be 'a great boon for sending urgent dispatches'.[22]

Across the river, a sequence of fifteen iron bridges slashed the new line between London Bridge and Charing Cross across existing roads, presaging the wider defacement and blight that South London was to suffer from overhead railways.[23] But when the line opened in January

1864, there was as yet no second station at Waterloo, let alone the grand terminus once promised. Waterloo Junction Station, as Waterloo East was first called, only opened five years later. A single-line connection by bridge across Waterloo Road linked up with the LSWR's Waterloo Station, but was little used. This Waterloo Link, as railway enthusiasts call it, was dismantled when the main Waterloo Station was rebuilt in the early twentieth century.[24] The bridge is still there, another barrier across Waterloo Road just below the viaduct-bridge of the Charing Cross line. It now serves foot passengers making the awkward transition between the two stations – which are, inevitably, on different levels.

It remains to ask what effect the railway's arrival made upon Waterloo Bridge's fortunes. Just as the opening of the original Nine Elms Terminus boosted the income received from tolls over Vauxhall Bridge, so the LSWR's extension to Waterloo in 1848 caused a drop in takings at Vauxhall and a rise in revenues at Waterloo Bridge.[25] But the increase was not great. Pressure from a Metropolitan Anti-Bridge Toll Association had already forced the bridge company to reduce tolls in 1841–2, while the creation of the Hungerford Bridge and its successor offered foot passengers an alternative route to and from Waterloo Station.

The Waterloo Bridge Company's revenues held up during the 1850s and 1860s due to a general intensification of London's traffic, not least between the main-line stations. In 1864 the company's chairman confirmed that two-thirds of the traffic crossing the bridge had to do with Waterloo Station.[26] Penny horse-buses were also becoming numerous, but the company had no power to exact extra income from them beyond the normal vehicle tariffs.[27] There was no thought as yet of putting tram lines across the bridge: that proposal lay in the future. But overshadowing the morale of the company throughout this period were persistent rumours that Waterloo Bridge, along with London's other toll bridges, would imminently be taken over and made free for the public. Who would pay for that, and would the company get a fair price when the day came?

8

Bridge of Sighs

> *Poor unfortunate Ellen Fearen is now no more. Her body now lyes in the river Thames, which has put an end to all her troubles. God forgive her! Peace to all.*

This message was found in one of the seat-recesses of Waterloo Bridge one night in August 1843. The tide was 'running very strong at the time', so that Ellen was probably carried far downstream; her body seems not to have been recovered. Nobody saw her jump, but before so doing she had been 'observed to be in grief'. Another young woman, the same issue of the *Illustrated London News* reported, had 'precipitated herself from Lambeth Palace Stairs' into the river and drowned, eluding a man who tried to save her.[1] Another newspaper claimed that three attempts at suicide by women had been frustrated at Waterloo Bridge that week.[2]

In October 1822 a 'very fine looking person', identified from pawnbrokers' tickets just as 'Wilson', flung herself into the water from the northern steps of Waterloo Bridge. Her body, found by a waterman floating near a coal wharf, was washed and conveyed to the Church of the Savoy. At the inquest her predicament emerged. A naval officer who had been keeping her severely cut her allowance when he decided to marry, deputing a shopkeeper to dole out the money. This she had supplemented by taking in washing, 'preferring hard labour to prostitution'. Overwhelmed by debt, she bade a tearful farewell to the shopkeeper and walked straight to her death in the river, leaving her bonnet, muff, silk handkerchief and gold pin upon the steps, to be taken in by the toll-keeper.[3]

Just one more in what could be an endless litany of pathetic cases. In 1846 the body of an unusually large woman was found in the water off

75 The original Bridge of Sighs, Venice, depicted in an engraving by Edward Finden after J.M.W. Turner for *The Life and Works of Lord Byron*, 1833. Turner's original drawing is lost

Red House, Battersea. Papers identified her as Mme de Letzi, alias the Swiss Giantess, real name Eliza Laurence, aged 51. She had been taken round in a caravan and exhibited for her exceptional girth and height. No longer in demand, she fell into 'dissipated habits' and begging. Poor and hungry, she told people she would go to Waterloo Bridge 'and had a great mind to stop there and make a hole in the water' – a common euphemism for drowning oneself. She had certainly been seen on the bridge. But that it was her point of escape from desperation could not be proved.[4]

No surprise, then, that Waterloo Bridge became infamous as the Bridge of Sighs. The phrase, now familiar, was not old. It was coined by Byron in the closing stanzas of *Childe Harold*, published in 1818, the year after the bridge opened.

I stood in Venice, on the Bridge of Sighs,
A palace and a prison on each hand:
I saw from out the wave her structures rise
As from the stroke of the enchanter's wand . . .

The pretty footbridge, built high over a little canal around 1600 to link the Ducal Palace with the Prison (fig.75), had not been called by the name before. The invention must have pleased Byron, because he repeated it in his *Marino Faliero* (1821). By then it had already caught on, and soon went international. 'Ponte dei Sospiri' was taken up by the Venetians. It even became the title of an Offenbach operetta, *Le pont des soupirs*. Nowadays the name is applied to any picturesque footbridge (preferably one lifted up over navigable water) under which lovers may kiss. The dark side of the coinage has disappeared.

The first traceable uses of 'bridge of sighs' beyond Venice were not to do with suicide. A flippant newspaper item of 1828 suggested the name might apply to Waterloo Bridge because of its cost ('I think the shareholders would nod assent'), or because of the '*sighs* as well as shouts' once uttered upon the battlefield commemorated.[5] Gradually the phrase's range extended. It was used to refer to Westminster Bridge on the day that New London Bridge was opened because it was so deserted; to Old London Bridge when it was doomed to destruction; even to a little wooden bridge where riders in a hunt came to grief.[6]

Then the tone changed. The crucial text, from *Bentley's Miscellany* for 1839, is worth giving in full:

> WATERLOO--BRIDGE. Sailing onwards from the Temple, we arrive at that magnificent structure which spans the bosom of the Thames at its widest breadth within metropolitan limits, and is named in honour of the great battle which at last gave peace to Europe. Around its arches clings half the romance of modern London. It is the English "Bridge of Sighs," the "Pons Asinorum," the "Lover's Leap," the "Arch of Suicide." Well does it deserve all these appellations. Many a sad and true tale might be told, the beginning and end of which would be "Waterloo-bridge." It is a favourite spot for love assignations; and a still more favourite spot

> for the worn and weary, who long to cast off the load of existence, and cannot wait, through sorrow, until the ALMIGHTY GIVER takes away his gift. Its comparative loneliness renders it convenient for both purposes. The penny toll keeps off the inquisitive and unmannerly crowd; and the foolish can love or the mad can die with less observation from the passers than they could find anywhere else so close to the heart of London. To many a poor girl the assignation over one arch of Waterloo-bridge is but the prelude to the fatal leap from another. Here they begin, and here they end after a long course of intermediate crime and sorrow, the unhappy story of their loves. Here also, wary and practised courtezans lie in wait for the *Asini*, so abundant in London, and justify its cognomen of the *Pons Asinorum*. Here fools become entrapped, and wise men, too, sometimes, the one losing his money, the other self-respect. But, with all its vice, Waterloo-bridge is pre-eminently the "Bridge of Sorrow." There is less of the ludicrous to be seen from its smooth highway than from any in the metropolis. The people of London continually hear of unhappy men and women who throw themselves from its arches, and as often of the finding of bodies in the water, which may have laid there for weeks, no one knowing how or when they came there – no one being able to distinguish their lineaments. But often as these things are heard of, few are aware of the real number of victims that choose this spot to close an unhappy career – few know that, taking one year with another, the average number of suicides committed from this place is above thirty.[7]

Charles Mackay, author of this piece, was a journalist in the Dickens circle, best known for his *Memoirs of Extraordinary Popular Delusions and the Madness of Crowds* (1841). He went on to publish a sonnet about Waterloo Bridge suicides in 1844, so his interest in the phenomenon was more than fleeting.[8]

Dickens himself had been the editor of *Bentley's Miscellany* until just before Mackay's piece appeared. He may even have inspired it, for he had a lifelong obsession with death and the Thames. It first surfaces in 'A Drunkard's Death'. This piece originally gave the dark concluding touch to *Sketches by Boz* (1836), otherwise so affirmative about London street-life. The miscreant sot resolves to make away with himself and so directs himself to the stairs of Waterloo Bridge.

> The stream stole languidly and sluggishly on. Strange and fantastic forms rose to the surface, and beckoned him to approach; dark gleaming eyes peered from the water, and seemed to mock his hesitation, while hollow murmurs from behind urged him onwards. He retreated a few paces, took a short run, desperate leap, and plunged into the water.

All his life, Dickens's mind was possessed by the lure of the Thames, from the bleak finality of this early story to the terror of the estuary marshes in *Great Expectations*. Even cheery Sam Weller, before he meets Mr Pickwick, has endured a fortnight's 'unfurnished lodgin's' under the dry arches of Waterloo Bridge, amid the 'worn-out, starving, houseless creeturs as roll themselves in the dark corners o' them lonesome places'. *The Chimes*, *David Copperfield* and *Bleak House* all feature pursuits to save lost women from casting themselves into 'the dreadful river'. In *Bleak House* Esther Summerson and Inspector Bucket search frantically for Lady Dedlock up and down the night-time waterfront. They pass a 'Found Drowned' notice and end their fruitless search on a bridge which can only be Waterloo:

> In my memory, the lights upon the bridge are always burning dim; the cutting wind is eddying round the homeless woman whom we pass; the monotonous wheels are whirling on; and the light of the carriage-lamps reflected back, looks palely in upon me – a face rising out of the dreaded water.

Dickens's last completed novel, *Our Mutual Friend*, might well have had some watery title like *Ebb and Flow*. It starts out with a solitary boatman who seeks and reclaims bodies anywhere between Southwark Bridge and Limehouse (fig.76). Gaffer Hexam makes a living from this ghoulish pursuit by selling clothes and possessions from the corpses, or by claiming the reward for finding a missing person. At the other

76 'The Bird of Prey', Lizzie and Gaffer Hexam searching for bodies in the Thames, illustration by Marcus Stone for Dickens's *Our Mutual Friend*, 1864–5

end of the book, we are spirited upstream to a spot where the water flows tranquilly beyond the reach of the tides and detritus of London, and Hexam's daughter, Lizzie, has found a new life working in a rural paper mill. But here too there is horror, for in the culminating scene two accursed wretches, Bradley Headstone and Rogue Riderhood, tumble fighting into a lock and are discovered bound dead together 'under the ooze and scum behind one of the rotting gates'.

There was journalism too. 'Down with the Tide', in *Household Words* for 1853, develops into a dialogue between Dickens and 'Waterloo' in which the bridge is callously personified:

> 'If people jump off straight forards from the middle of the parapet of the bays of the bridge, they are seldom killed by drowning, but are smashed, poor things; that's what *they* are; they dash themselves upon the buttress of the bridge. But,' said Waterloo to me, putting his finger in a buttonhole of my great coat; 'you jump off from the side of the bay, and you'll tumble, true, under the stream of the

> arch.' . . . I asked Waterloo if there were a favourite side of his bridge for this dreadful purpose? He reflected, and thought yes, there was. He should say the Surrey side.[9]

Likewise 'Night Walks', an insomniac's ramble of 1860, directs Dickens back unerringly to Waterloo Bridge, where he pays the toll for

> a halfpenny worth of excuse for saying 'Good-night' to the toll-keeper, and catching a glimpse of his fire. A good fire and a good great-coat and a good woollen neck-shawl, were comfortable things to see in conjunction with the toll-keeper; also his brisk wakefulness was excellent company when he rattled the change of halfpence down upon that metal table of his, like a man who defied the night, with all its sorrowful thoughts, and didn't care for the coming of dawn. There was need of encouragement on the threshold of the bridge, for the bridge was dreary . . . the river had an awful look, the buildings on the banks were muffled in black shrouds, and the reflected lights seemed to originate deep in the water, as if the spectres of suicides were holding them to show where they went down. The wild moon and clouds were as restless as an evil conscience in a tumbled bed, and the very shadow of the immensity of London seemed to lie oppressively upon the river.[10]

Neither Dickens nor Mackay did the most for sensationalising the suicides of Waterloo Bridge. That was reserved for Thomas Hood. Towards the end of his sickly life, Hood turned from satire and comedy towards the lives of the distressed and dispossessed. 'The Song of the Shirt' addressed the misery of seamstresses; 'The Workhouse Clock' the rigour of the Poor Laws; 'The Lay of the Labourer' the grimness of agricultural toil; and 'The Bridge of Sighs' ('the purest poem of these public verses') suicide by drowning. This last appeared in 1844. The case which had drawn Hood's notice was in fact a canal suicide, as common as a Thames drowning, and nor was the victim a deserted young woman, but that hardly mattered.[11] The famous poem must be given in full. Its haunting rhythm, its simplicity and its moral-religious ending added to its immense popularity.

One more Unfortunate,
   Weary of breath,
Rashly importunate,
   Gone to her death!

Take her up tenderly,
   Lift her with care;
Fashion'd so slenderly
   Young, and so fair!

Look at her garments
Clinging like cerements;
Whilst the wave constantly
   Drips from her clothing;
Take her up instantly,
   Loving, not loathing.

Touch her not scornfully;
Think of her mournfully,
   Gently and humanly;
Not of the stains of her,
All that remains of her
   Now is pure womanly.

Make no deep scrutiny
Into her mutiny
   Rash and undutiful:
Past all dishonour,
Death has left on her
   Only the beautiful.

Still, for all slips of hers,
   One of Eve's family –
Wipe those poor lips of hers
   Oozing so clammily.

Loop up her tresses
   Escaped from the comb,
Her fair auburn tresses;
Whilst wonderment guesses
   Where was her home?

Who was her father?
   Who was her mother?
Had she a sister?
   Had she a brother?
Or was there a dearer one
Still, and a nearer one
   Yet, than all other?

Alas! for the rarity
Of Christian charity
   Under the sun!
O, it was pitiful!
Near a whole city full,
   Home she had none.

Sisterly, brotherly,
Fatherly, motherly
   Feelings had changed:
Love, by harsh evidence,
Thrown from its eminence;
Even God's providence
   Seeming estranged.

Where the lamps quiver
So far in the river,
   With many a light
From window and casement,
From garret to basement,
She stood, with amazement,
   Houseless by night.

The bleak wind of March
   Made her tremble and shiver;
But not the dark arch,
Or the black flowing river:
Mad from life's history,

Glad to death's mystery,
Swift to be hurl'd –
Anywhere, anywhere
Out of the world!

In she plunged boldly –
No matter how coldly
The rough river ran –
Over the brink of it,
Picture it – think of it,
Dissolute Man!
Lave in it, drink of it,
Then, if you can!

Take her up tenderly,
Lift her with care;
Fashion'd so slenderly,
Young, and so fair!

Ere her limbs frigidly
Stiffen too rigidly,
Decently, kindly,
Smooth and compose them;
And her eyes, close them,
Staring so blindly!

Dreadfully staring
Thro' muddy impurity,
As when with the daring
Last look of despairing
Fix'd on futurity.

Perishing gloomily,
Spurr'd by contumely,
Cold inhumanity,
Burning insanity,
Into her rest. –
Cross her hands humbly
As if praying dumbly,
Over her breast!

Owning her weakness,
Her evil behaviour,
And leaving, with meekness,
Her sins to her Saviour!

Where writing led, pictures followed. Meg from *The Chimes*, the first of Dickens's forlorn women to be rescued on the river brink, had been sentimentally illustrated (by Dicky Doyle) in 1844 (fig.77). George Cruikshank ramped up the agony in *The Drunkard's Children*, one of two series of etchings about the perils of drink which he published in 1848, accompanied with poems by none other than Charles Mackay. The last plate, coarsely effective, shows the drunkard's daughter in precipitate fall, outlined by a bridge arch (fig.78).

G.F. Watts, as emotional as any painter in an age suffused with emotionalism in art, now took the lead. He was much taken by Hood's social poems, depicting *The Song of the Shirt*. But his responses to *The Bridge of Sighs* are more powerful. Both his chosen scenes are set below a bridge. *Under a Dry Arch*, of 1849–50, shows an anguished woman shivering against unrelenting stonework, with St Paul's in the

77 Meg and her baby at the river's brink, illustration by Richard Doyle for Charles Dickens's *The Chimes*, 1844

78 Final plate to George Cruikshank and Charles Mackay's *The Drunkard's Children*, 1848

79 G.F. Watts, *Found Drowned*

background. *Found Drowned*, its more familiar pendant, features the sacrificial body of a young girl, implausibly clean, unblemished and richly dressed, indeed morbidly seductive. In the final version, dating from 1867, a shot tower and Hungerford Bridge loom in the murky backdrop, framed by an arch which can only belong to Waterloo Bridge (fig.79).

Nothing in *Found Drowned* intimates that the woman is a prostitute. But amid the many ambiguities in Rossetti's *Found* (1854) there can be no ambiguity about that. When he painted the picture (fig.80), Rossetti was living with Lizzie Siddal on the north side of Blackfriars Bridge, so it was naturally Lizzie who modelled for the woman. This is not a modern London scene; the bridge and river are generic, the costumes half-mediaeval. Rossetti stated that his theme was 'the rescue of the fallen', just as in the Dickens novels. But he himself seems to have been undecided what that meant. The tethered calf in the cart hints that suicide may not be the worst of fates. He came back repeatedly to the theme of *Found*, even composing a late sonnet which he thought of appending to the painting's frame, suggesting that the man and woman had previously been lovers.

When Hood's best poems were republished with illustrations in 1858, John Everett Millais was chosen to etch *The Bridge of Sighs*. In his simple composition, a young woman stands staring at the river's brink, while the gaslights on Waterloo Bridge glow and reflect in the placid water. Some commentators like to think that the woman's ample cloak conceals a baby. It is at any rate another token of the Pre-Raphaelite fascination with the theme.

80 Dante Gabriel Rossetti, *Found*, 1854

81 J.R. Spencer Stanhope, *Thoughts of the Past*, 1859. Waterloo Bridge can be seen through the window

A latecomer to the series is Spencer Stanhope's *Thoughts of the Past* (1859). Stanhope, who had studied with Watts, was obsessed, like his fellow artists, with the theme of prostitution at a social level high enough to be set off by beautiful accoutrements and clothes (fig.81). To paint this Thames-side scene, he rented a studio near Blackfriars Bridge below Rossetti's, whose *Found* he must have known. A conventional 'modern' Pre-Raphaelite picture, rigid in arrangement, it tells the usual story of desertion. The unhappy girl, *en deshabille*, is in a reverie. She has been brushing her long red tresses and probably crying. Through the open window behind her we see the traffic of London River with Waterloo Bridge in the distance, beckoning.[12]

* * *

It is time to take distance from these works of imagination and establish some facts. First, only a small proportion of the dead picked up by Gaffer Hexam would have been suicides. The Thames in London was, as it remains, a very dangerous river. In the days before high embankments, when access to the water was easy and the port crowded and chaotic, mishaps, collisions and other accidents yielded a high annual toll of fatalities. Boys in particular loved to lark about on boats and floating timbers, to leap or swim riskily between them. Often they ended up crushed or drowned. Lightermen and watermen died too. Such cases were regularly reported, but with little feeling. Frequently, bodies were dumped surreptitiously in the river – murder victims sometimes no doubt, more often inconveniences or embarrassments whose funerals might otherwise have had to be paid for.[13]

Nor was Waterloo Bridge the only preferred bridge for suicides. A low bridge on the Regent's Canal near the Zoo was another favourite. So too was access-free Blackfriars Bridge; it earned notoriety in 1841, when a magistrate, told by the police that attempts were made there every night, tried to deter the practice with hard sentences for the survivors.[14] Years before, Pierre-Jean Grosley's vivid account of Georgian London includes an excursus on the 'eternal disposition of the English to suicide', inspired by 'the shocking sight of twenty skulls' found in the foundations when Blackfriars Bridge was being built, and set out in a yard there by its architect, Robert Mylne.[15]

The English were probably no more addicted to suicide than anyone else. One early psychiatrist, Dr Forbes Winslow, even produced figures suggesting that in 1834 it was ten times more common in Paris than London – as improbable a claim as Grosley's.[16] The Seine in Paris was certainly famous for its drownings, accidental or intentional. For a hundred years the public morgue on the Île de la Cité, opened in 1804 and relocated in 1864, offered a free display of unidentified bodies, many picked out of the river in the early morning by fishermen's nets at St Cloud. Baudelaire, Rimbaud and Zola all made play with the Paris Morgue. English tourists too were keen visitors. Dickens, on trips to Paris, made straight for the morgue like an arrow. Browning's 'Apparent Failure' reflects on the corpses of the day laid out before him there, before concluding with complacency:

It's wiser being good than bad;
It's safer being meek than fierce:
It's fitter being sane than mad.[17]

What can be said is that most of those who leapt from Waterloo Bridge or waded into the river from its stairs were young women. Olive Anderson's excellent study of Victorian and Edwardian suicide shows that about three times more men committed suicide than women. But the women preferred drowning to hanging or other more violent forms of death, which were the regular masculine route to oblivion. Later, poisons and coal gas came into favour. Women also threw themselves increasingly in front of trains, a less considerate method of self-destruction.[18]

The association of Waterloo Bridge suicides with prostitution was also accurate. Great numbers of prostitutes lived in 'Whorterloo', as Flora Tristan had observed. They crossed the bridge on the way to and from the Strand and other West End places of assignation, or simply plied their trade on the bridge itself. Drunkenness, thinks Anderson, was a commoner precipitant to end it all than remorse. But despair played its part. In 1840 two sisters threw themselves off the bridge. They were said to be the daughters of a Manchester businessman who had been seduced and brought to London by married men. One of the men died, the other left the girl to shift for herself, so they turned to the 'gay life', ending up in Waterloo Road. There, 'in consequence of the steps taken by the inhabitants', they became friendless. Whereupon the sisters made up their minds to die together.[19]

The occasional middle-class suicides garnered the most publicity. Alice Blanche Oswald's case occupied the press for more than the usual day or two. It took place in 1872, when the vogue of jumping from Waterloo Bridge may have been on the wane. She leapt in silence from a parapet but screamed frantically for help when she hit the water, as was common. A steamer and a boatman both tried in vain to rescue her, and her body was recovered 'with the grapnel drags'. Oswald left a long letter expressing her hopelessness and destitution, which the newspapers published. She was an American, it said, not quite twenty, who had gone first to Australia to work in a hotel, then came to Britain to try for a job under a new name as a nursery governess. Her burial plot was paid for and her funeral attended by an 'assemblage of ladies unmistakeably American', including the poetess Estelle Anna Lewis ('Stella').[20] Later it was claimed that the story the victim had told was 'a far from truthful one. She was nothing more than an adventuress.'[21]

The outpouring of sympathy over Alice Oswald's suicide – far from universally shared – did not prevent a string of copycat attempts in the days following. But the incident does seem to mark a slow shift of emphasis from condemnation of sin to a more humane and pragmatic attitude to bridge suicides.

The police in particular became geared up for prevention and rescue work. There had long been a police force of kinds on the river, directed almost exclusively to protecting property; the quick and the dead could be left to the likes of Gaffer Hexam. After the Thames Police was amalgamated with the Metropolitan force in 1839, things gradually changed. By the 1890s the river police had three steam launches and as many as 28 rowing boats, known as galleys. Among their tasks was searching for missing persons. As in Gaffer Hexam's time, much of this work took place after dark. Every time the night patrol stopped on the water, wrote Arthur Pask, 'the thought of an almost nameless horror comes to me with a swift chill, which makes me turn my eyes the other way, and then by a horrid fascination compels me to bring them back'.[22]

In 1874, soon after the Oswald case, a floating police station with a resident duty officer was established just east of Waterloo Bridge along the recently completed embankment, as a subsidiary to the main river station at Wapping. Here blankets, towels, medicine and the invaluable hot bath were available – rough and ready stuff, but better than nothing.[23] A few newspaper articles covered its work. One such of 1891 described the procedures for resuscitation.

> Close at hand is a little medicine chest, containing numerous medicine phials, a flask of stimulants, and a smelling-bottle. A dozen or so of tins, of all shapes and sizes, are handy. These are filled with hot water and placed in contact with the body of the person rescued from the river. It is often an hour before anything approaching animation makes itself visible, and even four hours have elapsed before any sign has been apparent. The rescued one is laid upon a wooden board, below which is a bath, and rubbed by ready hands according to Dr. Sylvester's method, whose instructions are prominently displayed upon the wall, and are understood by all the police.

82 Lobby card for the original *Waterloo Bridge* film, 1931, directed by James Whale after a play by Robert E. Sherwood and starring Mae Clarke and Kent Douglass

83 Tidal Thames Water Safety Forum, *Drowning Prevention Strategy*, 2019. The railings of Waterloo Bridge are recognisable

This article pointed out that the staff of the floating police station were all men, whereas there should have been women on hand to help with the female victims.[24] Another account claims that because of the floating station's work, out of one hundred attempts at suicide in the vicinity, seventy-five were saved – 'a very creditable record'.[25] The station survived in various forms till after the old bridge disappeared, when it was abandoned in favour of one at Wapping. Today there is still a lifeboat station on the site.

Thames suicides naturally continued, perhaps reported less sedulously. Some figures for bodies received at the floating police station in 1892 seemed to reverse the old tally in favour of women.[26] But the count may well be inaccurate or unrepresentative, and include accidental drownings. Writers too continued to consign their hapless protagonists to London River, on the whole less sentimentally than Dickens and his contemporaries. Examples are Gissing's *The Last Half Crown* and Somerset Maugham's *The Merry-Go-Round.*

If sensational interest in women leaping from Waterloo Bridge ebbed away, its association with prostitution lasted longer. 1931 saw the release of a successful feature film, *Waterloo Bridge*, starring Mae Clarke and Kent Douglass. Based on the First World War experiences of the American playwright Robert E. Sherwood, it told the story of a 'girl of the streets' who plied her trade on the bridge, only to be killed in a Zeppelin raid. The film (fig.82) invested the dying years of the old bridge with a glamour and romance which could hardly survive its reconstruction. Other versions on the same theme followed.[27]

Men and women still throw themselves or just fall into the Thames. According to an estimate in 2024, about thirty bodies are recovered each year in the London area by the Marine Policing Unit, or about one a week along the full course of the river.[28] These are lesser numbers than in Dickens's day. But the issue remains urgent enough for the various authorities to have come together in launching the Tidal Thames Water Safety Forum. The cover of that body's *Drowning Prevention Strategy*, published in 2019, shows a young woman looking out over the river, with only the scanty railings of modern Waterloo Bridge between her and the water (fig.83). The echo of the bridge of sighs has not faded away.[29]

9

Free but Fragile

It was, as it should have been, a joyful day. The turnstiles had been dismantled, the gates loosened for removal. A few flags stretched across Waterloo Road. There was 'jovial bantering' as the last paying customers crossed. At midday on Saturday, 5 October 1878, the great bridge was thrown open at both ends and the crowds streamed freely and gaily through (fig.84). 'You, as ratepayers of London, are now the possessors of Waterloo Bridge', pronounced Edward Dresser Rogers, who presided for the Metropolitan Board of Works over a brief ceremony. From there the Board's delegation proceeded to the Charing Cross Bridge, where a similar if quieter ceremony took place for the footpaths beside the railway. Two London bridges had been freed from tolls on the same day.[1]

The change was immediately apparent. The next Monday morning, every arriving train at Waterloo Station disgorged a host of pedestrians heading straight for a bridge that they would previously have shunned, crossing without payment via Blackfriars or Westminster Bridge despite the extra time and effort involved. Cabs followed suit. As it was market day at the Metropolitan Livestock Market in Islington, droves of cattle and sheep likewise reaped their doubtful advantage from the new regime.[2]

It had been a long haul – over sixty years. London had maintained tolls over its major river bridges beyond the rest of the world's great cities. A sense of iniquity and shame over this state of affairs had grown as South London coalesced into a destination for working and living far behind the Thames frontage, cementing a mutual dependence between the two shores. The working classes, for whom a daily penny or halfpenny toll was a significant sum in household expenses, had suffered most. The small, degraded houses of the Waterloo Road district were just one sign of it. Wherever toll bridges were the main means of communication,

84 Waterloo Bridge is freed from tolls, *Illustrated London News*, 12 October 1878

property on the South Bank depreciated. In the early 1870s new houses in Battersea were alleged to be failing to find tenants because of the toll on Chelsea Bridge. Wives, it was also said, would prepare their husbands' lunch during the morning and entrust it to a stranger at the toll gate so that they did not have to pay to deliver it to their spouse, waiting hungrily on the other side.

Protests against tolls on bridges were as old as toll bridges themselves. But a co-ordinated response surfaced only towards the end of the 1830s. Waterloo Bridge was the prime target. A Metropolitan Anti-Bridge Toll Association argued that the bridge 'had the claim of being national as well as public property' on account of its name alone.[3] It made some progress. Petitions from coach and omnibus proprietors and from workmen's bodies piled up in Parliament, and in 1841 the pedestrian charge on Waterloo Bridge was reduced from a penny to a halfpenny. That was still more or less equivalent to what the working man paid for daily fuel, claimed the association. Meanwhile, 'all the other evils of the imposts, viz., depression of trade and property, and deprivation of public stages in these districts, still continue; coupled with the demoralised state of the Waterloo-road, and over-burdened state of traffic, east and west, and over the free bridges.'[4]

The association soon fizzled out. It is easy to see why. If the tolls were lifted, someone would have to take over the bridges, pay off the companies that had built them, and maintain them. Who should that be? The City? There was no enthusiasm from that curmudgeonly quarter, for all the City Corporation's claim to authority over London River. It would not yet even take over underused and loss-making Southwark Bridge, as was frequently urged. The Crown? Through the agency of the Office of Works, the Crown was girding up its loins to build a suspension bridge from Chelsea to Battersea and its new park, but it had no other stake in London's river crossings. The County Justices? That might make sense for upriver toll bridges in semi-rural districts, but it could not apply to Central London. Until the legislature created the Metropolitan Board of Works in 1855, there was no obvious body in which the bridges could be vested.

And where was the money to come from for all this? Governments of all hues were chary about doling out funds for London improvements. If new rates were to be imposed for the cost of freeing and maintaining the bridges, on which local authorities should they fall? Confronted with this minefield, continuing with the tolls looked almost attractive.

There was just one source of revenue which looked plausible – the coal and wine duties. This mysterious and intricate topic cannot be neglected if the financing of London's bridges in the Georgian and Victorian years, and indeed London improvements as a whole, are to be understood.[5]

* * *

The London coal duties went back to mediaeval times. (The comparable wine duties, which brought in much less money, can be ignored for present purposes.) On every 'chaldron' (a measure of 3,148 pounds) of coal arriving into the Port of London, a tax or taxes had to be paid. With few exceptions, until well into the nineteenth century this duty was appropriated by the City Corporation. It paid for orphan establishments;

it funded much of the rebuilding of the City after the Great Fire, including, famously, St Paul's Cathedral;[6] often it was used to underwrite or clear other items of City expenditure. From the 1760s the coal dues helped pay for major City improvements, notably the costly approaches on both sides of the river to the Rennies' new London Bridge.

As London grew and coal came in by canal and then railway as well as river, the boundaries within which carriers had to pay the coal duties were vastly enlarged. After several changes they became co-extensive with the Metropolitan Police District as established in 1829, which stretched miles beyond the built-up area. Most people in this wide expanse of territory were indirectly paying a tax on their coal but not getting anything back from it – certainly no infrastructural improvements. Many were also having to pay to cross the Thames. Recognition of these injustices led to the application of money from the coal duties after 1839 to help pay for the limited street improvements undertaken by the Crown in the West End of London and Clerkenwell. But these did not help residents in the outer suburbs.

The coal tax was always unpopular. It put a burden upon the poor and upon manufacturing industries. It was inequitable and inflationary. Governments frequently pledged to abolish it or, rather, not to renew it. But they kept failing to do so. That was because the money it raised proved handy in various respects and saved the Government from having to sort out a proper taxation system for London.

The Metropolitan Board of Works (MBW) was created in 1855 to deal with matters which were not being adequately addressed by the constituent vestries and other bodies governing London.[7] Drainage was its most urgent priority. The commission advising on the MBW's formation recommended that the coal duties should be assigned to the new body. That did not happen because of the City's opposition. But in due course the Board acquired the lion's share of the income and was allowed to spend it on its improvement projects.[8] In 1869 it took direct control of the coal duties. The Board of Works' area was still much smaller than that over which the duties were levied, so inequities remained. All this while the tax seemed to be on the brink of abolition, yet lingered on.

The chances of applying the coal dues to freeing the London-area toll bridges hoved into view at last when representatives of the western suburbs revolted in 1868 against their use to subsidise the heavy costs of the Victoria Embankment, which offered them no benefit. They were assuaged by a promise that the dues would also be used to free the bridges at Kew, Kingston, Hampton, Walton and Staines. It took time to go through the legalities, but in 1873 Kew Bridge, the last of the five, was opened with much the same ceremony as Waterloo Bridge was soon to enjoy, in the presence of the Lord Mayor of London and the Chairman of the MBW.[9]

With the system of turnpike roads and tolls on its last legs, toll bridges too looked like an anachronism. 'Tollgates have been swept from the roads, and they must now be taken from the bridges', called the *Daily Chronicle*. 'Waterloo Bridge is conveniently situated. It is one of the finest pieces of architecture in the metropolis . . . yet the bridge is like a quiet street which lies out of the route of traffic and business.'[10] Even the City Corporation had at last been persuaded to take over and free less-frequented Southwark Bridge.

So a fresh pressure group, the Metropolitan Free Bridge Association – founded in 1871 with strong support among MPs – was pushing at an open door. Once again its prime target was Waterloo Bridge. All the meetings held by this vigorous body seem to have taken place south of the river. It brought a Bill before Parliament in 1877 to free London's remaining toll bridges – Waterloo, Charing Cross Footbridge, Vauxhall, Chelsea, Albert, Battersea, Hammersmith and Putney. The City tried to kill it because it objected to the MBW becoming the body that would own and manage the bridges. But after some amendments the Bill passed at last.

* * *

If the freeing of Waterloo Bridge was a joyful day, especially for the South Bank populace, for the Metropolitan Board of Works, now the bridge's owner and manager, there can have been little joy. While the lawyers were arguing how much should be paid to the old bridge company (some of them got 'smeared with mud' on a boat trip to view the property at issue),[11] an examination of its foundations revealed a grave state of affairs.

Months before the opening, the *Illustrated London News* reported that Sir Joseph Bazalgette, the Board's well-known engineer, together with a consultant, Henry Law, had assessed the bridge as in an extremely critical condition and liable to collapse at any moment. Bazalgette estimated a figure of £33,000 to 'prop up the tottering piers on the Middlesex side with iron cylinders'.[12] Law then clarified his own opinions. He had never said the bridge was likely to fall, but he had identified the fourth, fifth and sixth piers from the Middlesex side as in a critical state, because the scour of the river, more pronounced since the rebuilding of London Bridge, had dropped the level of the ground by up to 10ft, so that the base of the sixth pier, for instance, which Rennie had left '4ft 6in under the bed of the river, is now 5ft 6in above the same'.

Law went on to cite two documents. One was from the original contractors, Jolliffe and Banks, who had characterised the river bed at this point as 'loose gravel and sand, a more porous strata does not exist, the slightest breach in it would destroy all that we have hitherto effected, and we have our fears of such an event if precautionary measures are not adopted'. The other was a letter dated 28 January 1847 and addressed to the bridge company by Sir John Rennie and John Plews, who had both worked on the original construction. It referred to 'operations' – presumably dredging – then proceeding which had caused scouring of up to 3–4ft under the second and third arches, and urged the company to make good the damage by filling up the excavations with Kentish ragstone (as appears to have been done). If this remedial operation was requisite in 1847 when the scouring amounted to 3–4ft, 'how much more necessary is it when the bed is 5ft 6in below the same?' To cap his remarks, Law added that the foundations at London Bridge were a full 19ft 6in lower than the sixth pier at Waterloo, showing how drastic the scouring had been at the latter since the date of construction.[13]

Rennie junior and Plews had been loyal to Waterloo Bridge ever since its construction, sitting as directors on the company's board. In his old age, Sir John had even visited the Victoria Embankment works every day to ensure that they did not damage the Middlesex end of the bridge.[14] But their advice had not been enough to induce the impecunious company to counteract the effects of scouring. As a result the bridge, renowned for its supposedly solid construction, had been handed over to the MBW in a dire state. And it was now going to have to bear much more traffic than before. Therefore, arbitrators assessed the final figure which the Board had to pay the Waterloo Bridge Company at £475,000, as opposed to the £750,000 that the company had claimed.

To put the crisis of 1878 in perspective, the Board faced similar issues with the bridges it inherited further up river. Lambeth Suspension Bridge, only opened in 1862, was already in trouble. Chelsea Bridge (1858) and even the recent Albert Bridge (1874) both needed strengthening. The shaky old wooden Battersea Bridge and Putney Bridge were both waiting to be rebuilt in the 1880s by the industrious Bazalgette, as was the pretty fifty-year-old suspension bridge at Hammersmith. In several of these cases the ability of their superstructures to bear modern loadings was more at fault then their foundations. Whatever the cause, the Board of Works faced a repair and rebuilding bill for its Thames bridges far exceeding any potential revenue from the coal dues. Loans had to be taken out to cover the costs.

In view of this litany of defects, it is fair to point out that not even the most skilfully constructed and admired of the older road bridges across London River endured very long. Tides, scour and the intensity, weight and grind of traffic saw to that. The seeming exception, Old London Bridge, was in a chaotic state long before its destruction. Old Westminster Bridge enjoyed just over a hundred years of life, Blackfriars a little less; both were in trouble long before they were replaced, having been patched, propped and derided for decades. Waterloo Bridge, subject to the same cycle of praise, precariousness and disdain, just made it to 120. Southwark Bridge, stable but impractical, lasted just a century; Vauxhall Bridge only 82 years. Even the Rennies' New London Bridge, which took up and improved on the foundation techniques used at Waterloo, survived less than 140.

Compare these lifespans with such old French bridges over wide rivers as are still going strong at Blois and Saumur on the Loire, or in Paris. If they faced less formidable natural conditions, their maintenance régimes may also have been more systematic. Curiously, the road bridge over London River that has endured longest is one that has never been much admired – Thomas Page's new Westminster Bridge, opened in 1862 and

85 Thomas Page's Westminster Bridge. Photograph by Frederick York taken *c.*1870

still heavily used (fig.85). Perhaps the main reason for that is that it was much wider than the others from the start – 84ft, as against Waterloo's meagre 42. By contrast London's Thames railway bridges, designed for heavier loadings, have all fared well.

To return to the challenges facing the Board of Works after it took over at Waterloo Bridge, not a great deal happened until 1880. Then, in the wake of the sensational Tay Bridge disaster the year before, the MBW's Bridges Committee took up the cudgels. Its chairman acknowledged that piles beneath some of the piers were visible at very low tides. Bazalgette undertook a fresh examination in 1881 and recommended building coffer dams at 20ft distance round each of the faulty piers, the worst of which were now identified as towards the Surrey side. The remedial work was carried out under Bazalgette's son Edward in 1882–3 by William Webster, one of the contractors for the Victoria Embankment. Water was pumped out, soil was poured in and concrete blocks were laid to protect the damaged piers and piles. Thus repaired, and with new granite paving laid in 1880, the increased traffic could bowl or trundle merrily across the bridge. Even so, everyone knew that Waterloo Bridge was on the sick list. It was to remain so till the end of its life.[15]

86 *By the Balcony*, lithograph of a sketch by Whistler of his wife Beatrice lying sick on a couch in the Savoy Hotel overlooking Waterloo Bridge, 1896

87 Hungerford Bridge, etching from Whistler's 'Thames Set'. The view shows the bridge being readied for demolition in 1861, with workmen clambering up the chains. Access to the steamboat pier is by means of a temporary gangway

10

Pictorial

Whistler the painter married late, at the age of fifty-four. His bride was Beatrice, daughter of the sculptor Birnie Philip and widow of the architect E.W. Godwin, Whistler's close friend. He called her Trixie or by various pet nicknames. An artist in her own right, she was only eighteen when she married Godwin and twenty-nine when he died in 1886. Her marriage with Whistler less than two years later was somewhat hugger-mugger, because she supplanted his difficult mistress Maud Franklin.

Everyone agrees that they were very happy. Whistler calmed down and became less prickly. After four years in Chelsea, the couple moved to Paris. They made trips, for instance to Amsterdam. Then in 1894 Trixie fell ill with cancer and they returned to England. After a wretched year at various addresses, in January 1896 they installed themselves at the Savoy Hotel.[1] Still quite new, the Savoy boasted services then unique in a London hotel. No doubt the Whistlers hoped to secure better comforts and nursing there than in a private hospital or home. Their suite overlooked the Thames. Hence, looking down on Waterloo Bridge and the Embankment, Whistler did desultory sketches, some of which were later translated into lithography. Most touching is the drawing he made of Trixie resting or sleeping on a couch beside the balcony, with the great indifferent bridge below (fig.86). They moved out towards the end. Trixie died that May. Whistler was said to be 'never the same again'.[2]

The artist's long affair with London River began in Wapping and Rotherhithe amidst the hubbub of port activity, matured into experiment and exoticism during his Chelsea years, and reached its close beside Waterloo Bridge. For lovers of realism, nothing can beat the early etchings, started in 1859, not long after he came back from his art-study years in Paris, full of Charles Meryon's bristling images of

Whistler 1862

88 Whistler's *The Last of Old Westminster*, 1862. The title is confusing: the new bridge in erection is in the foreground, but people can be seen crossing the old bridge still behind

the Seine and its bridges. These celebrated scenes open a window on the downstream river life of the time, but they do not stand alone. The 'Thames Set' as finally published included Old Westminster Bridge on its last legs, and Hungerford Bridge also on the verge of demolition, with workmen clambering up its chains and steamboats clustering messily around its pier (fig.87). All these, plus some other river scenes (but not Waterloo Bridge), date from 1859–61. There is also an oil painting of 1862 showing the reconstruction of Westminster Bridge, with a misleading title (fig.88).[3] A stylised version of Battersea Bridge – under the name of Chelsea Bridge – slipped into the Thames Set as an afterthought in 1871. By then Whistler was plunging into the fantasy world of his nocturnes, in which Battersea Bridge and the looming profiles of industry across the river were translated into the realm of the personal imagination. The painter's old duty of record was fading away.[4]

Whistler kept in touch with the fellow-spirits from his early Paris years. When the Franco-Prussian War and the Commune of 1870–71 sent the avant-garde painters scuttling into brief exile across the Channel, he welcomed them as allies against English earnestness in art. Even before then there had been some interest in the Thames among French artists. Charles Daubigny, for instance – a painter happiest with rural scenes and rivers – was in London in 1865 and 1866, lunched with Whistler and executed a number of Thames scenes. Among them is a dashed-off sketch of the Victoria Embankment in the making, with Waterloo Bridge in the background (fig.89).[5] A fuller Daubigny painting, now in the National Gallery and showing St Paul's and Blackfriars Bridge as a backdrop to the smoky Thames, probably dates from the exile years. During those testing times the glue which kept the French painters together was supplied by Paul Durand-Ruel, who opened a gallery and gathering place for them in London. There Daubigny introduced the famous dealer to Monet, a meeting crucial for the latter's fortunes.[6]

Having fled France to avoid conscription, Monet too was already painting the river. There is something quaint and amiable about his *Thames below Westminster*, made at this time (fig.90). The viewpoint is low and humble, two boats ply on placid, rippling water, while Lowry-like stick-figures potter about on a jetty in front of a toy-town

89 A sketch of 1866 by Charles Daubigny showing works for the Victoria Embankment, with Waterloo Bridge and a shot tower behind

90 *The Thames below Westminster* by Claude Monet, 1871

91 Claude Monet, *Waterloo Bridge, Temps Gris*, 1903

92 Claude Monet, *Waterloo Bridge, soleil dans le brouillard*, 1903

Houses of Parliament. There is none of the provocation that Whistler contrived to inject into his river scenes. Only the acidic fog portends the pictures to come.

In 1887 Monet was back to exhibit at the Royal Society of British Artists, which Whistler was then promoting. They probably met several times. Afterwards, Monet told a friend that he was tempted to go back and paint the *effets de brouillard* on the Thames. During the exile period he and his first wife, not having the language, had disliked London, but he had evidently got over that. There was another trip in 1891. Then, in 1898, Michel, Monet's teenage son, came over to study English. He fell sick, and his father dutifully visited until Michel was better. He, his second wife Alice and stepdaughter Germaine next planned a longer trip to London. This took place in autumn 1899 when the Monets, comfortably off by now, installed themselves in a sixth-floor suite at the Savoy. The recommendation must surely have come from Whistler, present in similar rooms but sombre circumstances. For Monet, surveying the great bend in the river, the embankment and the bridges below in all their unstable moods of time and 'idiosyncratic' weather, the itch to paint from this Olympian eyrie was irresistible.[7]

As often with Monet, the thing became an obsession. He returned alone for almost three months in 1900. He could not get the same suite again because the sixth floor of the Savoy was full of officers convalescing from the Boer War, so he had to make do with the fifth floor with a different prospect, turning one of the rooms into a studio. There was a final two-month stint in 1901. For these return visits Monet chose early months of the year as best suited to his purposes. He evolved a schedule: in the morning he painted the bridges, Waterloo and Charing Cross, and on some afternoons he would cross the river to tackle the Houses of Parliament from St Thomas's Hospital, where he borrowed a balcony. Despite his intensity of work in all weathers, he managed to have a social life. Well-known by this time and epicurean by nature, he went out to dinner or entertained at the Savoy. His stays there have not been forgotten. At the time of the big Royal Academy exhibition of his paintings in 1998–9, a 'Monet package' could be purchased at the Savoy, including tickets to the show and a 'complimentary Monet cocktail' exclusively created by the head barman.[8]

93 Claude Monet, *Waterloo Bridge*, 1903

94 Thames scene with Waterloo Bridge by André Derain, 1905

Monet worked fast, so the bag of paintings which went back for finishing at Giverny was big. The best estimate is ninety-five: forty-one of Waterloo Bridge, thirty-five of Charing Cross Bridge and nineteen of Parliament. A few may have been destroyed. Durand-Ruel was allowed to sell a handful early on but had to wait till 1904 for a larger batch, which he exhibited together to great acclaim. Monet continued to fiddle with many of the pictures in his studio, sometimes indeed referring back to photographs. Now scattered all over the world, those which are not in art-museums attract fabulous prices.

There is little of the lightness of 1871 in any of these 'stridently horizontal' pictures (figs 91–3).[9] The mood is set by air, water and smoke, and the chemistry that turned them into the noxious, shifting London atmosphere of yore, mercifully irrecoverable today. Mostly it is sombre, sometimes it is baleful, occasionally apocalyptic, as in some of the Parliament pictures where the late winter sun burns through the sky. The buildings, bridges and chimneystacks that punctuate or frame the elements take on contrasting and exaggerated tones: blue when they are back-lit, dark-green or pink when they reflect the water. Sometimes the effect is gaudy.

What there is not is any attempt to discriminate between structures beyond their qualities of outline, depth and mass. Viewed from on

95 The Thames with Waterloo Bridge looking upstream, by Emile Claus, 1916, private collection

high, Charing Cross Bridge looks no better or worse than Waterloo Bridge. They are merely manmade interjections under the thumb of an overruling sky and river. Buses and horses bunch up on Waterloo Bridge, stick-figures no more but in an unpitying blur of colours. Monet depicts London perceptively but without loyalty or love. It is all about extracting beauty from drabness.

In 1906–7 André Derain followed Monet to London, as his dealer Ambroise Vollard encouraged the younger painter to repeat the success of Monet's Thames paintings.[10] Derain dutifully concentrated on the river but, less settled and more questing, shifted around much more. Boats, traffic and human activity featured often. He portrayed Waterloo Bridge at least twice. One scene is an exercise in Fauvist wonkiness, brighter and gayer than any Monet. A red and gold sky showers down upon a dappled breadth of water, while the bridge and the shot towers lurch sideways in blue. The quieter picture looks the other way, with the river in pink and St Paul's just a pile-up behind (fig.94). In both, we are a further step away from representation for its own sake.

One other painter is worth adding to the tally of foreign artists who tackled Waterloo Bridge. Emile Claus, a Belgian from Antwerp, became a First World War exile late in life. Hitherto he had mainly painted rural life. But in 1916 Claus found the new subject he was looking for in the Thames. By taking an upper-floor studio in a block just east of the bridge, he followed Monet's lead. His series, *Réverbérations sur la Tamise*, was almost equally prolific. In his portrayals of livid skies or fog-piercing sun over bridge and water he likewise paid homage to the impressionist master. If lacking the latter's powers of selection and drama, Claus has his own worth for his atmospheric depictions of Waterloo Bridge in its twilight years of utility, not to mention other buildings forming the backdrop to London River (fig.95). He took 'great consolation', he said, from this wartime work.[11]

Illustration brings us to a broader category of paintings and engravings of the bridge, with less or more independent value – or, in other words, varying degrees of subordination to the structure or event they depict. That tension informs the greatest of the early paintings of the bridge, Constable's *The Opening of Waterloo Bridge (Whitehall Stairs, June 18th 1817)*. This vast canvas (fig.49) belongs to the artist's late period when he was expanding his subject-matter and scale. It is almost a history painting: but who would have expected Constable to take on a subject associated with vainglory, war and the unpopular Prince Regent?[12] That may partly be why the picture caused him such trouble, taking fifteen years to complete after various trials (fig.96). Denys Sutton calls it his 'most perplexing and exacting task'. The long process was punctuated by outbursts of frustration: 'I may as well produce this abortion as another', Constable wailed at one point, 'for – who cares for landscape?'[13]

A distaste for celebration may be one of the reasons why the bridge itself sits so far back in the splendid composition. A long bridge seen head-on must always be hard to fit into a painting. In fact Constable had recently tried something of the same kind, for during the years when he was meditating the Waterloo picture he painted his *Chain Pier, Brighton*. It is similar in arrangement, perhaps indeed a rehearsal, with the full length of the structure central yet far away. The picture was not very well received. This time Constable again included the bridge's entire proud length and horizontality, but reduced its size to fit into less than half the width of his canvas. It stretches lankily out in the distance beneath a changeable sky (less gusty in fact than in the preliminary study in the Tate, and not the fine weather recorded on the opening day). Meanwhile all the 'business' takes place in the shady foreground,

96 John Constable, *The Opening of Waterloo Bridge*, a trial version dating from the early 1820s. For the finished version see fig.49

97 Charles Deane, *Waterloo Bridge and the Lambeth Waterfront from Westminster Stairs*, 1821

98 A dredger with Waterloo Bridge, watercolour sketch by E.W. Cooke

where Lord Liverpool and his entourage prepare to embark amid a flurry of flag-bedecked vessels and oarsmen. Their pomp and bustle look insignificant in the face of sky and river. The painting is rather like one of those Claudes in which the story depicted is dwarfed by the magnificent landscape. Yet allowing for the claims of imagination, Constable has illustrated the event with a measure of faithfulness.[14]

Other comparisons reinforce the point. Around the same time, for instance, Charles Deane produced an agreeable view of the Thames with Waterloo Bridge in the background (fig.97). In Deane's hands river craft and their crew hold centre stage, whereas Constable, like Monet, consigns boats and bridge alike to the lap of the weather-gods. Among other versions of the bridge's opening, much the liveliest is the anonymous coloured etching published by Ackermann (fig.50). But the background is coarse, the architecture does not look special and quite what is going on is unclear. The flags, the gunfire, the soldiers and the crowds on land and water are all packed in there to play up the glamour and excitement of the day.

The earliest views of Waterloo Bridge, working drawings apart, were made by Edward Blore, not yet an architect in his own right but a freelance draughtsman working for the Cooke family of artists and engravers, whose depictions of Thames structures and boats in their time are invaluable.[15] Blore must have had access to the Rennie office as his fine perspective of the bridge is dated March 1814, when construction had a

99 Cabs waiting on the Embankment next to Waterloo Bridge, etching by Willem Witsen, 1890. The view is reversed

long way to go (fig.51). The lamp standards apart, the details are accurate. The one criticism that might be made is that the elliptical character of the arches is not well conveyed. Blore followed on in 1815 with a graphic drawing of the first of the mighty arch centres in place on the Surrey side, as masonry begins to be laid. These along with elevations, plus another version of the opening ceremony by R.R. Reinagle, were engraved by the Cookes for their *Plates of Thames Scenery . . . from Original Drawings by Eminent Artists*, published in 1818. Informative though these are, they do not come up to the standard of the superb drawings made by Edward Cooke, George Cooke's son, depicting the dismantling and reconstruction of London Bridge in the next decade (fig.65). Regrettably, this great marine artist seldom turned his hand to Waterloo Bridge. Only a little watercolour showing a few arches with a dredger in front (fig.98) and a print featuring the two shot towers seem to be known.

London River has been an endless source of allurement for artists and illustrators. Taking just the old Waterloo Bridge, so many pictures were made of it that it would be impossible to run through them all. Willem Witsen from Amsterdam, for instance, was in London around 1890 and seems to have found it hard to tear himself away from bridge, river and embankment, especially at dusk, picking up in his many Whistlerian views 'a mood of seriously heavy fatigue' (fig.99).[16]

Just a few examples and themes may be picked out. For reasons already explained, attempts to depict the whole length of the bridge

100 C.R.W. Nevinson, *Waterloo Bridge From a Savoy Window*, 1924–6

101 Waterloo Bridge from the Embankment at night, lithograph by Jan Poortenaar, *c.*1925

102 Waterloo Bridge approach with west wing of Somerset House, print by Francis Dodd, 1911. The view is reversed

seldom succeeded, though many such were made to illustrate early Victorian topographical publications. It was wiser to abbreviate or choose an angle. One of the little Whistler lithographs shows six of the nine arches before tailing away. A drypoint by Nevinson, also taken from high up in the Savoy Hotel, likewise shows five and a half arches but is more powerful and ominous, with the bridge black against spidery trees and a shining river (fig.100).

Other illustrators chose to pull in closer. An angled viewpoint in one of an inter-war series of lithographs by another Dutch artist, Jan Poortenaar, emphasises the lonely cavernousness of the great arches (fig.101). Then there was the lure of the monumental staircases which attracted Clarkson Stanfield and others. Few artists resisted the drama of arch and water altogether. One such was Francis Dodd who, in an etching of 1911, shows the roadway next to Somerset House with commercial horse-and-cart traffic still prevailing (fig.102). But the prize for the most observant upper-level scene must surely go to the French illustrator Jules Arnout (fig.103). For *Grande Bretagne*, a picture-publication, Arnout depicts just a few yards of bridge-pavement over the expanse of river, but these are packed with human incident. A father and child nestle in the corner of one of the niches over the piers, exaggerated in breadth. Among other hangers-on, a man gazes over the balustrade, perhaps with thoughts of ending it all – who knows? – and a pair of women look pertly about them as if on the alert for a pick-up – who knows?

The predominance of black-and-white treatment is striking among these later images. That was conditioned by the strong market for affordable prints and book illustrations, which stimulated an international flowering of etching and lithography. River and bridge scenes were among the beneficiaries of this movement. Naturally there were artists who never ceased to explore the subtle and varying coloration of the Thames. The river was a favourite in transport posters, for instance (fig.104). And the prolific William Wyllie had an unbounded affection for the many crafts, activities and moods of London River. Waterloo Bridge was not a special favourite of Wyllie's, but he has a fine view of its dying days, seen from the angle of steam tugs sitting low in the water.

The last of the old bridge was also depicted in oils. There is a lively high-level Kokoschka of 1926 revealing the temporary bridge built behind the

103 Somerset House and the Thames, looking downstream from Waterloo Bridge, lithograph by Jules Arnout for *Grande Bretagne*, 1847

Jules Arnout 1847

104 Poster for London County Council Tramways featuring Charing Cross and Waterloo Bridges, designed by Herbert K. Rooke at the Central School of Arts and Crafts, 1924

ailing structure, before the latter finally succumbed (fig.105). Thirty years later Kokoschka was back to interpret its replacement (fig.106). The old bridge's final moments of agony were caught by the topographical artist Charles Cundall, RA. Cundall's two views, taken from either side of the river in 1935, are tinged with nostalgia. The parapets have crumbled, cranes with wrecking balls attack from either side, while gulls circle the wounded victim beneath a yellowish sky (fig.131).

Last, there are photographs. The earliest of them, by W.H. Fox Talbot in about 1846 and by Roger Fenton (or so it is claimed) in about 1857, must be long-exposure plates taken early in the morning (figs 52, 107). The bridge appears silent and dreamy, devoid of shipping or traffic. The 'Fenton' view is particularly valuable because it shows the structure emerging over messy wharves on the north side, before the Victoria Embankment was created. Another photograph of these early years captures the bridge in profile, with soot under the arches and on the columns. Perhaps the most beautiful early photograph is one in Lambeth Archives, showing moored boats and the Charing Cross

105 Oskar Kokoschka, Waterloo Bridge with temporary steel bridge, 1926

106 Oskar Kokoschka, Waterloo Bridge, 1959

107 The earliest known photograph of Waterloo Bridge, by W.H. Fox Talbot, *c.*1846

108 Waterloo Bridge, north face of pier no. 3 in 1924, photo by Ernest Milner

109 Boys and gulls on Waterloo Bridge, 1923

Bridge before it was widened in the foreground, and the loping arches of Waterloo Bridge behind (fig.73).

All these images have an aura of chill, mist and poetry about them. Later photographs are more prosaic, if equally or more informative. From them we learn details which paintings and engravings do not so clearly convey: about radical changes in the bridge's environment; about the precise channelling of the arch stones (fig.108); about the harsh discoloration and punishment meted out by wind, frost and tide, even upon granite; and about the unremitting bleakness of the wintery Thames before industry was banished from it. A series taken in the 1870s shows how the Victoria Embankment impacted on the north end of the bridge, consigning the northernmost arch to the land, and also records something of the steamboat traffic (fig.44).

Towards the end of the bridge's life, the London County Council took copious photographs, as in 1923–4 when the bridge was closed to traffic for repairs but left open for pedestrians. In just a few of them there is some humanity. Men, almost as many as over London Bridge, cross purposefully to work sporting a variety of headgear (fig.117). In one shot, three boys who hardly come up to the height of the balustrade watch the antics of swooping gulls (fig.109). But there is a sadness about the record, as the temporary bridge goes up alongside, shoring appears beneath, and the great bridge is made ready for destruction.

11

Battle of the Bridges

Worn, soot-stained and patched up below the surface, for forty-five years after 1878 Waterloo Bridge fulfilled the destiny that its first authors had hoped for, as a major artery for metropolitan traffic. South London having spread outwards and Waterloo Station correspondingly inflated, it bore a heavy burden of carts, lorries, omnibuses and pedestrians. Road traffic worsened yearly. The Strand was one of many jammed-up thoroughfares, with a notorious pinch-point where Wellington Street (Lancaster Place today) debouched into it, causing blockages back over the bridge.

In 1903–4 a Government-appointed Royal Commission on London Traffic grappled with the Gordian knot of issues. About Thames bridges, it was agreed that they were too few and too narrow. Maurice Fitzmaurice, recently appointed as the London County Council's chief engineer after long service as its deputy, was among the witnesses. As a young man Fitzmaurice had worked on the Forth Bridge, and at the time he was rebuilding Vauxhall Bridge. These were his comments on Waterloo Bridge:

> 'Waterloo Bridge is narrow, is it not?' 'Yes, Waterloo Bridge is very narrow indeed; it is 27ft. 6in. only between the footways. It is the same, practically, as Putney Bridge. There are a number of them about the same width.'
>
> 'Is there a very large traffic across Waterloo Bridge?' 'Enormous.' . . .
>
> 'Do you call attention to the fact that either Waterloo Bridge must be widened, or there must be a new bridge between

> Waterloo and Blackfriars?' 'Yes, I think it is very necessary to provide a new bridge.'
>
> 'Which would you prefer?' 'I should much prefer a new bridge.'[1]

As successor to the Metropolitan Board of Works, the London County Council (LCC) at this time owned and managed all the Thames road bridges in Central London upstream of Blackfriars Bridge, but the City Corporation was still in possession of the four further down river, including the brand-new Tower Bridge. Nor was the LCC the overall traffic authority for London; indeed no such body existed. The Royal Commission's main recommendation was that such an authority should be created. It would have made sense to confer such powers on the LCC, but the Tory Government was never going to do that while the Council was in the hands of the Progressive Party, so the idea lapsed. Traffic management in London, not least public transport, continued chaotic for another generation.

Still, the LCC could do a good deal, and had already done much during the Progressives' years of control, 1892–5 and 1898–1907. In terms of roads, its outstanding initiative was the long-meditated Kingsway–Aldwych improvement, which destroyed swathes of slums and created a wide north–south thoroughfare, bypassing Wellington Street and Bow Street and thus linking Waterloo Station via the bridge with Bloomsbury and Euston beyond (fig.110). After Edward VII opened Kingsway in 1906, the frontage buildings intended to fund this great scheme followed slowly on. Until the rents from these came in, the debt burden imposed on the Council was very onerous, while the new route added to the traffic on the narrow bridge.

The LCC was well aware of the bridges issue. After many different designs, the great ellipse of the Aldwych fixed on in 1898 was so contrived that the eastern 'horn' could lead down to a new bridge across the river that was to be a counterpart to the existing bridge already attached to the western horn. Thus would Waterloo Bridge's weakness be relieved and its integrity safeguarded.[2] This was the new crossing hinted at by Fitzmaurice in his evidence. He had to admit that it would have involved a costly roadway on the south side of the river, probably aimed

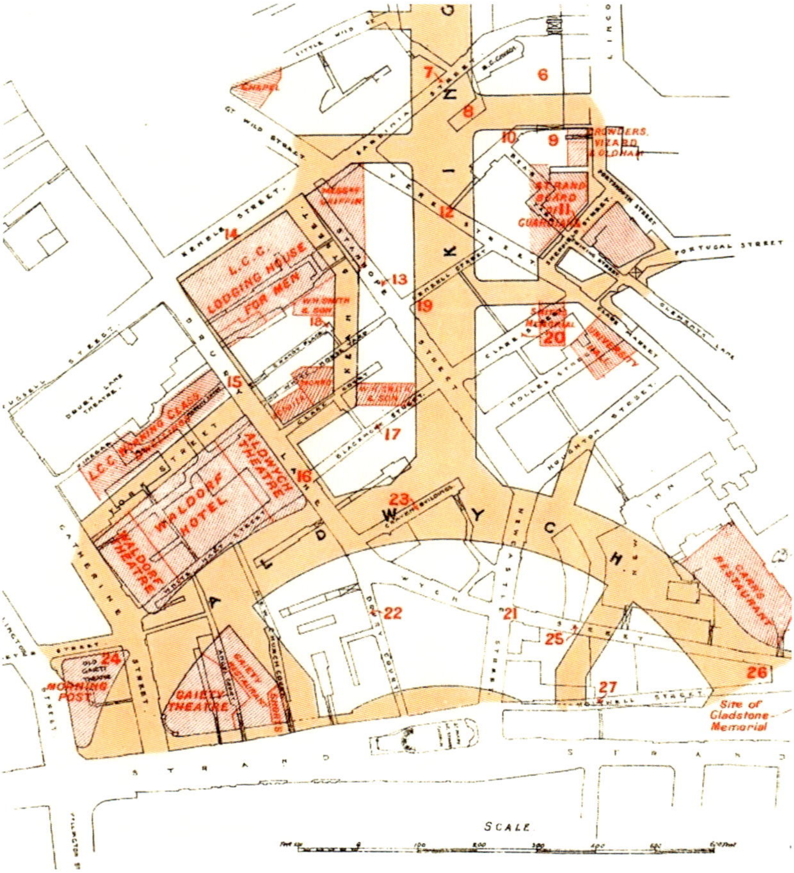

110 Plan of the south end of the London County Council's Kingsway–Aldwych scheme in its final version, 1905

towards Elephant and Castle, but the LCC had not got as far as working out the details.[3] The idea had been a bridge too far, as the saying goes, for the Council to add to its Kingsway–Aldwych project approved by Parliament in 1898. So it lay on the table, to be picked up now and again when fresh crossings for London River were mooted over the next fifty years. Sometimes it was called the Temple Bridge scheme.

In the heyday of Progressive enthusiasm for municipal enterprise, the LCC also plunged into public transport in the shape of tramway ownership, so that cheap fares could allow working men and women to commute from healthy houses in the suburbs to their employment in Central London. Unluckily, the Council backed the wrong ticket. Two revolutions in powering vehicles – first, electric traction, followed hard on its heels by the internal combustion engine – transformed urban

111 London County Council trams beneath the north end of Waterloo Bridge, 1906. To the right, double-decker trams scrape the final arch of the bridge; to the left, a tram emerges from the Kingsway Tunnel

transport between 1890 and 1910. Trams, if powered by clean electricity instead of messy, space-consuming horses, appeared to be an advanced form of conveyance at the start of this period. But soon enough they looked dated before the advent of deep-level tube lines and flexible motor buses.

The intersection of the LCC's policies on tramways and on bridges came about in this way. Against dogged opposition, the Council was finally permitted to buy up existing tramway routes from 1896. These were mainly south of the river and all still horsedrawn. The LCC took them over with a view to modernising them and reforming labour practices. Its first electric trams, using the conduit system – neater but costlier than overhead wires – were proudly inaugurated in 1903. But they could still not pass the Thames bridges. A parliamentary tussle over the issue in 1905–6 saw the coining of the phrase 'The Battle of the Bridges'. Then the Liberals replaced the Tories, the LCC veteran John Burns (of whom more shortly) became President of the Local Government Board, and the trams took possession of the bridges. That meant Blackfriars Bridge, soon to be widened, the rebuilt Vauxhall Bridge and, most prestigiously, Westminster Bridge. Hence the trams swept along the Victoria Embankment as far as Waterloo Bridge. There some of them carried on along the riverside, while others ducked left into a special subway under Aldwych and Kingsway devised by Fitzmaurice and colleagues on the precedent of American tram tunnels, to emerge into daylight at Southampton Row (fig.111).

It was an ingenious but twisting route. Why could the trams not take Waterloo Bridge? Simply, because it was too narrow and clogged by buses and goods vehicles. This caused vexation in go-ahead LCC circles. Long after they had ceased to be the cutting edge of urban public transport, Herbert Morrison, future Labour leader of the Council, insisted that he would never accept a widened Waterloo Bridge unless it could take trams.

Why not widen the bridge? Mediaeval bridges had often been broadened, but there were few precedents for widening urban bridges over major rivers to accommodate modern intensities of traffic. The Rennies' London Bridge was the first Thames crossing to undergo the treatment. Horace Jones, the City Corporation's architect, devised a scheme back in 1875, but it was opposed by the Royal Institute of British Architects on the prophetic grounds that it would deface an important monument, though the bridge was then less than fifty years old.[4] The creation of Tower Bridge postponed the idea, but the City came back to London Bridge in 1903–4. Iron projections having been ruled out, the City's surveyor and engineer caused the granite corbelling to be pushed out by 6ft on either side. Many regarded that as a disfigurement.[5] Blackfriars Road Bridge followed in 1908–9 after the City, in a rare flash of co-operation, agreed to widen it to accommodate the LCC's trams. Here the bridge's looks mattered less, but the operation was more complex. It was engineered by Sir Benjamin Baker of Forth Bridge fame and taken up after his death by Basil Mott; the work was carried out by Sir William Arrol & Co., the contractors for Tower Bridge.[6] These names will recur.

112 A large boat negotiates Waterloo Bridge, *Illustrated London News*, 8 February 1925

No one yet dared suggest such treatment at Waterloo Bridge. Besides altering its proportions and tampering with the famous elevations, there were practical objections. Account had to be taken of the bridge's questionable foundations. Also, the 120ft arches, at the culmination of the great river bend, were already tricky for vessels to navigate. Boats, like road vehicles, were getting larger and harder to manoeuvre (fig.112). If the arches were effectively deepened into tunnels, they would be more perilous still. The Port of London Authority, created in 1909 to impose fresh order on London River and London Docks, was proving restive about the scale of arch openings available to upriver navigation. It would have preferred to substitute suspension bridges for arched bridges up and down the river.

Under these conditions Waterloo Bridge soldiered on into the 1920s, battered by traffic of every weight and type except trams. But there was hope yet for its salvation in the form of a new relief bridge – not down river, as the LCC had foreseen, but up river, in place of the unlovely Charing Cross Railway Bridge. The drawn-out saga of the Charing Cross road bridge that never was must dominate the rest of this chapter.

* * *

The campaign to replace the railway bridge begins with the larger-than-life personality of John Burns. Burns was not quite the one-dimensional character he has often been made out to be. A rabble-rousing socialist orator in the 1880s, then an ideologue of the LCC's Progressive Party and its mouthpiece in the House of Commons, he became the token working-class minister in the Liberal administrations of 1906–14, in which role he is judged to have failed. Burns resigned from the Government when war was declared, one of only two cabinet ministers to do so. He stayed on in Parliament for a while before retiring with his books and his grudges to his native Battersea.

Missing from this picture is that Burns was something of an aesthete, as well as a life-long lover and student of London. He had known Oscar Wilde in his youth and he always admired good architecture. So it is plausible that, as he later claimed, Burns and his fellow LCC Progressive, the pacifist W.H. Dickinson, interviewed the directors of the South Eastern Railway (SER) in 1891–2, begging them to abolish Charing Cross Station and the bridge leading to it and to stop their line short at Waterloo. If the date is right, that was soon after the railway bridge had undergone its first increase in girth and obstructiveness.[7]

The pair got a polite refusal. But the idea did not go away. The SER was soon bent on widening its London lines to take increased commuter traffic. In 1900 the company announced that it would be rebuilding Waterloo Junction (now Waterloo East) and enlarging Charing Cross Station, and asked Parliament to let them broaden its bridge by a further 54ft 6in. Around this time the engineers of the LCC and of the company visited the South Bank together to scope out a site for a new terminal station somewhere alongside the existing South Western terminus. According to the SER's chairman, they agreed the idea was out of the question.[8]

After some delay the railway company obtained powers to widen its bridge. But it did not yet take them up, as that would have involved recasting Charing Cross Station too. In 1904, Burns, this time supported by another LCC member, H.J. Greenwood, again raised the idea of abolishing the railway bridge. This was now explicitly linked with the notion of a new road bridge instead, as part of the strategy of advancing the trams across the river without widening Waterloo Bridge. It got as far as various LCC committees before the railway company came down hard on it and a Charing Cross road bridge was dropped as a fantastic wheeze.[9]

The anti-railway lobby enjoyed some *Schadenfreude* when part of the roof of Charing Cross Station collapsed the next year, destroying the Avenue Playhouse below. The havoc set back the company's plans, but it showed no sign of abandoning either bridge or station, despite renewed calls to use the opportunity to get rid of both. T.E. Collcutt, the RIBA's incoming president, urged the company to shift its terminus to the south side, suggesting a covered bridge across the river to minimise inconvenience to travellers. Collcutt followed this up with a sketch for a Charing Cross road bridge lined with shops – seemingly the earliest of many such projects to come.[10]

* * *

Thus far the dispute had been parochial. It was to revive as a cause bound up with the burgeoning movement for beautifying the metropolis. Architectural aesthetics seldom occupy centre-stage in London. But they did so at two self-consciously imperial moments, after the Battle of Waterloo and again in the years before the First World War. Why, patriotic commentators asked with fresh urgency, did the greatest city in the world have to suffer from such blatant ugliness? Why, in particular, was its noble Thames frontage so unprepossessing?

An international dimension now entered into these questions, transcending the old rivalry of London with Paris. In the United States the 'City Beautiful' movement was in full swing, as American civic leaders strove to repair decades of urban degradation. Across Europe, the theory and practice of urbanism, known quaintly in English-language circles as town planning, came to the fore. Britain was not wholly retrograde in these matters – its suburban housing was admired. But its city centres and industrial districts were behindhand, largely because its urban authorities had weak powers. The LCC was doing its best. It had even offered a lead by resolving, in 1908, after several false starts, to build its own headquarters on the blemished South Bank beside Westminster Bridge. But there was only so much the Council could do when its policies and visions were obstructed, as so often, by governments at Westminster; and its drive faltered after the Progressive Party lost power in 1907.

The 1910 Town Planning Conference held in London was a pivotal moment. By hosting this international event, Britain showed its eagerness to contribute to the new urbanism. The theories of Patrick Geddes and the suburban housing of Raymond Unwin offered a lead to the world.

Complex though town planning might be, few doubted as yet that it should be led by design – by architects, in other words. It was the RIBA that hosted the 1910 conference. From its aftermath emerged the London Society, a voluntary organisation created in 1912–13 with the aim of improving and beautifying the capital. Many European cities could boast similar, old-established civic societies, but London's size and elaboration had prevented any previous such body from gaining traction. As often with pressure groups, the London Society was most dynamic in its early years. Its broad membership included influential figures, John Burns among them. But it was dominated by architects, and soon chaired by the establishment architect Sir Aston Webb.

As regards the river, Captain George Swinton ushered in the enlarged vision with a letter to *The Times* of November 1910, renewing the call for a Charing Cross road bridge to replace the railway bridge as a memorial to Edward VII, recently deceased. Swinton's was among the most coherent of many ideas for a memorial. A leading Moderate councillor on the LCC with an interest in transport issues, he had been a key supporter of the plan for relocating the Council on the South Bank.[11] He was to become the most articulate advocate of a road bridge at Charing Cross. His original suggestion went beyond a simple anti-railway-bridge protest. The bend in the river, Swinton argued, made the South Bank and Waterloo area the 'central block of London', ideal for communication with both the City and Westminster. Two underground lines, the Waterloo and City Railway (opened 1898) and the Bakerloo Line (opened 1906), already linked Waterloo Station with the North Bank, while across Westminster Bridge lay 'the hub of the wheel of the LCC tramway system'. Now was the moment, while South Bank property was cheap, for Charing Cross Station to 'step over and join on'. Instead of one great railway terminus at Waterloo, there could be two.[12]

Swinton's appeal sowed seeds. In 1913 the London Society set up a South Bank committee. With the grand County Hall complete enough to house most of the LCC's staff, the dream was to displace more industry and wharfage and embellish the river front with further stone-faced blocks. Fresh vituperation against Charing Cross Railway Bridge now broke out: 'this beastly conglomeration of scrap iron . . . an eyesore of the most virulent kind', wrote *The Globe*; 'that awful nightmare of steel', Paul Waterhouse called it in a paper on 'The Surrey Side'. Once dismissed as visionary, the Charing Cross bridge project was coming into the realms of possibility, he prophesied. *The Times* supported the notion in weighty articles, while architects piled in with their designs.[13]

The dismal war year of 1916 saw no let-up in these minor metropolitan hostilities. The South Eastern Railway Company now came back to Parliament asking for a variation of the powers to enlarge its bridge once the war ended. Trains were getting heavier, some carrying 'their daily loads of wounded soldiers', claimed the Bill's supporters emotively.[14] Charing Cross Station was 'in the thick of things', employed not only for hospital trains but 'in constant use by ministers, high-ranging officials and their staff on their way to and from France'.[15] The wallpaper manufacturer Sir Walter Essex countered for the opposition, calling for the station's transfer across the river to 'a very much larger and wholly adequate site'. John Burns, who had maintained parliamentary silence since his resignation from the Government when war began, also rose to speak out 'with all his old vigour and force', quoting Wordsworth and referring to Canova's paean to Waterloo Bridge:

> Beauty is not a thing that materialists and cynics can brush lightly aside. It is paid for in solid cash by the people who value natural beauty in a city such as this river affords us, blended with architectural adornments, and the harmonious and symmetrical unity of commerce with civic pride, public taste, and fine public amenities.[16]

The company's Bill having been resoundingly rejected, the proponents of a new road bridge took the offensive. In newspaper articles reprinted as a London Society pamphlet, Burns, Aston Webb and a second architect, Reginald Blomfield, the main author, rehearsed the history of the case and put forward a plan for the new bridge. This showed a second Waterloo terminus on the opposite side of York Road from the existing one and fronting the river. Beside it, the new bridge leapt over the Victoria Embankment, slashed through the existing Charing Cross Station site and debouched into the Strand just east of Trafalgar Square (fig.113).[17]

The Burns, Webb and Blomfield scheme for the road bridge was far from the first. Unsolicited designs had been tossed around for years. As Swinton put it in a new article, 'no British architect worth the name has failed to build castles in the air about that glorious curve of the Thames'.[18] The tally of different bridge designs between 1908 and 1930 amounts to over a dozen (figs 114, 115).[19] Most were impractical, some foolhardy. Harold Falkner, for instance, wanted to move St Martin-in-the-Fields Church so as to get a good axis through to Charing Cross Road.

The difficulties were indeed formidable. A low-level bridge going over to the Embankment would not be much use. A high-level bridge and road to replace the station on the north side and connect with Trafalgar Square, as in the Burns-Webb-Blomfield pamphlet, was a more ambitious and costly proposition. It might compound traffic problems in the Strand. And where should the bridge land on the south side? It would have to relate to the terminuses, old

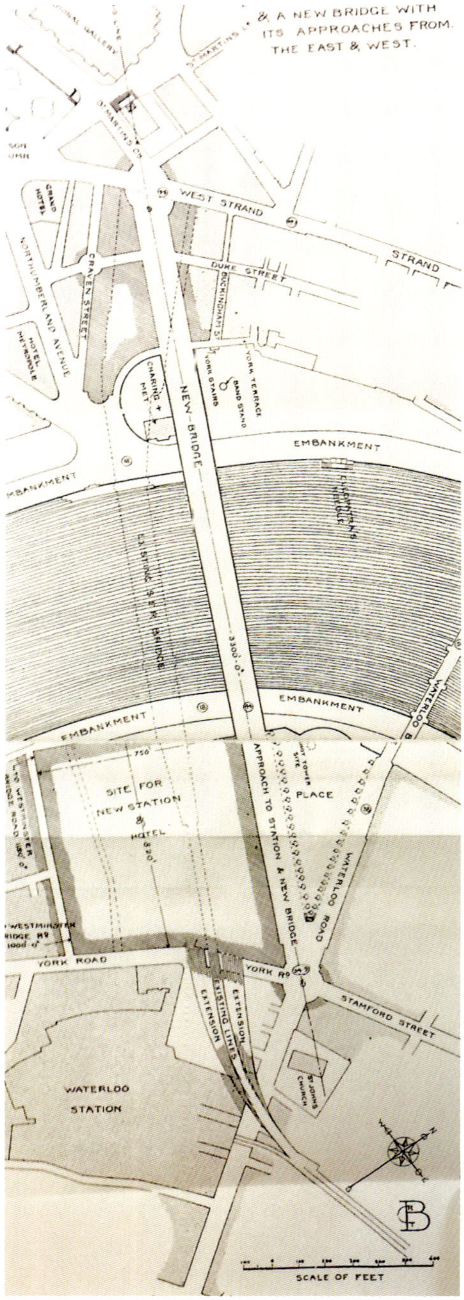

113 Plan for a Charing Cross Bridge from the London Society's pamphlet *The Charing Cross Improvement Scheme*, by John Burns, Aston Webb and Reginald Blomfield, 1916. The drawing is initialled by Blomfield

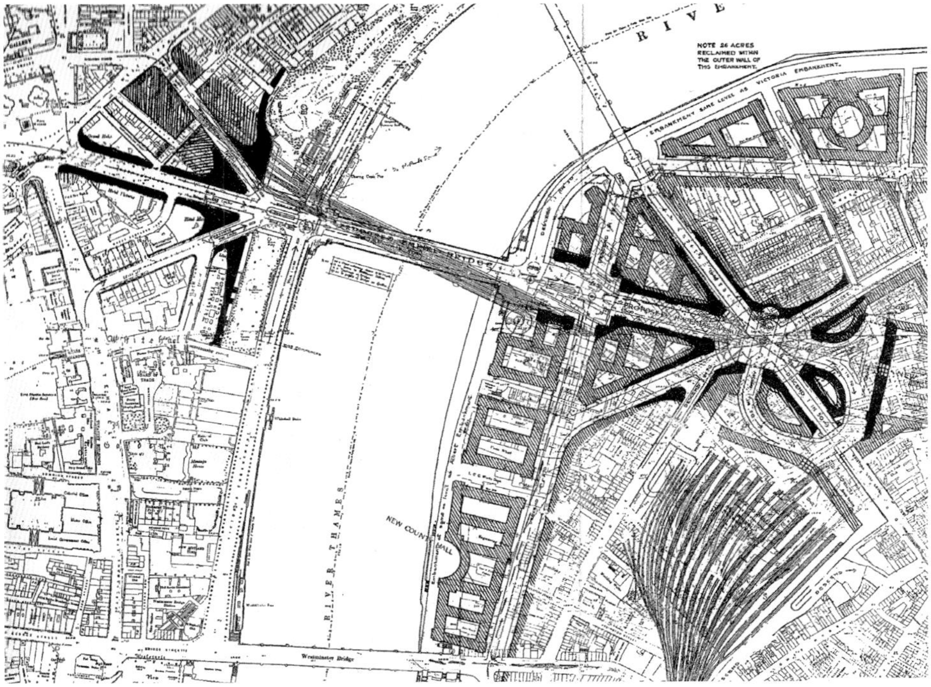

114 Plan for a Charing Cross Bridge by D. Barclay Niven, *c*.1914. One of many such plans, this one sets the bridge on the axis of Northumberland Avenue and ends at a new terminus for the South Eastern Railway

115 Perspective sketch by D. Barclay Niven and T. Raffles Davison, *c*.1914, showing avenues converging on a new place beside the Victoria Embankment on the north side of the proposed bridge

and new. Meanwhile the London and South-Western Railway had just embarked on a long campaign (1909–22) of rebuilding its ramshackle station to designs by its engineer, J.W. Jacomb-Hood. So any hope of getting the termini to relate *de novo* was scotched from the start. Swinton himself therefore abandoned the relocation faith and turned to advocating a two-level bridge with road traffic on top and trains underneath. That might leap handsomely over gorges, like Stephenson's High Level Bridge at Newcastle or Roebling's over Niagara Falls. But on the flattish Thames site it promised to be as obstructive as the bridge it aimed to replace.

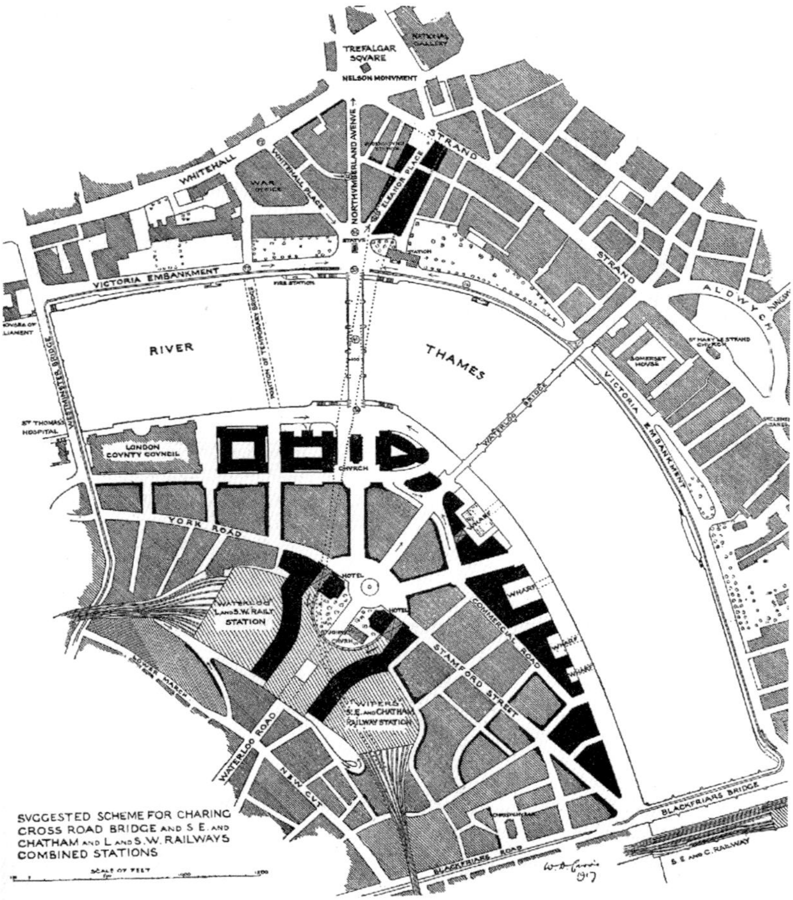

116 W.D. Caröe's plan for a Charing Cross road bridge, 1917, again using the Northumberland Avenue axis but ending on the south side at a circus, with the existing Waterloo Station on one side, a new 'Wipers' terminus for the South Eastern Railway on the other, and a raised platform between them

In view of the war, Swinton now wanted the bridge to commemorate the glorious dead. Herbert Baker suggested likewise in a letter to *The Times*, which the paper pompously endorsed.[20] The idea was taken up, for instance, by W.D. Caröe who wanted to cover over Waterloo Road and pair Waterloo Station with a second terminus to its east, sentimentally christened Wipers, the Tommies' name for Ypres (fig.116). Another fantasy dreamed of a 235ft-high monument on the site of Charing Cross Station, crowned by 'colossal statues of Liberty, Retribution, Peace and Victory'.[21]

Against this plethora of plans the railway company stood firm. Applying again to Parliament in 1917, it obtained fresh bridge-widening powers with a few provisos, but they could not be implemented till the war ended. Amidst post-war exhaustion and economic distress, there was an uneasy truce between the parties. As a sop to its detractors, the railway bridge was painted grey to blend with the river, instead of the old, staring, red oxide.[22]

* * *

In March 1923 the London Society put on an exhibition featuring some of the Charing Cross road bridge schemes. But attention was about to move abruptly down river. That autumn someone tipped off the *Architects' Journal* about the state of Waterloo Bridge. The pavement and roadway had started to undulate, rising at piers and falling at arch centres; the parapets were also leaning in and out, and exhibiting fractures and wide joints.[23] All the old problems of settlement were back. The focus was on the state of the third and fourth piers from the Lambeth side. The LCC responded urgently by injecting liquid concrete under pressure into the gravel round the piers. That exacerbated the problem; one of the piers sank two and a half inches in a week. As soon as the operation stopped, movement ceased.[24]

Next, Basil Mott was called in. By the following spring the engineers were reporting that the state of the bridge was 'extremely grave'.[25] Alarmed, the LCC's Improvements Committee decided to run up a temporary bridge and then rebuild the original, but to an 80ft width instead of the existing 42ft. The plan, as it emerged, was not to spoil the

117 Commuters crossing Waterloo Bridge on foot during its closure to traffic, 1924

elevations by corbelling out the flanks, but to create a new strip down the middle on fresh foundations; that, of course, would mean taking everything to pieces.[26]

A 'protest of the artists' against these plans erupted in *The Times*. The signatories were a mixed bunch. A few were architects, like Patrick Abercrombie, Ralph Knott the designer of County Hall, H.V. Lanchester and C.H. Reilly. More were literati and critics such as Arnold Bennett, Lawrence Binyon, E.V. Lucas, D.S. MacColl and St Loe Strachey. Lutyens agreed to sign but distanced himself from the suggested remedy of building a new bridge somewhere else. In the ensuing debate the LCC garnered some support, robustly from Blomfield, equivocally from Herbert Baker. Some thought that Waterloo Bridge might actually look better if it were wider. MacColl, soon to be central to the preservation campaign, pointed out that this would not meet the navigational objection to turning the arches into tunnels. Bernard Shaw, resident in nearby Whitehall Court, supported the widening lobby, adducing maverick arguments of his own. His only complaint about

Charing Cross Railway Bridge was noise: 'its appearance has never cost me a tear or a sleepless night'. As for Waterloo Bridge, 'I rather like the old thing. But it must go.' It was just a line of canal bridges laid end to end, Shaw added later.[27]

The bridge may have ceased to settle, but it had to be watched day and night.[28] It was actually shut to traffic except pedestrians for two months, between May and July 1924 (fig.117), causing chaos on the surrounding streets and bridges; schoolboys played marbles on the silent roadway.[29] The bridge then reopened with a weight limit, while the temporary bridge followed on quickly. Normal LCC tendering rules having been suspended, Sir William Arrol & Co. took the contract. Erecting the steel structure – which was to be on the downstream side – was no minor job. There were three spans, each of 75ft width, set on new cylindrical foundations in the river. The outer ones had to swing out from the line of the approaches, while the centre span was then slid across to join onto them. Complete by the late summer of 1925, after testing with motor buses packed with sandbags, this ugly makeshift was to continue in service for eighteen years (fig.118).[30]

118 Postcard with an aerial view of Waterloo Bridge looking north, with the temporary bridge beside it, *c.*1925. The old bridge is closed to traffic

Meanwhile the preservation lobby was mustering support. A reputable engineer, Harley Dalrymple-Hay, affirmed that Waterloo Bridge could be safely underpinned, against the opinions of Basil Mott and the LCC's engineer George Humphreys. The Royal Fine Art Commission (RFAC) was also stirring in the background. This government-sponsored body, invented to advise on any matters of public aesthetic interest it might care to consider, had just come into being. Its first chairman, the Earl of Crawford, was a stalwart of the London Society, whose work in many ways the Commission continued, only with an official voice and a national remit.[31] Its record was always chequered; in its early years there was much bickering between the high-rank architects who dominated its membership, notably Blomfield and Lutyens. From the time of its creation, consulting architects of lustre became a fixture in endowing large inter-war urban projects with acceptable faces, to greater or lesser success – and advantage to their bank balances. The Commission seems never to have taken on Waterloo Bridge formally. But in February 1925 it backed a delegation of societies and bodies which engaged with the LCC's Improvements Committee over what might be done to keep Rennie's masterpiece. The mood that summer was cautiously optimistic.[32]

The LCC responded by soliciting advice from one of the RFAC members, Sir Edwin Lutyens. Not even the eminent architect's most ardent admirer could say much for the ideas he came up with. Corbelling out the bridge to get extra width would not be right, Lutyens opined. Instead he proposed two bizarre options: either to build temporary suspension footpaths on either side of the structure, which could be removed once someone found a solution for the main bridge; or to construct a sweeping suspension bridge directly overhead, either for traffic or for pedestrians, as deemed best. As Lutyens admitted, these half-baked wheezes were tokens of failure: 'I deeply regret that I have failed to find a sure way of widening Waterloo Bridge by any method which does not, in some way, mar its brave appearance.'[33] Many interpreted these remarks as proof that the bridge would have to go. Meanwhile Reginald Blomfield, in one of his many trenchant letters to *The Times* about Waterloo Bridge, maintained that it could perfectly well be widened.[34]

Lutyens's hapless intervention stimulated a lobby now developing within the LCC to abandon compromise and go all out for a completely new, modern Waterloo Bridge of five arches to take six lanes of traffic. That became the stance of Herbert Morrison, the official Opposition leader after the 1925 LCC election boosted Labour numbers. The forthright Morrison called for the Council to free itself 'of all the cranks' and build a bridge to be 'a tribute to British architecture of the twentieth century'. After some dithering, that was adopted as official LCC policy in June 1926. There was talk of an architectural competition for the new bridge, with Sir Giles Gilbert Scott and Reginald Blomfield acting as two of four assessors.[35]

But the opponents of demolition were far from beaten. They pinned their faith on reviving the Charing Cross road bridge plan to take the traffic which could never be accommodated on Rennie's narrow bridge. They had also convened a standing conference of the official art-bodies opposed to the bridge's demolition. The chairman of this 'Thames Bridges Conference' was Arthur Keen, a decent elderly architect dating back to Arts and Crafts days.[36] In parallel, D.S. MacColl, another Royal Fine Art Commission member, assembled a powerful petition signed by a host of luminaries including both English archbishops, G.K. Chesterton, Arthur Conan Doyle, Rudyard Kipling, Earl Jellicoe and H.G. Wells. This called for 'further enquiry into the whole problem of London traffic and bridges, before the fate of Waterloo Bridge is finally determined'. The petition landed on Prime Minister Stanley Baldwin's desk in June 1926, the very month in which the LCC had resolved on a new bridge. A flurry of fresh letters appeared in *The Times*: one from nine French architects, reminding Britain that Waterloo Bridge enjoyed international renown; another from a group of engineers who maintained that 'there is a large preponderance of expressed engineering opinion in favour of underpinning'. Late signatories to the petition included Lloyd George, Ernest Rutherford, and Leonard and Virginia Woolf.[37]

* * *

Baldwin acquiesced and appointed a Royal Commission. That put paid to the LCC's idea of a competition for a new bridge. MacColl had already told Blomfield that it would be 'a blot on my escutcheon' to serve as an assessor, so he withdrew. With fresh wind in the preservationists' sails, he came round to the view that the LCC's decision to destroy the bridge was like 'the action of a doctor who, having first half-murdered his patient, decides to hide all trace of his incapacity by finishing him off'.[38]

Had the Royal Commission on Cross-River Traffic in London been set up years before, it might have done good. Instead, it was appointed in the context of a crisis. At least it had broad terms of reference, whence its name. Its chairman, Lord Lee of Fareham, had been among the signatories of the petition, while its membership of six included W.H. Dickinson, Burns's former colleague in the first protest against Charing Cross Bridge back in the 1890s. There was one engineer, the able Charles Inglis, but no expert on traffic or navigation, and no architect.

For all that, the Commission worked hard and swiftly, regardless of health or holidays, reporting after four months.[39] It encompassed issues up and down London River. It disposed neatly, for instance, of a St Paul's Bridge scheme, which the City Corporation, paddling its own canoe as ever, had been promoting for years, though no reputable traffic engineer or architect thought it anything but a vanity and distraction.[40] If the Commission's evidence and analyses were valuable, its recommendations were a surprise. It declined to endorse moving Charing Cross Station across the river. Instead, it suggested a two-level bridge for road and railway, slightly downstream of the old one. This was Swinton's idea, sketched out for the Commission as a steel bridge by the engineer Sir Owen Williams.[41] On Waterloo Bridge, another independent engineer, Sir Alexander Gibb, assured the Commission that it could be successfully preserved and strengthened. The report, published in December 1926, recommended a new compromise whereby its roadway would be widened into four lanes – less than the LCC had envisaged. A six-lane widening, it was argued, would exacerbate traffic problems at both ends, especially in the Strand.[42]

The aftermath of the Royal Commission was many further years of confusion, ignominy and farce. They will be dealt with as concisely as possible. The Government sent these conclusions for study to a committee of engineers, supposed to consist of Humphreys, representing the LCC, Basil Mott's firm of Mott, Hay and Anderson, and A.W. Szlumper from the Southern Railway (as it now was). The railway company sulked and would only let Szlumper advise the others.[43] Progress was slow, while critics carped on the sidelines. The rumour emerged that the double-decker bridge for Charing Cross was being costed at twice as much as had been predicted and would be dropped. No one liked it anyway: 'the effect on the scenery of the river of this great barrier of a bridge . . . would have been disastrous'.[44] It seemed that the Council would have to revert to its rebuilding scheme for Waterloo Bridge: 'the LCC are likely to win the second battle of Waterloo next month', said the *Daily Chronicle*.[45]

When the engineers reported in April 1928, they duly scrapped the double-decker scheme and reverted to the idea of moving the station to the South Bank and building a road bridge only at Charing Cross. At first the second terminus was to be on the Waterloo Junction site. The railway company would not have that; instead it reluctantly accepted moving to the Lion Brewery site, in other words the position of the present Royal Festival Hall. To develop this new bridge scheme and champion it before Parliament, the LCC appointed the consultant engineer Frederick Palmer, marking the first appearance of this important figure in the saga.

At this point a new howl of protest broke out, led by Keen and the Thames Bridges Conference. The chief objections were the mishandling of the roads behind the South Bank (Waterloo Road, for instance, became a dog's dinner of bridges and tunnels) and the want of good new building frontages. As before and since, plans for rebuilding on this side of the river were bedevilled by the different levels.[46]

The LCC, now in alliance with the Ministry of Transport (since the appointment of the Royal Commission the Government had become fatally embroiled in the tangle of issues), tried to mollify the critics by calling back Lutyens.[47] His second intervention was even less helpful than before. He was employed not to style the Charing Cross bridge, which he might have done well, but to cheer up the engineers' road schemes on either bank. He eventually came up with some paintings showing how the gloomy tunnels under the South Bank viaducts might be alleviated with good lighting and shops, and a model of the area around Charing Cross.[48]

Perhaps he hardly believed in these gestures himself. They were overshadowed by a row between Lutyens and his fellow architects which led to his resignation from the RIBA. The background was a want of scrupulousness and etiquette on Lutyens's part towards colleagues, or so they saw it. A letter from Arthur Keen to Lutyens, suggesting that he would do well for his reputation to give up the appointment, lit the fuse. It was meant as a private communication, but Keen made the mistake of writing on RIBA-headed paper. Lutyens saw it as an opportunity to checkmate his envious opponents. He sent the letter on to Herbert Morrison, who had now crossed the river and presided as Minister of Transport in the second Labour Government. Poor Keen, the mildest of men, must have been appalled to hear that his letter had been read out and roundly condemned as improper by Morrison during a Commons debate on the 'official scheme'.[49]

Though Morrison and the Government won the debate with a solid majority, when Palmer's Charing Cross road bridge scheme went to a Select Committee in March 1930, it underwent tough questioning and failed, the Committee chairman curtly telling the LCC: 'it is rejected'. A last-minute scramble between different schemes for the approaches seems to have irked the Committee, which thought the displaced station had been allotted the wrong South Bank site, or should not have faced the river front at all.[50]

Once again it was back to zero. The whole costly project looked less and less plausible. Everyone was exhausted. On the LCC the Municipal Reform Party, in power since 1907, was nearing the end of its tether, while the country's economic condition was deteriorating. The Council wearily appointed a broad-based Advisory Committee to take up the Charing Cross scheme again. It was chaired by a retired lawyer, assisted by Frank Pick, the ubiquitous Blomfield, Giles Scott, Raymond Unwin, Sir Frederick Palmer, Sir Herbert Walker from the Southern Railway, and some others. Palmer and Scott will feature prominently in the next chapter. Meanwhile Arthur Keen published a book in October 1930 setting out the whole history of the hopes for Charing Cross road bridge.

The Advisory Committee did its best but failed to find a consensus.[51] It investigated a multiplicity of schemes for the South Bank, mostly based on the idea that Charing Cross Station should move to the Lion Brewery site. Walker, in alliance with Blomfield – by now a convert to keeping the station where it was – disagreed; at this stage Blomfield was plugging a project of his own for a suspension road bridge.[52] Eventually two schemes went across to Morrison at the Ministry in the spring of 1931, one of them concocted by the LCC's own architects, but neither formally endorsed by the Council.[53] These were the final tottering months of the 1929–31 Labour Government. Morrison was willing to support either scheme with a 75 per cent grant, if only the LCC would make up its mind. But the economy was in a parlous state and the Cabinet would not support him. At the end of July Morrison was obliged to slay the Charing Cross bridge dragon one last time, on the grounds that there was not enough money in the coffers for the Government to support it from the national Road Fund.[54] He had never been whole-hearted about the idea. A new Waterloo Bridge was what he had always wanted – and a new Waterloo Bridge was what he was to get.

That should have been that, as far as plans for a road bridge at Charing Cross went. It wasn't quite. In the study for the South Bank integrated into Abercrombie and Forshaw's *County of London Plan 1943*, the railway disappeared yet again in favour of a simple road bridge crossing over to the Embankment (fig.119); further downstream, a Temple Bridge was resurrected too.[55] The wartime Government followed that up by appointing a 'Railway (London Plan) Committee' under Charles Inglis, a veteran from the 1926 Royal Commission, to sketch out broad plans for the future of railways in the London region. Not content with demolishing Charing Cross Station and Bridge all over again, Inglis's Committee recommended getting rid of Blackfriars, Cannon Street and Holborn Viaduct stations too, and burying every single Central London cross-river railway in tunnels.[56]

No wonder, then, that in some early sketches for the Festival of Britain – for instance Misha Black's 1946 notion of a megastructure enveloping the whole South Bank site – a road bridge was shown.[57] The

119 Excerpt from a drawing by William Walcot for Abercrombie and Forshaw's *County of London Plan 1943*, with a sketch of a proposed road bridge in replacement of Charing Cross Railway Bridge

idea even got as far as the first LCC drawings for the Royal Festival Hall. It was, of course, the railway that survived, its sonorous proximity inspiring the wrapping of the auditorium within a protective outer layer – the so-called 'egg in the box'.

* * *

Downstream, the agony went on. Would Waterloo Bridge be widened or replaced? That was the only question left. Early in 1932 the veteran dockers' leader, Ben Tillett, launched the most ferocious tirade yet against this 'Absalom of the bridges, the most useless that ever cursed a river by crossing it – this wretched bridge has obstructed river traffic for a hundred years.' Landlubbers had 'done their best to choke the river with obsolete bridges and many arches, obstructing, harassing traffic, piling danger on the top of difficulty in navigation for all craft and river workers.' Vessels had increased in size prodigiously, so that tugs could sometimes haul up to 3,000 tons on as many as six heavily laden craft behind them. Instead of a multiplicity of arches, narrow or widened, Tillett called for 'one huge span'. Much of this was rhetoric. The Royal Commission had looked into the issue and found that over a three-year period, 'not one single accident had occurred there which caused loss of life or even of cargo'.[58] Yet the *Daily Herald* endorsed Tillett, reminding its readers that 'It is London River that has made London.'[59] In like mood, the *News Chronicle* quoted from *Timon of Athens*: 'Down with it flat: take the bridge quite away.'[60]

The LCC was persuaded. In February 1932 its Leader, Sir Percy Simmons, announced a fresh beginning. Without competition, without further ado, there was to be a new Waterloo Bridge, to be designed by Sir Giles Scott in partnership with the engineer Sir Frederick Palmer of Rendel, Palmer and Tritton.[61] Here begins the story of the present Waterloo Bridge, to be recounted in the next chapter. Despite a distracting intervention from Owen Williams – who now came up, for anyone who would listen, with his own arch-free design in concrete which he costed at about half that of Scott's scheme[62] – it looked as if things were decided at last.

Not a bit of it. There was a warning rumble in March when, in a Lords debate, the preservationists proved as obdurate as ever and the LCC came in for some kicking. Lord Lee, in a bitter speech, pointed out that if his Commission had only been heeded, London would have acquired ten lanes of roadway across the Thames, six at Charing Cross and four at Waterloo. Now they were to lose 'a great architectural monument' while 'that red iron behemoth' at Charing Cross was to survive. And all because the friends of Waterloo Bridge had 'filled the newspapers and the platforms with their discordant criticisms of the [Commission's] scheme on the ground that it was not the particular scheme which they individually favoured'. So the LCC had concluded: 'Really this kind of thing cannot go on any longer.' Now everyone, said Lee, was confronted with a bridge which was to be an unnecessary six lanes wide just to get trams across, although trams were outdated.[63]

In June 1932 the clause in the LCC's annual Money Bill relating to the new bridge was thrown out in the Commons by a clear majority. This time the leader of the charge was Sir William Davison, who professed that Waterloo Bridge was as sacred to the generation of 1815 as was the Cenotaph today. He advocated a return to the corbelling-out policy, which would give the bridge four lanes at a modest cost – less than that of the freelance Williams scheme.[64]

Morrison (no longer Minister of Transport, he was now back leading the LCC opposition) urged the Council to go ahead with the

120 Herbert Morrison, cigarette in mouth, takes a symbolic mallet to start the demolition of Waterloo Bridge, 20 June 1934

new bridge, regardless of Government subsidy.[65] Briefly it looked as if that might happen. Then prudence prevailed, the LCC crumbled and sought to negotiate. At the end of 1932 the old options were back on Prime Minister Stanley Baldwin's table: reconstruct the present bridge to three or four lines, or build a new one with six according to the Scott-Palmer design.[66] The Government recommended the former option, with advice from the Royal Fine Art Commission and the employment of an architect. Rendel, Palmer and Tritton were accordingly put back on to the reconstruction job alongside Scott, who picked up a tidy 1,000 guineas for his unbuilt bridge design.[67]

Reluctantly, the LCC set about the task. The bridge would have to close for four years ('Four Years More!' howled the *Daily Mirror*[68]), while four piers were underpinned, and two piers and three arches completely rebuilt; all traffic would have to use the temporary bridge.

Operations of this kind were unpredictable, so a detailed specification had first to be written, after which contractors' tenders would set out how they intended to tackle the job. Sir Henry Maybury, the Government's heavyweight former Director General of Roads, was called in; his advice would help to guarantee the promised subsidy. It was February 1934 before tenders were finally called for. Uncertainty still prevailed as to the road's width. The LCC's own architects, for instance, came up with a solution for corbelling out the bridge slightly so as to get a modestly increased width, on the lines of Dalrymple-Hay's ideas ten years before. But the Council said it would consider any reasonable scheme. Meanwhile Morrison, intransigent in the background, demanded an end to all the folly.[69]

He it was who won out. In the LCC elections of March 1934, Labour trounced the Municipal Reformers, ending with a clear majority of sixteen, for the first time in London's history – a momentous victory. As the new Leader of the Council, one of Morrison's first actions was to scrap the refurbishment scheme and reinstate the Scott design. Who cared if a penny-pinching Government would not subsidise the scheme? London could manage its own destiny. Three months later, Morrison was out in the rain with his deputy George Strauss, cigarette dangling from mouth, wielding a symbolic mallet and attacking the granite parapet (fig.120). The curse of Waterloo Bridge was lifting at long last.[70]

12

A New Bridge

The battle of the bridges was a battle of generations. The protagonists who pressed for a new Charing Cross bridge and fought to keep Rennie's masterpiece – Blomfield, Burns, Keen, Lutyens, MacColl and Swinton – were thorough Victorians, dating from the 1850s or 1860s. Giles Gilbert Scott, the new bridge's architect, was born in 1880; Herbert Morrison, who cut the Gordian knot by peremptorily decreeing the demolition of the old one, in 1888. Barely thirteen when the old queen died, Morrison was forty-six when he won power for Labour at County Hall in 1934, ousting the Municipal Reformers whose lacklustre leadership of the London County Council went back to before the First World War. Morrison's brusque solution of the Waterloo Bridge question stood for a gust of change ruffling London's whole polity.

There was one exception to this shift in age-group. The engineers appointed to work alongside Scott were Rendel, Palmer and Tritton. The London principal of this long-established business was Sir Frederick Palmer (1862–1934). The forceful Palmer did not survive to play much part in the bridge's design, which was to be ably taken up by his juniors. Yet he was crucial in the run-up to the project, as in the inter-war strategy for other Thames bridges.[1]

After the death of James Meadows Rendel in 1856, his firm's fortunes became identified with imperial undertakings, especially in India where it monopolised infrastructural tasks for the East Indian Railway Company. Palmer made his name as principal engineer for that company's ninety-three-span Upper Sone (now Nehru Setu) Bridge, said, when it was completed in 1900, to be the second longest bridge in the world. He then took charge at the port of Calcutta. On the strength of his strategic skills he returned to England, winning the post in 1909 of chief engineer to the Port of London Authority, newly created to bring order and direction to the facilities of the tidal Thames. Palmer put all his drive into formulating a future for London's outmoded docks. But the PLA was a troubled body. He resigned in 1913 to rejoin his old firm, now Rendel, Palmer and Tritton, taking with him copious consultancy jobs related to the docks and indeed all along London River.

Seven Thames bridges downstream of Teddington were built or rebuilt between the world wars.[2] Of these, four came within the County of London. Lambeth and Wandsworth were engineered by the LCC's own staff, but Chelsea and Waterloo ended up with Rendel, Palmer and Tritton. These jobs followed on from Palmer's role in devising and championing the LCC's abortive Charing Cross road bridge of 1930 and his membership of the hapless Advisory Committee which tried to sort things out thereafter (pp 209–10). He and his firm were also hired to help with one of the schemes to save and widen the old Waterloo Bridge around that time.[3]

The story of Chelsea Bridge is instructive. The 1926 Royal Commission had recommended rebuilding this shaky Victorian suspension bridge. Five years later the LCC announced its reconstruction, with the Ministry of Transport paying 60 per cent of the cost. Palmer was singled out by name as the engineer and awarded a favourable contract. If there was ever talk of an arched bridge, it soon gave way to a scheme for a six-lane suspension bridge. Later, the Rendel engineers justified this choice by arguing that the closely spaced Thames bridges further downstream were 'rightly' of the arch type, whereas at Chelsea there was a good straight stretch of open river; besides, it was better for navigation not to prolong the tunnel effect produced by the nearby Grosvenor Bridge taking trains in and out of Victoria Station – another of the obstructive railway bridges that encumbered London River.[4]

These were dire times for the national economy, so the first Chelsea Bridge project fell away when the Government grant was withdrawn. It revived in November 1933, not long before Morrison came to power at County Hall, when the Ministry agreed to renew its grant if the width came down from six lanes to four and associated roadworks were omitted. With Palmer's health failing, the contracts for Chelsea and the other Thames works which had been awarded to him personally

121 Chelsea Bridge in 1937, looking south towards Battersea Park

were transferred to Rendel, Palmer and Tritton. The design was now recommenced from scratch under engineers lacking Palmer's public profile.

One of these, J.R.H. Otter, is said to have suggested that they should apply to Chelsea Bridge the principle of the self-anchored suspension bridge – in other words a structure in which the traditional massive anchorages for the suspension cables at the bridge's two ends are omitted and the forces within them resolved by high-tension steel girders within the deck. This system had been first employed over a wide river at the Deutz Bridge over the Rhine at Cologne (1913–15) and was subsequently adopted in a famous trio of bridges over the Allegheny River in Pittsburgh.[5] It says something about British engineering at this time that the method had not been previously tried in the United Kingdom.

Be that as it may, the new Chelsea Bridge as reconstructed in 1935–7 was a success, and at £310,737 cost about half the estimate for the original design. The LCC's architects added only a few light decorative touches to Rendel, Palmer and Tritton's structure. Obelisks were preferred to old-style arches for the steel pylons; if the junction between the tops of the pylons and the prestressed cables is more curious than elegant, that holds true for many suspension bridges (fig.121).

Who designed Chelsea Bridge? Besides Otter – mainly a technician – we have the names of Ernest Buckton and Harry Fereday, who wrote it up for the *Journal of the Institution of Civil Engineers*. Both were senior figures within the Rendel firm. Fereday had presided over its bridge and steelwork department and was an expert on Indian bridges, but he was over sixty when the revised Chelsea design was made and retired in the year the bridge opened.[6] More likely the overall leadership came from Buckton, who had been assisting Palmer at the time of the Advisory Committee on Charing Cross bridge.[7] He was also to be heavily involved at Waterloo – to which we now come.

* * *

As recounted in the last chapter, the opening moves for designing the new Waterloo Bridge took place early in 1932, again in the days of the pre-Morrison London County Council. Herbert Morrison was then in the doldrums, having lost his powerful position as Minister of Transport and then his parliamentary seat after the general election of October 1931, when the National Government came in to cope with the economic crisis. The new minister was John Pybus, a Liberal. As at Chelsea, the Ministry offered a 60 per cent grant, but here only on condition that the LCC employ 'an architect of high standing and repute'. The odds were that the mantle would fall on Sir Giles Gilbert Scott, working with Sir Frederick Palmer.[8] The LCC formally confirmed that in mid-February.

How was it that Scott slipped into the job? One must go back. He had been approached, with Reginald Blomfield, to be an assessor for the 1926 competition for a new Waterloo Bridge which never took place. Then in May 1930, when the Select Committee had summarily rejected the LCC's scheme for a Charing Cross bridge, he wrote at length to *The*

122 Sir Giles Gilbert Scott's sketch design for a masonry road bridge at Charing Cross, 1931

Times to defend the architects involved against Frank Pick, who had claimed that they had devoted insufficient study to the planning and traffic issues. That was unfair, responded Scott. Architects indeed should be planners and not just ornamentalists, as people still seemed to think. The trouble was that they had not been given the data they needed.[9]

So when Lord Crawford approached Scott later that year to represent the Royal Fine Art Commission on the LCC's Advisory Committee which was trying to rescue the Charing Cross bridge project, he could hardly say no. He worked diligently at the nightmare brief. His instinct was to solve the problem by putting the new South Bank railway terminus underground, as the Americans had been doing since the advent of electrification, but he knew that would never wash because it would mean displacing two underground lines. So, like other members

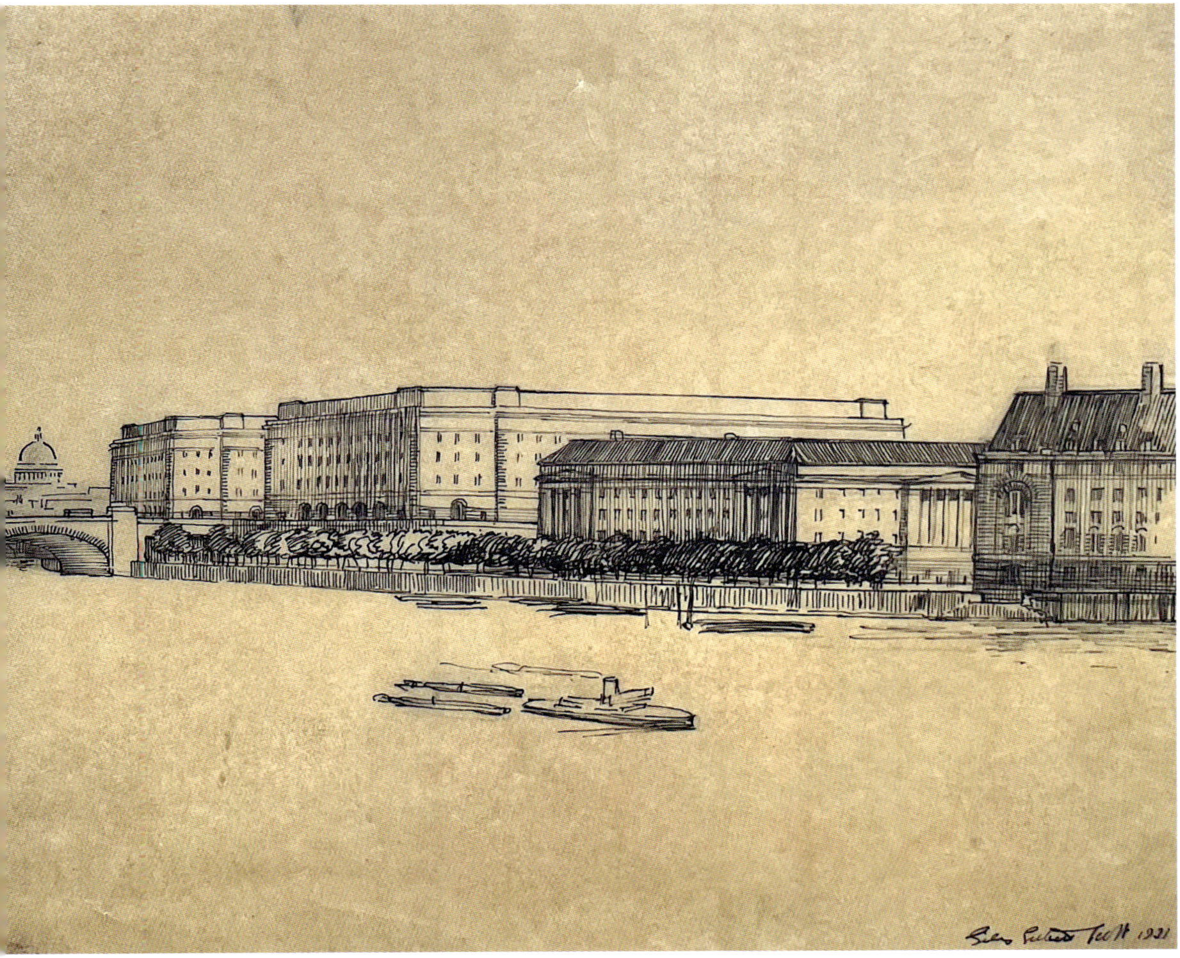

of the Advisory Committee, he came up with dutiful proposals for a new road bridge and a new South Bank terminal for the railway. For the bridge, he first (in November 1930) suggested a fairly obstructive steel bowstring truss structure, then (in January 1931) a conventional arched masonry design – of five arches, like the future Waterloo Bridge (fig.122). Though he upheld his schemes against others, he cannot have been surprised when they were set aside. At any rate, his work on the Committee brought him into contact with Sir Frederick Palmer and his deputy, Ernest Buckton.[10]

Sir Giles Scott was a first-class and flexible designer, skilled in modern versions of all the traditional styles and cautiously committed to architectural development. He was also known to be tractable, courteous and reasonable, more so than many of his rivals. He personally answered all the many letters he received, preposterous ones included, in a polite and accommodating tone, though he could also be firm. No doubt he was the same in committee work. So clients liked working with him. Naturally he made his compromises. He had been slippery on whether the old Waterloo Bridge should be kept, as the trenchant Blomfield enjoyed pointing out.[11] Nor – and in this he was not so singular – did he care to explain the purpose and logic, let alone the theory, behind his designs. His instincts were for reticence. At the same time Scott had a strong sense of his own value. The LCC's officers must have been apoplectic when apprised that his fee for the new bridge would be 8,000 guineas. He was beaten down to 7,000 and finally 5,000 guineas, of which a thousand went on the first, abortive design. Once that had been agreed, he stuck to his word.[12]

Once appointed, Scott and Palmer met several times, but we do not know what they said to one another.[13] Palmer was still then hyperactively embroiled in far-flung schemes like an expansion of the Port of Haifa. Probably even before he died in 1934, the main discussions were with his deputy, Ernest Buckton. The only evidence we have are some remarks made by Scott after the bridge had been completed, referring to conversations with Buckton. Here is the gist of them:

> The first thing which had to be decided was the type of bridge to cross the river at that point . . . The first design was of a more monumental structure, with pylons at the entrances at both ends, and it was much more of an architectural solution; but even before that design it had been necessary to decide upon the type of bridge to be erected. Mr. Buckton had shown him a sheet containing a large number of possible solutions for carrying the road traffic and satisfying the navigation requirements. Those were the primary practical requirements, and they could be met by about twenty types of bridges. Therefore, it was necessary to decide which type was the most suitable. He had felt strongly that the constructional elements of the bridge should be below the road-level, owing to the view down the river, with St Paul's in the background, and the general character of London and its bridges. It had seemed to him that anything in the shape of a suspension bridge or a

> bowstring bridge, or any type of bridge with a large quantity of superstructure, would be unsuitable for the position in question. It was also necessary to consider the question of the navigational headroom. A good height had to be provided for large barges, so that not much room was available for constructional work underneath the roadway, and that factor influenced the selection of the design and type. The positioning of the piers was dictated largely by the position of the navigation channel, which was a comparatively narrow part of the river; and another consideration was the relation of the appearance of the bridge to that of the adjoining buildings.[14]

That is a fairly typical Scott statement, precise, sensible and bland – qualities manifest in the bridge he designed. Given the fraught background to the project, the broad aesthetic choices must have been his. Beyond that, there is little sign of detailed collaboration with the engineers. It would be not without a grain of truth to suggest that Scott was embellishing the engineers' structure and behaving like the ornamentalist he had denied that an architect should be when responding to Pick. If so, was there harm in that? In Scott's other consultancy roles, at Battersea and Bankside Power Stations, for instance, he had a larger role in shaping the structures. But then a bridge is not a building.

Scott submitted his 'monumental' design to the LCC in May 1932. Seven arches in stone-clad reinforced concrete faced the river. The roadway, absolutely flat as in the Rennie bridge, was broad enough for six lines of traffic, including trams in case they were still thought necessary. Towards the ends of the bridge, pairs of square, Egyptian-type pylons reared up – mini-versions of the tower for the University Library at Cambridge that Scott was designing at the time. They were to be topped off with low-relief scenes from the Battle of Waterloo.

Surviving drawings (figs 123, 124) make clear that from the start the arches were shallow structures which did not run through laterally under the bridge.[15] The roadway between them was carried on a series of concrete cross-beams beneath the flat deck. The shallow arches and deck supported on beams helped to meet the navigational anxieties about a tunnel structure and save money. This substructure was the most visible

123 Perspective of north end of Sir Giles Gilbert Scott's 1932 design for Waterloo Bridge

124 Elevation, section and half-plan of Sir Giles Gilbert Scott's 1932 design for Waterloo Bridge

contribution of the Rendel, Palmer and Tritton engineers, and will be further described when we come on to the bridge's final design. All that need be said here is that this solution was present from the outset.

The monumental design was a hostage to fortune, given the political and economic straits of the time. No sooner had it been released than the Government killed the LCC Money Bill that was meant to pay for it. All hands, including Rendel, Palmer and Tritton's, now went back to trying to rescue the Rennie bridge, as recounted in the last chapter.

Only Morrison's victory in the LCC election of March 1934 resurrected the scheme from the long list of Thames bridge might-have-beens. But it would have to be pared down. There were rivals, too, lapping at Scott's heels, among them proposals by J.B. Mendham and by Oliver Hill, the latter a sweeping three-arch design promoted by a socialite, Freda, Lady Forres, with giant statues by Charles Sargeant Jagger (her sculpture-teacher) rising above the piers.[16] The steel industry was still lobbying for a suspension bridge. Above all there was the irrepressible, tactless but mightily able Sir Owen Williams, who had estimated his arch-free scheme of 1932 at half the price of the monumental design. Williams now came back with a fresh three-span bridge which he costed at £535,000, as against an estimate for Scott's project little short of £1,300,000 – almost four times the eventual cost of Chelsea Bridge.[17] All that had to come from the LCC's coffers, as Morrison had offended the Ministry by going it alone and could expect no government grant.[18]

In the event Scott and the engineers were able to persuade Morrison and his young lieutenant, George Strauss, chairman of the LCC's Highways Committee, to entrust them with revising their project. At that point, for the first and only time, the record reveals Ernest Buckton putting pressure on Scott. In a letter of June 1934 he begs the architect not to tone down his earlier effort, but to go instead for a functional design while retaining the twin-arch principle:

> Admittedly less 'life' can be introduced, but I feel your master hand can, by various subtleties, give life even to a purely functional bridge . . . I feel we may be led away at too early a date to a compromise between the monumental and the functional, instead of a really functional bridge.[19]

Buckton may have been pushing at an open door. At any rate he won. As agreed in October 1934, there were to be only five equal spans of 230ft instead of seven. As at Chelsea, the roadway came down from six lanes to four. All the ceremonial trappings went, while at the north end the first arch spanned simply over the Victoria Embankment and opened up the 'wonderful view' (Buckton's phrase) in place of the previous arrangement with a short straight span (fig.125).[20]

125 Northern arch of the new bridge, showing the revised embankment arch, from a drawing commissioned by Sir Giles Gilbert Scott and published in 1934

The change from seven arches to five did not alter the fundamental design of the structure. As before, the shallow arches concealed twin longitudinal girders in reinforced concrete below the deck, with stiffening cross-beams at regular intervals (fig.126). These hidden beams – the keynote of the structure – divided into continuous lengths over the two outer river spans, with short cantilevers at the two ends and a central span of almost 94ft.[21] This solution is said to have been worked out by Jack Cuerel, one of the Rendel engineers working with Buckton.[22] The idea of such a 'continuous beam' in concrete behind arches was not new, having been used, for instance, in the much shorter George V Bridge, Glasgow (1924–8).[23] The principle was explained to the public by Christian Barman in a short broadcast when the bridge opened.[24] It was not grasped by everyone. A.P. Herbert, the MP and panjandrum on many topics, not least the Thames, fatuously wrote: 'I once passed under

126 Under the arches of New Waterloo Bridge, from E.J. Buckton and J. Cuerel, 'The New Waterloo Bridge', *Journal of the Institution of Civil Engineers*, vol.20, no.7, 1943, p.170

the Bridge in a boat which carried Sir Giles, Sir Edward [sic] Lutyens and other architects. The top surface of the arches is not continuous: each is broken, I suppose for economy's sake, by a wide hiatus in the middle. I pointed up and said genially, "That's a skimpy bit of work, Sir". Sir Giles smiled ruefully and said, "I didn't mean it to be like that".'[25]

But why were arches needed at all? Why did not the authorities insist on a cheaper trabeated bridge of the kind that Owen Williams had repeatedly championed. The answer must lie in the painful record of Waterloo and Charing Cross Bridges. Parliamentarians, the LCC, the architects and Scott himself all expected an arched bridge, and an arched bridge was what they got. The changes from the monumental design did not in fact save a lot of money – perhaps £100,000. Even allowing for the greater width of the river at Waterloo compared to Chelsea, this was still a costly bridge.

Modernist taste is inclined to favour the revised design as simpler, sleeker, more rational. Maybe so; but a pared-down design allows the eye less to savour. At its best, the streamlined classicism in architectural vogue between the wars retains a certain nobility and formality. When the streamlining is scraped away, some weakening of identity results.

The mood of the moment being to get on with things, Scott's revised design received an almost universal welcome. It sailed through the

127 Vertical stone cladding of the arch faces and balustrade, with concrete eroding in between, 2024

LCC unopposed, contented the navigation lobby, and encountered little criticism. Bernard Shaw, always good for a captious comment, now thought all the Thames crossings ought to be suspension bridges. Blomfield, surprisingly, felt the bridge ought to have only three arches and objected to the Portland stone facing.[26] The LCC, probably briefed by the engineers, answered that the springings for a three-arch bridge would have to start lower, hindering navigation.

As to the facings, there has always been a broad aesthetic preference in London for Portland stone over concrete, and perhaps over granite as well. But it had not stood up well to the unremitting wind, wave and pollution of London River in earlier bridges. In fact some granite, reused from the old bridge, was redeployed at a low level to withstand the bite of the tides. Higher up, much depended on selecting the right Portland beds. After debate, 'Fine Roach' was chosen over 'True Roach' or 'Whitbed' on the grounds that it provided sharper arris edges.[27] The materials experts validated these choices. Today the stonework has lost its crispness and looks slightly raddled and shelly, but not too damaged (fig.127).

Of particular interest are the facings of the arches and spandrels. At the time of the monumental design, Scott seems to have intended to

128 Detail of the piers, arches and spandrels of the new bridge, looking north

set them out in conventional horizontal masonry. As late as January 1937 he was rethinking this and considering concrete, bush-hammered for relief. Feeling that concrete made with Portland cement looked drab, he came out 'dead against it'. He therefore consulted Maxwell Ayrton, architect of the recently completed Twickenham Bridge, which Scott admired. Ayrton replied that if the right sand and aggregate were used, the colour problem could be resolved.[28] Scott cannot have been convinced. Hence his decision to use thin Portland stone slabs deployed vertically, as if to say 'Look, we are only cladding!' It is pleasing enough for those who savour such gestures. They drop down upon a continuous brown concrete rim neatly defining the edge of the arches (fig.128).

* * *

Destruction had to precede construction. As the new bridge was to follow the exact same lines, the whole of the old one had first to come down, superstructure, arches, piers, footings and all. Past troubles meant there was never a chance of reusing any of the old foundations. The demolition of old Waterloo Bridge was one of the sights of London in 1934–6. No sooner had Morrison and his lieutenants administered their iconoclastic blows to the parapet in June 1934 than the bridge closed and Sir William Arrol and Co.'s men moved in. At this juncture the revised Scott design had yet to be approved. But Morrison was in haste to thwart yet another last-ditch attempt to rescue the Rennie bridge. So tendering was suspended. Arrols took the work on a 'value cost' basis: the LCC bore the expenditure, estimated at over £200,000, and paid a percentage plus overheads to the contractors.[29]

The intricate and dangerous demolition work probably cost the engineers – once again Rendel, Palmer and Tritton, working with the

129 Removing balusters from the old bridge

130 Demolition work on Waterloo Bridge looking south, July 1935, showing the hangers from the superstructure keeping the arches in place, and the temporary bridge behind

LCC – as much pains as the new bridge's design. Getting rid of the superstructure was the easy part. The granite balusters, some 1,500 of them (fig.129), were sold off by the LCC at a pound a piece or donated to public bodies all over the Empire, as were the lamp standards. The great issue was how to take down Rennie's deep and precisely balanced arches. The decision was to set up lines of trussed steel girders above them from which were suspended new steel centerings fitting tightly to the shape of the arches (fig.130). These girders were made by Arrols in Glasgow, shipped by sea and river barge, and assembled on site. They dominate images of the scene, for instance, Charles Cundall's paintings of the dismantling operations (fig.131). Once the arches had safely been removed, stone by stone, and taken to a field in Harmondsworth for storage, the men could construct new steel coffer dams round the old piers and foundations, and the engineers could finally assess their state

131 Old Waterloo Bridge in demolition, a painting by Charles Cundall, 1935

before they were removed. They found the masonry of the piers in good condition. The wooden piles were mostly sound too, but those below Pier 5 were parlously out of plumb, with little strength left to their core.

Buckton and Fereday presented a detailed account of the operations to the Institution of Civil Engineers in October 1936 – the first time the Civils had hosted such a paper. The demolition was then nearing completion. The authors assessed Rennie's bridge fully and frankly. They were impressed that it had been constructed so speedily and admired the quality of the masonry. But they denied that it had ever been a 'national monument':

> Viewed from the Embankment it was a beautiful bridge, but passing under or over it was a disappointment. It had had its day and had lived its life. Apart from its failure and consequent propping, it had passed from utility to obstruction by the changing

> conditions around it. Its beauty remained, but was marred by a broken back.[30]

Despite a few demurrers, most of the audience accepted the fait accompli and eagerly awaited the new bridge.

* * *

The story of the new bridge's construction has been told with authority by Christine Wall.[31] The main contract went not to Arrols but to Peter Lind and Co., whose lower tender of £647,624 was accepted in July 1937. It covered the bridge proper, not the approaches. After repeated failures to get a curmudgeonly Government to subsidise the project, Morrison threatened to delay various road improvements in London desired by the Ministry of Transport. That caused the Government to give in and vote £400,000 towards the bridge that December – a 'Christmas box for London'.[32] So the LCC ended up paying much less than the £1.3 million that had once been feared, though the costs of demolition and the approaches must be allowed for.

Peter Lind was one of several Danish-born engineer–contractors who made inroads into the inter-war British construction industry on the basis of their grip on concrete technologies. The design and connections of the reinforcement within the concrete work was the key. Instead of a plethora of conventional hooked and overlapping steel bars, Lind and the engineers opted for arc-welded bars joined at the butts, which reduced weight to a minimum and promoted the development of welding skills among the workforce. Lind himself was riding high when he won the contract for Waterloo Bridge; he now embarked on a grand house for himself at St George's Hill, Weybridge, in which the floorboards of the principal rooms consisted of elm salvaged from the piles of the old bridge. Some quantity of stonework and cobbles also made their way to St George's Hill.[33]

Operations began in October 1937 with the erection of a high-level gantry for cranes on the downstream side, next to the temporary bridge, while the foundations and piers were being built up. The office of the site engineer, H.F. Nolans, filled up with souvenirs dragged up from the mud: 'an ancient cannon ball, a pair of handcuffs, a service rifle (probably jettisoned by a soldier in the last war), an anti-aircraft shell of the same period, an empty cash-box, a pair of leaden dumb-bells and, most interesting of all two nautilus shells belonging to a species that exist only in tropical countries'.[34]

The contract encountered many problems. There were strikes in both 1938 and 1939, arising in the first instance from attempts to use non-unionised labour for the steel fixing. As Lind's responses were reasonable, the disputes were soon settled. A copper cylinder containing newspapers, coins and stamps of the day was buried in the northern abutment in May 1939, when completion was expected the following year.[35] To cope with the anticipated increase of traffic the LCC now planned a roundabout, or 'Waterloo Circus', at the north end of the bridge which would have destroyed the Lyceum Theatre and Inveresk House. Mercifully that never happened. The fate of the bridge's southern end has been, as always, less happy; the 'bullring' roundabout here dates from the 1960s (fig.132).

With war looming (a large National Service slogan, 'We've Got To Be Prepared', went up on the temporary bridge), ambitions had to be curtailed. The pool of labour shrank. By 1940–41 the workforce had fallen to between 50 and 150 men from an initial 500; the structural work on the south end of the bridge was complete but the north end lagged behind. Changes had to be made to the welding methods because of the shortage of skills. All London's bridges became obvious targets during the Blitz – as Morrison remarked when the bridge finally opened, it was a miracle that none was destroyed. Such were the perils of the Waterloo site that operations became hazardous and intermittent. 'The bridge and adjacent works were hit nineteen times', says Christine Wall. A direct hit at the north end by a high explosive bomb in May 1941 killed five people sheltering in the tram tunnel beneath. To this has to be added the damage suffered by Peter Lind and Co., their subcontractors and suppliers, at depots up and down river.

Today, Waterloo Bridge is celebrated as the 'Ladies' Bridge'. As their boats pass beneath, tourist guides invariably proclaim that it was built by women. Since women feature elsewhere in this book chiefly as the sick, the sex workers and the suicidal, all possible amends should be

132 Bullring roundabout at the south end of the bridge, completed in 1965. St John's Church, Waterloo is at the far right

made here. Christine Wall has looked scrupulously into the question. Altogether about 25,000 women worked in the British construction industry during the Second World War. From reminiscences gleaned from members of the male workforce, Wall concluded it to be highly likely that some women, perhaps not that many, worked on the finishing stages of Waterloo Bridge around 1941–3. Definitely, women worked on dismantling the temporary bridge in 1943–4, after the new bridge had opened to two lanes of traffic; photographs from the *Daily Herald* archive show three face-shielded women cutting steel (fig.133). The dismantled elements, one newspaper assured its readers, would 'soon be hurled at the Germans as shells, tanks, and other kinds of munitions'.[36] More constructively, some of the girders went to repair bridges in Holland damaged during the war.[37]

With traffic trickling along the two completed lanes, the final stages of construction dragged on under Peter Lind and Co. into 1945 (fig.134). Temporary tubular railings were affixed to the parapet. Scott must have been disappointed because he had always been interested in the balustrade design, and in 1945–7 he was still busying himself designing

133 Women cutting up steelwork from the temporary bridge on the South Bank, 1944

134 Applying the finishing touches to the new bridge

135 New Waterloo Bridge, north stairs on the downstream side, 1946

136 New Waterloo Bridge completed, 1943. The temporary bridge remains in place, with only two lanes of the new structure in use

special lamp standards.[38] None of this transpired. The temporary railings have never been replaced and continue to be admired, but they must be easier to slip across than those on any other Thames bridge in London. Notices offering help for the afflicted now feature; so the ghost of old Waterloo Bridge lingers on. At both ends, Scott designed stone-lined public staircases down to ground level worthy of their august predecessors (fig.135). On the Victoria Embankment side, even the old stink of urine was carried over.

The bridge (figs 136, 137) had been in full use for over a year when Herbert Morrison, now Lord President of the Council in the new Labour Government, came to open it formally on 10 December 1945. There was a subdued ceremony in the fog (fig.138).[39] A worn inscription at the northern end, downriver side, records the occasion. The completion seems to have been greeted without much enthusiasm. A grudging *Architectural Review* had only this to say: 'The foil this bridge provides to the superb accidental effects in which London is so rich, is a hint of possible future triumphs and reconstructions.'[40] Enthusiasm had to await Ian Nairn, writing twenty years later:

> This is still the best modern bridge in Britain. The only sad thing is that it replaced a masterpiece by Sir John Rennie [Nairn got

137 New Waterloo Bridge completed, *c.*1950. A similar view looking downstream, but with all lanes open and the temporary bridge gone

> that slightly wrong] . . . In its bridge-ness it must outdo even Rennie. The rhythm of the five arches is like a coiled spring, catapulting you from one bank to the other. Physically, it is supported by piers; spiritually the bridge hardly seems to notice them. The arches are split longitudinally and a magnificent view of the space between them can be got from the Embankment, directly underneath.[41]

Scott still longed to make one final effort and shoe in some sculpture. Once the grand pylons of his 1932 design had bitten the dust, the approaches were left only with modest plinths at the heads of the end stairs. They had originally been destined to carry lions couchant, but they were too small and far apart for anything they carried to respond visibly to one another across the length of the bridge. In 1935 the veteran Captain Swinton contacted Scott, supporting a suggestion from Lady Forres whereby some fine lions devised by her old master Sargeant Jagger for the British war memorial at Nieuwpoort in Belgium might be copied for deployment on the plinths. The gesture was partly to support Jagger's widow, who had been left in poverty when he died. Scott was accommodating and investigations took place, but the idea dropped away.[42] Instead, Scott's friend Sir William Reid Dick and

138 Herbert Morrison opens the bridge on an inclement day, 10 December 1945. His wife carries flowers. To Morrison's left, wearing the London County Council chain of office, is the Council's Chairman, Lord Snell

another sculptor, Richard Garbe, were asked to provide estimates for the lions; again nothing came of it.[43]

With the war over and the bridge complete, Scott returned to the charge. This time his choice fell on Charles Wheeler, another establishment figure. Wheeler came up with sketches and models for the Four Winds (fig.139). The LCC's Planning Committee gave its approval in 1946 and models went on display in County Hall, but no one seems to have been that keen on them. Next year, therefore, Scott set up a limited competition for six sculptors, to be judged by himself, Reid Dick, and Philip Hendy of the National Gallery, who was thought to be keen on the moderns. The list of entrants was balanced: Frank Dobson, Jacob Epstein, Barbara Hepworth, Eric Kennington, Henry Moore and Wheeler. No subject was prescribed.

Once again the outcome was abortive. Moore honourably pointed out that to devise four separate subjects on the four plinths would take him more time than had been made available and withdrew. Epstein failed to submit, while Wheeler's second effort did not improve on his original. Of the others' submissions little is known except for Hepworth's, which has been the study of an article by Alun R. Graves.[44] Abstract Hepworth compositions in stone at the ends of Scott's bridge, though odd, might have chimed in with the forthcoming Festival of Britain. As it was, the assessors were disappointed and made no award, which gave the LCC the excuse to drop the whole thing in February 1948.

Another sad coda must conclude this story of gallantry and high endeavour. Out of guilt or honour, it had been resolved to incorporate a memorial to John Rennie and his bridge within the new one. This was not quite a new idea. After Rennie died in 1821, the Waterloo Bridge Company talked of erecting obelisks at each end of the bridge in honour of the great engineer, but the idea came to nothing.[45] The new proposal took the form of two columns and some balusters from the old bridge tucked neatly beneath the end of the southernmost arch. It appears to have been ready when the bridge opened in 1942, but its lifespan was short.[46] It was there when the Festival of Britain transformed the South Bank. Then in 1957 came plans for a permanent National Film Theatre, to be built by LCC architects around and under the southern approaches to the bridge; the memorial had to go. In recompense the LCC constructed a makeshift platform below the other end of the bridge, where some foundations and piers from the old structure had been suffered to remain by the embankment shoreline. This pigeon-bespattered cave is now the shameful memorial to John Rennie's Waterloo Bridge.

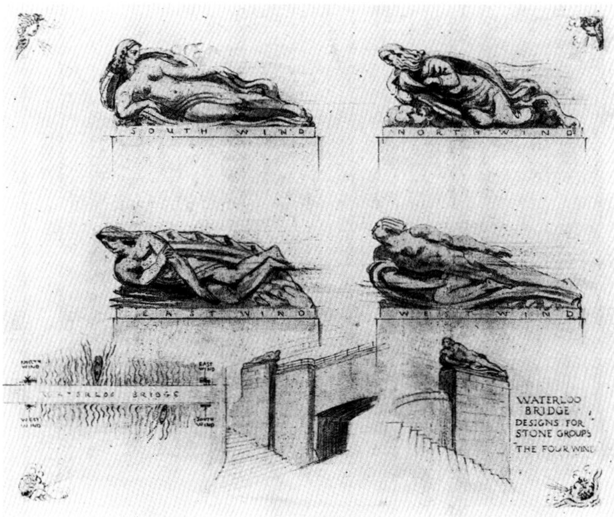

139 Sketches by Charles Wheeler for sculptures of the Four Winds, to be placed on the pedestals at the ends of the bridge, *c.*1945

13

Slack Water

I am standing on Waterloo Bridge. It is a bright autumn morning, and I am in the middle of the bridge, occupying the pavement on the downriver side. The road runs level and straight as a die in either direction, dropping away at the southern approach alone. Beneath me, the river is exceptionally still. The tide is about to turn, but just now we are at that moment of transition known as slack water. The Thames looks deep and wide – it is broader here than at any other crossing point in the centre of London. An expanse of moving water in the midst of any great city always takes one's breath away. This one seems alien, threatening almost, a challenge to the presumptuous manmade surface that sustains me. It is also empty, apart from a few shabby craft moored in midstream or along the banks. Everything is at rest.

Along the roadway it is different. Buses, cars and vans, not so many lorries, pass by, self-absorbed. They cannot race as once they did, since although the traffic is flowing freely, it has been squeezed into a single lane on either side since barriers were inserted between pavement and carriageway. These hideous 'Hostile Vehicle Mitigation' blocks were put up on London's seven most central bridges following terrorist incidents on two of them in 2017. Anchored in concrete at their ends, where lumpish gates across the pavements stand ready to close should emergency require it, they run in bumper-type metal panels along the length of each bridge. They have a sniff of expediency, of the door shut after the horse has bolted. Are incidents of the same kind likely to recur? But anxiety today always takes precedence over aesthetics. Only at Westminster Bridge, the tourist trap beside the Houses of Parliament, has a less defacing system of 'heritage' bollard-barriers been installed, as along Whitehall. The barriers also function as a way of demarcating cycle lanes. Like most cycle lanes in London, these are ugly too.

I turn to observe my fellow pedestrians. It is a long bleak trek across the bridge, unbroken by shelters or consumerist distractions. The only temptations to linger come from the wide-open view and the lure of the water below. Most walkers plough on regardless (fig.142). At this time of day most of them are crossing from south to north. Some will be commuters who have taken the train into Waterloo Station and relish the brisk walk before they settle to their tasks around the Strand and Covent Garden. But others are definitely visitors, for tourism nowadays is all year round. Mainly they seem to be young couples and families with pushchairs. Most take a casual glance at the river; a few look about them alertly and maybe pause at the engraved plaque in the middle which tells them what they can see. A young woman stops to take pictures. After all, downstream from here is among the finest views in Central London. The bridge bisects the Thames's stateliest curve in London, once known as King's Reach and gracefully fringed by the Victoria Embankment. There is plenty of open water between here and Blackfriars Bridge, beyond which one beholds as nowhere else so well the St Paul's dome, its nobility tarnished by the jostle of the City's misshapen office towers around it (fig.140).

Upstream the view is good too, though blocked by the bulk of Charing Cross Railway Bridge. Here the focus is on the south side as it presses gently forward into the convexity of the bend, tightly filled with the Festival Hall, the rebarbative South Bank Centre, and a miscellany of strollers, stallholders and skateboarders along the riverside walkway. Few in number as yet, they will turn on summer afternoons and evenings into a swarm of pleasure-seekers (fig.141). As an afterthought, the cluster extends downstream under the frowning concrete terraces of the National Theatre. All these are served by the bridge, which soars over them and can only link up with them via awkward steps and ramps. None of this medley of buildings and activities on the bank below had yet been thought of when the present Waterloo Bridge was completed. And none of them has the courtesy to face the back, towards South London. Only the river front is addressed – and that randomly enough.

140 Waterloo Bridge and the City skyline, 2024

141 The South Bank scene, 2024

How did this assortment of modern monumental attractions come about, I ask myself? Answer: they are the ultimate outcome of the South Bank's regeneration, long sought and fought for. The London County Council took the first steps when it built its proud County Hall, now a hotel and entertainment centre overshadowed and humiliated by the vertical circle of the London Eye. Alongside it, the LCC's County of London Plan (1943) envisaged a theatre and a concert hall, flanked by an array of office buildings which were to rub out grisly industry and wartime dereliction and become the staple of the South Bank's future. In front of it all, a formal walkway and gardens were to face the river, destined in these graver days for the health and diversion of a disciplined populace.

Then, in 1951, the Festival of Britain, that amalgam of pep-talk for an exhausted nation – a so-called 'tonic' – and of light-hearted entertainment and architecture, was parachuted in. Though it took over the South Bank site and was sponsored by that great mogul of London politics, Herbert Morrison, the Festival was about Britain, not London – screens at the back hid it from the blight of Waterloo. It had its serious side, like the exhibition of heavy industry in Glasgow, but that was, naturally, not popular.

142 Pedestrians on Waterloo Bridge, 2024

The dominant legacy of the Festival has been escapism. According to one commentator, it encouraged people to forget that 'a better life had to be worked for'. Arguably, the Festival marked the beginnings of a loss of seriousness. People seem to have felt instinctively that there was little to be gained, in a declining nation and port-city, by gravity. Virtue and respect for making things, for the harshnesses of physical work and duty, were ebbing away, however hard governments tried to impart them. The same has surely been true of London and Britain ever since. By the same token, any regret for heavy old Waterloo Bridge vanished long ago, while there is widespread nostalgia for the Festival of Britain.

The buildings that replaced the Festival on the South Bank site, the arts centre and the theatres, illustrate this, I can't help feeling. Instead of the humdrum office buildings foreseen by the LCC, they were dedicated to entertainment – culture, if you like. Given that high purpose, the harder their architecture paradoxically became, more unyielding and cheerless and imprisoning than the open-fronted Festival Hall. Perhaps only entertainment (or culture) was to be taken seriously anymore.

143 Tourist boats milling about in the water

No doubt redress was needed. As Sleary tells Mr Gradgrind in *Hard Times*, 'People mutht be amuthed. They can't be alwayth a learning, nor yet they can't be alwayth a working, they an't made for it.' I must remember that the South Bank has always been a place for escape and entertainment. Think of Vauxhall Gardens, or Cuper's Gardens, obliterated by the bridge's southern approach. The Thames, too, has always been a place of diversion and amusement, of regattas, trips and sheer fooling around with boats, not just in its upper reaches but in London too. But hasn't the balance now swung too far that way? Are we condemned to daily, perpetual frivolity? Must entertainment be the touchstone of everything now, even of politics?

I am diverted by some movement on the water. It is only the tourist boats, performing their pirouettes around the piers on both banks upstream of the bridge, waystations on the crowded cruise route between Westminster and Greenwich (fig.143). Even at this time of year there are sightseers enough to keep them in motion. They offer choices of style. The slick Thames Clippers owned by Uber run faster than the sedate City Cruisers, but have no outside seating. Speed and adventure are supplied by the little red Thames Rocket which likes to stick its nose up out of the waves and spray its adventurous, strapped-in customers.

144 The CORY tug *Regain* transporting waste on the Thames, from Wandsworth to Belvedere

Together they have the water to themselves. Queens of the depopulated river, they sweep brashly beneath the bridge's wide arches, skirting the drab barges anchored in the fairway.

So is the Thames just for tourists now? Thirty years ago, the planners were debating whether tourism could regenerate tired cities trapped by loss of industrial employment and in some cases of empire. Well, they have their answer now, at the cost of international homogenisation and destruction of local character. Venice and Amsterdam have become almost intolerable, other European city-centres little better. Luckily, London is too big and unappetising to be utterly eaten up. The swarms of tourists milling up and down Westminster Bridge have yet to colonise Waterloo Bridge. As for the river, any activity is better than none. The watery void cries out to be filled.

Yet, incorrigibly, I find myself reverting to the past. Where are the freight-filled craft of yore, I lament, the lighters, the barges and the tugs, even the precarious open rafts of timber, whose oarsmen had to ride the tides cannily as they took the tricky bend, if they were not to smash into one another on the crowded river, or come to grief on the cutwaters of old Waterloo Bridge? What, too, of the tumbledown wharves and muddy inlets, the upturned hulks and coal stores, the dismal factories and polluting power stations? All long gone. Good riddance to them, no doubt. It would be as preposterous to wish them back as to expect grain to be poled up the Thames from Oxfordshire in some *News from Nowhere* vision. Even Tilbury, far down river, is half-empty now. London's busiest port is Heathrow – an *air*port. But can the faithful river that brought the city into being and served it for two millennia no longer be of use to London and Londoners, one asks, except as a tatty source of foreign exchange?

One last question. Now that the river's banks are of so little practical significance, can there be any excuse for not making them handsome? On the cruise to Greenwich, I blench to see the appalling standard of architecture besetting the tideway on both sides. That is especially true below Tower Bridge. There are very few exceptions. It cannot be for lack of money, since many of the monstrosities are apartment blocks for the rich. Have we become so blind to beauty? For shame, London!

The river becomes restless, the tide starts to stir. Dispirited, I start to quit the bridge. Suddenly, out of nowhere, hope beckons. A launch named *Regain* pokes a pert nose through the arches, towing behind it two long barges packed with dirty-yellow containers of refuse bound for the waste-management facilities down river at Belvedere (fig.144). I am stirred by the humble yet honourable sight. London River is of use still after all.

Notes

1 LONDON RIVER

1 *The Times*, 26 March 1952.
2 Rufus Noel-Buxton, *Westminster Wader*, 1957, pp 42–3. Noel-Buxton was also obsessed with the river crossing at Brentford which, like others before him, he believed was where Julius Caesar crossed the Thames in 55 BC. His poem 'The Ford' was published on this subject in 1955, after his Westminster venture.
3 Gustav Milne, Martin Bates and Mike D. Webber, 'Problems, Potential and Partial Solutions: An Archaeological Study of the Tidal Thames, England', *World Archaeology*, vol.29, no.1, 1997, p.131.
4 Patrick D. Nunn, 'The Development of the River Thames in Central London during the Flandrian', *Transactions of the Institute of British Geographers*, vol.8, no.2, 1983, pp 187–213.
5 D.R. Stoddart, '"That Victorian Science": Huxley's Physiography and Its Impact on Geography', *Transactions of the Institute of British Geographers*, vol.66, 1975, pp 17–40.
6 See, for example, Ll. Rodwell Jones, *The Geography of London River*, 1931. Earlier uses can probably be found. The term was taken up by Basil E. Cracknell, *Portrait of London River*, 1968. Hilaire Belloc's 1912 book is simply called *The River of London*.
7 *The Star*, 19 June 1817.
8 Rodwell Jones, *Geography of London River*, p.34.
9 Cracknell, *Portrait of London River*, p.49.
10 Gustav Milne, *The Port of Roman London*, 1985, pp 79–86.
11 Samuel Smiles, *The Lives of the Engineers*, vol.1, 1861, p.12.
12 Wikipedia, 'Embanking the Tidal Thames', with a full bibliography.
13 Milne, *Port of Roman London*, pp 18–19.
14 John Timbs, *The Curiosities of London: Exhibiting the Most Rare and Remarkable Objects of Interest in the Metropolis*, 1st edn, 1855, p.707.
15 The evidence, expounded in a Channel 4 *Time Team* programme on 9 January 2002, consists of residual posts of a causeway or jetty above Vauxhall Bridge assigned to about 1500 BC, and an allegedly earlier series of posts just below the bridge and parallel with the shore, ascribed to around 4500 BC. See www.vauxhallandkennington.org.uk/firstbridge.shtml.
16 Chris Thomas, 'Roman Westminster: Fact or Fiction?', in *Londinium and Beyond, Essays on Roman London and its Hinterland for Harvey Sheldon*, Council for British Archaeology Research Reports, vol.156, Council for British Archaeology, 2008, pp 102–5; also Barney Sloane, Hedley Swain and Chris Thomas, 'The Roman Road and the River Regime: Archaeological Investigations in Westminster and Lambeth', *London Archaeologist*, vol.7, no.14, 1995, pp 359–70.
17 F.C.J. Spurrell, 'Early Sites and Embankments on the Margins of the Thames Estuary', *Archaeological Journal*, vol.42, no.1, 1885, pp 269–302.
18 *The Victoria County History of Kent*, vol.1, 1908, Appendix II (by Spurrell), pp 454–5.
19 H.R. Ormsby, *London on the Thames: A Study of the Natural Conditions that Influenced the Birth and Growth of a Great City*, 1924, pp 18–21; Cracknell, *Portrait of London River*, p.29. Anne V. Akeroyd, in 'Archaeological and Historical Evidence for

Subsidence in Southern Britain', *Philosophical Transactions of the Royal Society of London. Series A, Mathematical and Physical Sciences*, vol.272, 1972, pp 151–69, urges caution about some of these ideas.

20 Wikipedia, '1928 Thames flood'.

21 Dale H. Porter, *The Thames Embankment: Environment, Technology and Society in Victorian London*, 1998, p.26.

2 ABOVE BRIDGE

1 Hilaire Belloc, *The River of London*, 1912, pp 3–13. Belloc unluckily chose the Scheldt rather than the Maas as the future great trading rival of London.

2 Basil E. Cracknell, *Portrait of London River*, 1968, p.199.

3 Dick Fagan and Eric Burgess, *Men of the Tideway*, 1966.

4 See, for example, most recently, Peter Stone, *The History of the Port of London: A Vast Emporium of Nations*, 2017.

5 Bruce Watson, Trevor Brigham and Tony Dyson, *London Bridge: 2000 Years of a River Crossing*, Museum of London Archaeology (MOLA) Monograph Series, no.8, 2001.

6 Gustav Milne, *The Port of Medieval London*, 2003, pp 175–84; Brian Dietz, ed., *The Port and Trade of Early Elizabethan London*, 1972, pp x–xii.

7 Gordon Home, *Old London Bridge*, 1931, p.268.

8 For London Bridge and the weir effect, see especially Ll. Rodwell Jones, *The Geography of London River*, 1931, Chapter 5; and Robin Imray, 'The Perils of Old London Bridge: Travails Faced by the Watermen of the Thames', *London Topographical Society Newsletter*, no.99, 2024, pp 14–18.

9 M.[P.J.] Grosley, *A Tour to London: or, New Observations on England and its Inhabitants*, vol.1, 1772, p.27: French original of 1770, based on a visit of 1765.

10 Graham Gibberd, *On Lambeth Marsh: The South Bank and Waterloo*, 1992, Chapter 3.

11 *Survey of London: Battersea: Public, Commercial and Cultural*, vol.49, 2013, p.325.

12 Wandsworth Historical Society website.

13 Philip Banbury, *Shipbuilders of the Thames and Medway*, 1971, pp 278–86; H.G. Wells, *Tono-Bungay*, 1909, 4.3.

14 The authoritative account is Dale H. Porter, *The Thames Embankment: Environment, Technology and Society in Victorian London*, 1998.

15 Quoted in R.J.B. Walker, *Old Westminster Bridge: The Bridge of Fools*, 1979, p.140.

16 A.W. Skempton, 'Engineering on the Thames Navigation, 1770–1845', *Transactions of the Newcomen Society*, vol.55, no.1, 1983–4, p.153.

17 Fred. S. Thacker, *The Thames Highway*, 1914–20, 2 vols, 1968.

18 Skempton, 'Engineering on the Thames Navigation', pp 165–9. A remarkable 'half-lock' was added at Richmond in 1894 to prevent loss of water between Richmond and Teddington at low tide.

19 Peter Hounsell, *Bricks of Victorian London: A Social and Economic History*, Studies in Regional and Local History, Vol. 22, 2022.

20 For the Grand Junction, see Alan H. Faulkner, *The Grand Junction Canal*, 1973, especially pp 16–18, 47 and 75–9.

21 *Daily Courant*, 19 July 1717. I am very grateful to John Greenacombe for this reference.

22 Henry Mayhew, *London Labour and the London Poor*, vol.3, 1861, pp 327–36. The original article on watermen, lightermen and so forth appeared in *Morning Chronicle*, 17 October 1850.

23 Captain Marryat, *Jacob Faithful*, 1834, Chapter 1.

24 Donald Maxwell, *A Pilgrimage of the Thames*, 1932, pp 43–7.

25 Fagan and Burgess, *Men of the Tideway*, p.31.

26 Harry Gosling, *Up and Down Stream*, 1927, pp 32–7, 59–60.

27 See Hervey Benham, *Down Tops'l: The Story of the East Coast Sailing-Barges*, 1951; Edgar J. March, *Spritsail Barges of Thames and Medway*, 1970. I am grateful to John Scott for help with this paragraph.

28 Fagan and Burgess, *Men of the Tideway*.

29 *Morning Chronicle*, 24 June 1816.

30 Banbury, *Shipbuilders of the Thames and Medway*, p.59.

31 Robert J. Harley, *London's Victoria Embankment: A History of the Embankment and its Bridges*, 2005, pp 40–43.

32 Porter, *The Thames Embankment*, p.119.

3 THREE BRIDGES

1 A full and valuable list by Malcolm Tucker of Thames river crossings in London is supplied in Bridget Cherry and Nikolaus Pevsner, *London 2: South*, 1983, pp 706–16.

2 Dale H. Porter, *The Thames Embankment: Environment, Technology and Society in Victorian London*, 1998, pp 137–41. In 1908 the Thames Conservancy ceded responsibility for the Thames below Teddington to the Port of London Authority.

3 R.J.B. Walker, *Old Westminster Bridge: The Bridge of Fools*, 1979, p.37.

4 Gordon Home, *Old London Bridge*, 1931, pp 65, 76 and 258–9, cites toll charges for London Bridge going back to 1212–13.

5 Walker, *Old Westminster Bridge*, p.223.

6 ibid., pp 225–6.

7 Bruce Watson, Trevor Brigham and Tony Dyson, *London Bridge: 2000 Years of a River Crossing*, Museum of London Archaeology (MOLA) Monograph Series, no.8, 2001, pp 156–71; Charles Welch, *History of the Tower Bridge*, 1894, p.126; *Whitehall Evening Post*, 24–27 February 1759; *London Chronicle*, 5–7 February 1767.

8 *Evening Post*, 5–7 February 1782; *Public Advertiser*, 9 January 1783.

9 An excellent discussion of the financing of public infrastructure in this period is given in M.J. Daunton, *Progress and Poverty: An Economic and Social History of Britain 1700–1850*, 1995, pp 287–97.

10 Quotations from Bishop Carleton Hunt, *The Development of the Business Corporation in England, 1800–1867*, 1936, p.15.

11 *Morning Post*, 7 December 1807.

12 For the first Vauxhall Bridge Act, 49 Geo. III, c.142, with a list of proprietors, see https://www.legislation.gov.uk/ukla/Geo3/49/142/pdfs/ukla_18090142_en.pdf.

13 J.G. James's excellent 'Ralph Dodd, The Very Ingenious Schemer', *Transactions of the Newcomen Society*, vol. 47, no.1, 1977, pp 161–78, is supplemented by articles by Mike Chrimes on the three Dodds in *Biographical Dictionary of Civil Engineers*, vol. 1, pp 183–6.

14 *Morning Advertiser*, 4 August 1809; *Morning Herald*, 5 August 1809.

15 *The Satirist*, October 1809, pp 368–75.

16 *Mechanics' Magazine*, vol.4, 1828, p.445.

17 James Perry in *Morning Chronicle*, 10 October 1821.

18 This on the authority of *The Autobiography of Sir John Rennie*, 1875, p.6.

19 *St James's Chronicle*, 11 May 1811.

20 Peter Cross-Rudkin, *John Rennie – 'Engineer of many splendid and useful works'*, 2022, p.88.

21 *The Pilot*, 10 May 1811.

22 *Public Ledger and Daily Advertiser*, 30 December 1812.

23 For the Bentham design, see Cross-Rudkin, *John Rennie*, p.89. The second Vauxhall Bridge Act was 52 Geo. III, c.147 (https://www.legislation.gov.uk/ukla/Geo3/52/147/pdfs/ukla_18120147_en.pdf).

24 *Morning Chronicle*, 12 August 1816. The chief engineer for the Pont d'Austerlitz was in fact not Gauthey but Becquey de Beaupré. The original bridge, which indeed had iron arches, proved inadequate and was reconstructed in the 1850s.

25 *Morning Advertiser*, 7 May and 2 November 1827.

26 John Martin Robinson, *The Wyatts: An Architectural Dynasty*, 1979, pp 14–16. For John Wyatt's origination of the Southwark Bridge project, see, notably, *Law Chronicle, Commercial and Bankruptcy Register*, 13 April 1815.

27 On Hutton, see *Biographical Dictionary of Civil Engineers*, vol.1, and now also Benjamin Wardhaugh, *Gunpowder and Geometry: The Life of Charles Hutton*, 2019. Wardhaugh's edition of Hutton's letters, *The Correspondence of Charles Hutton (1737–1823)*, 2017, contains a severe missive sent in 1802 to Rennie, whom he evidently did not then know well, about the latter's early designs for the Menai crossing. Hutton's 'History of Iron Bridges' is no. 6 of his *Tracts on Mathematical and Philosophical Subjects*, 1812. The paper is undated but was clearly written before Southwark Bridge was conceived.

28 On Young and bridges, see Santiago Huerta, in Santiago Huerta, ed., 'Thomas Young's Theory of the Arch', in *Essays in the History of the Theory of Structures, in Honour of Jacques Heyman*, 2005, pp 189–234.

29 *St James's Chronicle*, 3 November 1821.

30 51 Geo. III, cap 166: https://www.legislation.gov.uk/ukla/Geo3/51/166/pdfs/ukla_18110166_en.pdf.

31 *The Autobiography of Sir John Rennie*, 1875, pp 10–15.

32 *Architects' Journal*, 8 June 1921.
33 *London Chronicle*, 29 May 1815.
34 *Commercial Chronicle*, 30 March 1819.
35 Quoted by Cross-Rudkin, *John Rennie*, p.101.
36 *The Era*, 1 May 1853.

4 STRAND BRIDGE

1 John Gwynn, *London and Westminster Improved*, 1766, sections 83–4 and 98.
2 Ted Ruddock, *Arch Bridges and Their Builders, 1735–1835*, 1979, pp 64, 66, 110–14.
3 *Public Advertiser*, 4 June 1768, 8 June 1770.
4 See the entry by Jill Lever in Sir John Soane's Museum Collection Online.
5 Moira Anne Rudolf Ockrim, 'The Life and Work of Thomas Harrison of Chester 1744–1829', PhD, Courtauld Institute, 1988, pp 335–6. The description is quoted by Ockrim as coming from Michaud's *Biographie Universelle Ancienne et Moderne*, 1857, vol.18, p.496. The ascription of the design to the Waterloo site comes from the memoir of Harrison by G.C. Blomfield in *The Builder*, 21 March 1863, p.205.
6 Drawings for Sandby's bridge are divided between the RIBA, the V&A and Sir John Soane's Museum. It is illustrated in Samuel Ireland's *Picturesque Views on the River Thames*, vol.2, 1792, pp 185–9, which describes it as running from the western extremity of Somerset Place.
7 *Morning Post*, 18 June 1778.
8 *St James's Chronicle*, 21–23 October 1779.
9 *Public Advertiser*, 4 November 1784.
10 *Morning Post*, 4 November 1788.
11 *Kentish Gazette*, 11 November 1788.
12 Other references: *Public Advertiser*, 16 August 1777, 17 April 1784, 11 September 1784, 22 June 1785, 30 June 1786, 4 May 1787, 1 May 1790, 11 July 1791; *Morning Post*, 13 November 1778; *Morning Herald*, 5 September 1782; *Gazette and New Daily Advertiser*, 6 January 1787; *Star & Evening Advertiser*, 6 February 1789. Later, in 1806, the young Jesse Hartley, then of Pontefract, produced designs on behalf of the 11th Duke of Norfolk for a seven-arch bridge stretching across the river from Arundel Street (east of Somerset House). The Dukes held property both here and in the Pontefract area of Yorkshire. I am grateful to Carol Morgan for telling me about this scheme, the drawings for which are in the Institution of Civil Engineers' Archives, ref PCA D2.
13 J.G. James, 'Ralph Dodd, The Very Ingenious Schemer', *Transactions of the Newcomen Society*, vol.47, no.1, 1977, pp 164, 166.
14 *Morning Chronicle*, 27 October 1808; also *The Sun*, 6 July 1809.
15 James, 'Ralph Dodd', p.167. For Capon's involvement, James cites T. Hughes, *The Steamboat Companion from Queenhithe to Richmond*, 1824, p.12; and for Bond's, *Literary Gazette*, 11 November 1837.
16 For example, *Public Ledger and Daily Advertiser*, 24 November 1809; *Morning Post*, 23 March 1810.
17 Ruddock, *Arch Bridges*, pp 178–9.
18 *Gentleman's Magazine*, May 1829, pp 469–70.
19 *The Builder*, 1 March 1863, p.205.
20 These drawings, in the collections of Cheshire Museums Services, are illustrated in Moira Ockrim's thesis, cited above.
21 *Morning Chronicle*, 20 June 1810; *Evening Mail*, 22 June 1810.
22 *Morning Post*, 23 June 1810.
23 Samuel Smiles, *The Lives of the Engineers*, vol.1, 1861, Chapter 6.
24 'Henry Swann' entry in R.G. Thorne, ed., *The History of Parliament: The House of Commons, 1790–1820, Vol.1*, 2006.
25 Ruddock, *Arch Bridges*, p.22, etc.
26 Peter Cross-Rudkin, *John Rennie – 'Engineer of many splendid and useful works'*, 2022, p.158.
27 The early processes of granite extraction in the Penryn district were the subject of a memo by Herbert L. Wettern of Cooper, Wettern & Co. sent to Sir Giles Scott in April 1932: see RIBA Manuscripts, ScGG/90/1. Wettern ascertained that most of the granite came from the parishes of Stithians, Mabe and Constantine.
28 The best source for the modern history of Cornish and Devon granite is Peter Stanier, 'The Granite Industry of South-West England, 1800–1980', PhD, University of Southampton, 1985. For Penryn granite, see also *Royal Cornwall Gazette*, 29 August 1818, summarising an article from *Transactions of the Royal Geological Society of Cornwall*, vol.1, 1818,

pp 231–4; and for Swann's part in providing local employment in the industry, *Morning Herald*, 16 June 1818. For early uses of Dartmoor granite in London, see Linda Clarke, *Building Capitalism: Historical Change and the Labour Process in the Production of the Built Environment*, 1992, pp 200–201, 244–5.

29 *The Globe*, 12 October 1811.

30 *Survey of London*, vol. 43, 1994, p.273.

31 Besides Vauxhall, Waterloo, Southwark and London Bridges, Jolliffe and Banks rebuilt the granite-faced Staines Bridge under George and John Rennie (1829–34). The extant Serpentine Bridge between Hyde Park and Kensington Gardens was also their work, again under George Rennie (1824–7).

32 See Anthony Burton, *The Canal Builders*, 1972, Chapter 14; and J.R. Ward, *The Finance of Canal Building in Eighteenth-Century England*, 1974.

33 The standard article is H.W. Dickinson, 'Jolliffe and Banks, Contractors', *Transactions of the Newcomen Society*, vol.12, no.1, 1931, pp 1–8. Fuller biographies of Banks can be found in *Oxford Dictionary of National Biography* (Michael Port) and *Biographical Dictionary of Civil Engineers* (David Brooke). For a list of Jolliffe and Banks's civil engineering contracts in London, see Greater London Industrial Archaeology Society, *Notes and News*, August 1982.

34 Peter McGow's extensive 'Notes on the Surrey Iron Railway', 2001, to be found on the Wandle Industrial Museum site, https://wandle.org/surreyironrailway/header.html, argues that Banks was not the contractor for the railway extension, as earlier sources had claimed.

35 Peter Cross-Rudkin on Rennie, *Biographical Dictionary of Civil Engineers*, p.564.

36 *Morning Post*, 6 September 1823.

37 For information on the Banks family and Sheerness, see https://sussexhistoryforum.co.uk/index.php?topic=17050.0.

38 Robert Wilkinson, *Londina Illustrata*, vol.2, 1834, p.110.

39 *The Autobiography of Sir John Rennie*, 1875, pp 5–6.

40 Ancestry, genealogical data on Henfrey. His residence is given as Waterloo Bridge in the registers of Christ Church, Southwark, 28 August 1816, when his son Henry was baptised.

41 *Morning Advertiser*, 14 June 1825.

42 For the affairs of the Haytor Granite Company, see *New Times*, 12 July 1825; *Morning Herald*, 11 July 1827; *The Globe*, 11 July 1827; *London Courier*, 9 August 1827.

43 Obituary of Henfrey in *London Courier*, 26 July 1827; sale of his furniture, *Morning Herald*, 10 October 1827 etc; will, TNA, PROB 11/1730/242.

44 A mysterious early contributor to the progress of the bridge was a certain Alexander Hay, probably a Scot. Hay was the recipient, on 11 June 1812, of a silver mounted snuffbox 'for his faithful conduct at the Strand Bridge'. The donors were JP, JH, JM and RS, initials difficult to identify: see *The Builder*, 23 November 1934, when the snuffbox was in the possession of Alexander Hay Lamont of Edinburgh.

45 *The Globe*, 12 October 1811.

46 See Terry Coleman, *The Railway Navvies: A History of the Men who Made Railways*, 1965.

47 *Caledonian Mercury*, 18 October 1813.

48 The following paragraphs are deeply indebted to Ruddock, *Arch Bridges*, pp 178–86, and Cross-Rudkin, *John Rennie*, pp 89–91, which offer full professional engineers' accounts of the bridge's construction methods.

49 *The News*, 24 July 1814.

50 Quoted in Ruddock, *Arch Bridges*, pp 178–9.

51 *The Examiner*, 27 October 1816.

52 *St James's Chronicle*, 19 June 1817.

5 WATERLOO BRIDGE

1 Brian Cathcart, *The News from Waterloo: The Race to Tell Britain of Wellington's Victory*, 2015.

2 ibid., p.5.

3 *Morning Post*, 9 January 1852.

4 R.L. Stevenson, 'On the Sombre Canalised', in *An Inland Voyage*, 1878.

5 *The Times*, 1 and 21 July 1815.

6 For a fuller account of the various attempts to commemorate Waterloo, see Luke Reynolds, *Who Owned Waterloo? Battle, Memory, and Myth in British History*, 2022, pp 175–211. The earliest monuments completed seem all to have been in Scotland. They included a cairn erected by the Marquess of Huntly at Kinrara, Inverness-shire; a tower built by the Marquess of Lothian on Peniel

Heugh, Roxburghshire, which soon fell down and had to be replaced; and a tower built by public subscription near New Abbey, Kirkcudbrightshire. A column was also started on the Plas Newydd estate of the celebrated Lord Uxbridge, later Marquess of Anglesey, who lost a leg at Waterloo; and an obelisk in Wellington's honour was erected on the Blackdown Hills in Somerset. The so-called National Monument on Calton Hill, Edinburgh, was first suggested in 1816, not as a Waterloo monument but as a tribute to Scottish soldiers who had fallen in the Napoleonic Wars. Paid for by private subscription, it was properly begun only in 1826 and never finished.

7 *Commercial Chronicle*, 20 May 1819.

8 Reynolds, *Who Owned Waterloo?*, p.181; *Morning Chronicle*, 15 January 1816. Few submissions seem to survive, apart from a varied set of designs by Robert Smirke in the RIBA Collections. The design by Benjamin Wyatt for a massive pyramid, now in the Royal Collections and illustrated in Reynolds, p.180, may be another, but it is more likely to have been separately submitted by Wyatt to the Duke of Wellington.

9 *Evening Mail*, 7 February 1816.

10 Farington Diaries, XIV, 4787–8, 21 and 24 February 1816.

11 This Committee of Taste may have been a continuation of the Committee for the Erection of Monuments chaired by Long from 1802 and concerned chiefly with St Paul's Cathedral: Roger Bowdler and Ann Saunders, 'The Post-Reformation Monuments', in Arthur Burns, Derek Keene and Andrew Saint, eds, *St Paul's, The Cathedral Church of London, 604–2004*, 2004, pp 277ff.; and Holger Hoock, *Empires of the Imagination: Politics, War, and the Arts in the British World, 1750–1850*, 2010, Chapter 3.

12 *London Chronicle*, 3 May 1816.

13 The winning Smirke design appears to be one of several by this architect preserved in the RIBA Collections (SC92/23, RIBApix 21490). The catalogue states that it was probably intended for Greenwich Park.

14 *Public Ledger and Daily Advertiser*, 3 June 1817; *Morning Herald*, 6 June 1817; *National Register*, 9 June 1817; also *Commercial Chronicle*, 22 November 1817; Hoock, *Empires of the Imagination*, pp 361–72.

15 *The Globe*, 26 June 1815; *Morning Chronicle*, 26 June 1815.

16 *The Globe*, 29 July 1815.

17 *London Courier*, 21 December 1815.

18 Rennie notebooks, 11 February 1816, National Library of Scotland, kindly communicated by Peter Cross-Rudkin.

19 53 Geo. III, c. 63, clause 22.

20 M.H. Port, *Six Hundred New Churches: The Church Building Commission 1818–1856*, 2006, Chapter 2, especially pp 38 and 43. The generic phrase 'Waterloo churches' seems not to predate the 1870s. As the author points out on p.253, it was sometimes restricted to the four erected in Lambeth, including St John's, Waterloo.

21 Quoted in ibid., p.84.

22 *Bury and Norwich Post*, 26 March 1817.

23 *Commercial Chronicle*, 17 June 1817.

24 *London Courier*, 13 June 1814.

25 ibid., 7 May 1817.

26 *Morning Post*, 14 June 1817.

27 *Morning Chronicle*, 9 June 1817.

28 Elizabeth Longford, *Wellington, Pillar of State*, 1972, p.44.

29 The following description of the opening of the bridge, including the quotations, is taken mainly from *The Star*, 16 and 19 June 1817.

30 Longford, *Wellington*, p.44, says there were Waterloo veterans in the procession on the Admiralty Barge, but this seems unlikely.

31 According to Harry Gosling, *Up and Down Stream*, 1927, p.103, new light standards briefly replaced the originals when electricity came in, but the public clamoured for the return of the old lamps: 'They were discovered on the municipal scrap heap and only saved in the nick of time.'

32 *Morning Herald*, 20 June 1817.

33 *London Courier*, 20 August 1817.

34 *Morning Post*, 22 January 1817.

35 *St James's Chronicle*, 19 June 1817.

36 *Trades Free Press*, 17 November 1826.

37 *The Sun*, 12 November 1818.

38 *Cobbett's Weekly Political Register*, 16 January 1819.

39 *The Sun*, 10 October 1818.

40 ibid., 1 December 1815.

41 *Military Register*, 21 August 1816; *Commercial Chronicle*, 17 June 1817.

42 From an article by Pite on 'The Architecture of the Bridges of London', *RIBA Journal*, vol.15, 1908, p.427.

6 TROUBLED TOWNSHIP

1 *London Chronicle*, 4 November 1816.
2 *The Star*, 4 September 1816; *Public Ledger and Daily Advertiser*, 4 June 1817; *The Sun*, 28 August and 11 November 1817.
3 *Morning Post*, 23 September 1818.
4 *Survey of London*, vol.36, 1970, p.226.
5 Geoffrey Tyack, *Sir James Pennethorne and the Making of Victorian London*, 1992, pp 52, 64.
6 *RIBA Journal*, vol.15, 1908, p.445.
7 Robert Wilkinson, *Londina Illustrata*, vol.2, 1834, p.109.
8 58 Geo. III, c. 28.
9 R.J.B. Walker, *Old Westminster Bridge: The Bridge of Fools*, 1979, pp 253–6.
10 Basic information about the development of the Waterloo district is given in *Survey of London*, vol.23, 1951, to which Mireille Galinou, *London's South Bank: The History*, 2023, now provides an admirable supplement.
11 *Morning Advertiser*, 6 October 1818. For reports of Usher's various forays, see *Morning Advertiser*, 1 July 1818 and 30 September 1818; *New Times*, 20 September 1818; *Weekly Dispatch*, 27 September 1818; *British Press*, 29 September 1818; *General Evening Post*, 1 October 1818.
12 Terry Coleman, *The Old Vic: The Story of a Great Theatre from Kean to Olivier to Spacey*, 2014, p.3.
13 *British Press*, 26 May 1818.
14 *General Evening Post*, 12 May 1818.
15 For the early history of the Old Vic, see particularly George Rowell, *The Old Vic Theatre*, 1993, Chapter 2. The laying of the foundation stone is reported in *Public Ledger and Daily Advertiser*, 16 September 1816. The completed theatre is described and illustrated in Robert Wilkinson, *Londina Illustrata*, vol.2, 1834, pp 187–8. See also Galinou, *London's South Bank*, pp 422–9; and Diane Piccitto and Terry F. Robinson, *The Visual Life of Romantic Theater, 1780–1830*, 2023, pp 290–98.
16 Jim Davis and Victor Emeljanow, *Reflecting the Audience: London Theatregoing 1840–1880*, 2001, Chapter 1.
17 F.G. Tomlins, *A Brief View of the English Drama*, 1840, p.60, and *Remarks on the Present State of the English Drama*, 1851, pp 12–13.
18 *Public Ledger and Daily Advertiser*, 16 November 1822.
19 Peter Jefferson Smith, 'Waterloo Parish: A History', unpublished text kindly communicated by the Revd Giles Goddard, Vicar of St John's, Waterloo.
20 *Public Ledger and Daily Advertiser*, 16 November 1822.
21 Janet Myles, *L.N. Cottingham 1787–1847: Architect of the Gothic Revival*, 1996, pp 117–19; *Oxford Dictionary of National Biography*; Howard Colvin, *A Biographical Dictionary of British Architects 1660–1840*, 3rd edn, 1995; *Survey of London*, vol.23, 1951, pp 28–30.
22 Myles, *Architect of the Gothic Revival*, p.118.
23 *The Representative*, 22 July 1826.
24 *The Atlas*, 25 January 1829.
25 London Picture Library, 91878–9, 91946, 91970–1.
26 *Morning Herald*, 4 September 1839.
27 George Prior, ed., *Flora Tristan's London Journal: A Survey of London Life in the 1830s*, 1980, pp 74–5. I have substituted 'pimps' for 'fancy men', the word used sometimes in the Prior translation. In the original Tristan has 'souteneurs', the normal French word for pimps.
28 For the Roupell Street district (*c.*1825–40), see Galinou, *London's South Bank*, pp 402–3.
29 *Survey of London*, vol.23, 1951, p.27, quoted from Albert Smith, *The Struggles and Adventures of Christopher Tadpole*, 1848, p.93.
30 Modern accounts of the South Bank shot towers mostly derive from *Survey of London*, vol.23, 1951, pp 16, 47. Two articles by Sarah Mulcahey on the Layers of London website are also informative. However, the suggestion on p.16 of the survey that the Lambeth shot towers were preceded by one further east in Southwark – built in about 1758 by Henry Raminger, who took out a patent for lead shot that year – is disputed by D.J. Rowe, *Lead Manufacturing in Britain: A History*, 2018, who argues that it derives from a misinterpreted statement in Manning and Bray's *History and Antiquities of the County of Surrey*, vol.3, 1814, p.536.

All that is certain is that Raminger had a base 'near the Falcon Stairs', in the Bankside district of Southwark. The third South Bank shot tower, built around 1808, was near St Olave's, Tooley Street.

31 Samuel Ireland, *Picturesque Views on the River Thames*, 1791, p.194.

32 Charlotte Bronte, *Shirley: A Tale*, 1849, 'The Winding-Up' (last chapter).

33 *Trades Free Press*, 17 November 1826.

34 *Household Words*, 26 June 1858; and *Strand Magazine*, July–December 1891, pp 205–9. The Hollingshead piece was reprinted in the author's *Odd Journeys In and Out of London*, 1862, pp 121–9; it is sometimes incorrectly attributed to Dickens.

35 Gerald Barry, 'Recollections of the Festival', in Mary Banham and Bevis Hillier (eds), *A Tonic to the Nation: The Festival of Britain 1951*, 1976, p.20; Barry Turner, *Beacon for Change: How the Festival of Britain Shaped the Age*, 2011, p.58.

7 ENTER THE RAILWAYS

1 Hammersmith Bridge is the only one of these bridges to have earned a printed history: Charles Hailstone, *A History of Hammersmith Bridge*, 1987, augmented edition, 2022.

2 *Morning Herald*, 27 June 1836; *Morning Advertiser*, 29 August 1836.

3 *Morning Advertiser*, 29 May 1838 and 13 December 1844.

4 *Morning Herald*, 30 and 31 May 1845.

5 For the Royal Commission on Metropolitan Termini, see Jack Simmons, *The Railway in England and Wales, 1830–1914*, vol.1, 1978, pp 116–18; also *Lloyd's Weekly Newspaper*, 5 July 1846.

6 *Morning Advertiser*, 13 December 1844; *The Sun*, 9 January 1845; *Railway Bell*, 18 January 1845, which adds that William Hawes and Chadwick were both directors of the Richmond extension of the LSWR, also under way at this time.

7 Information in this paragraph comes mainly from *The Builder*, 12 April 1845, p.169; also 8 May 1845, p.209.

8 I am grateful to Steven Brindle for informing me about Brunel's sketch designs for the Hungerford Bridge towers.

9 *Illustrated London News*, 1 July 1848. The best account of Waterloo Station is given in Alan A. Jackson, *London's Termini*, 1969, pp 210–42, which supplies details of its development simplified or omitted here.

10 *Evening Mail*, 5 January 1846.

11 *The Autobiography of Samuel Smiles, LL.D.*, 1905, pp 232–44.

12 Jackson, *London's Termini*, pp 243–53, again gives the best account of Charing Cross Bridge and Station.

13 *Daily News*, 22 April 1862; Smiles, *Autobiography*, p.239.

14 *Morning Herald*, 1 September 1866.

15 *The Graphic*, 30 July 1870, quoted in Jackson, *London's Termini*, p.246.

16 *The Sun*, 9 September 1861.

17 The name Hungerford Bridge is still sometimes used for the railway bridge, but I have used 'Charing Cross Bridge' throughout to distinguish it from its predecessor, Brunel's suspension bridge.

18 *Building News*, 14 November 1862. For an invective against the first Blackfriars Railway Bridge, see 'Railway Eye-Sores on the River', *Weekly Dispatch*, 17 May 1863.

19 *London Observed: A Selection from the Letters of Jacob Burckhardt*, 1997, p.9.

20 *The Echo*, 12 June 1899; *The Globe*, 24 July 1899.

21 Smiles, *Autobiography*, pp 241–2.

22 *Morning Herald*, 23 March 1859.

23 ibid., 3 December 1863.

24 Jackson, *London's Termini*, pp 216–17.

25 *Standard of Freedom*, 4 November 1848; *Herapath's Railway Journal*, 9 December 1848.

26 *The Standard*, 2 December 1864.

27 *The Globe*, 3 December 1869.

8 BRIDGE OF SIGHS

1 *Illustrated London News*, 19 August 1843.

2 *Weekly Chronicle*, 19 August 1843.

3 *Morning Post*, 9 and 10 December 1822.

4 *The Standard*, 12 October 1846.

5 *High Life in London*, 10 February 1828.

6 *The Star*, 2 August 1831; *South Eastern Gazette*, 31 January 1832.

7 *Bentley's Miscellany*, vol.5, 1839, p.378. Reprinted in *Morning Herald*, 6 April 1839, and *Morning*

Chronicle, 8 April 1839, and then in Charles Mackay, *The Thames and its Tributaries*, 2 vols, 1840, pp 34–6.

8 *Ainsworth's Magazine*, June 1844.

9 *Household Words*, 15 February 1853. This grisly information is elaborated by another journalist who visited 'the Bridge of Sighs' for *The Dial* in 1860. Here the interlocutor is a policeman who adds: 'Now, I should say that Hungerford-bridge would be twice as good as this. But 'tis all a matter of fancy, I s'pose.'

10 *All the Year Round*, 21 July 1860, reprinted in *The Uncommercial Traveller*, 1868.

11 John Clubbe, *Victorian Forerunner: The Later Career of Thomas Hood*, 1968, pp 171–4, 226–7.

12 Other paintings in the genre include Augustus Egg, 'Past and Present no. 6', 1858, where the scene is set at the Adelphi arches; and Abraham Solomon, 'Drowned, Drowned', exhibited in 1860. The modern literature on death by drowning and the Victorian arts is extensive. Titles include Dixie Lee Larson, *The Motif of the Drowned Woman in Nineteenth-century Literature and Art*, 1998; and Barbara T. Gates, 'Not Choosing Not To Be: Victorian Literary Responses to Suicide', *Literature and Medicine*, vol.6, 1 January 1987, pp 77–91.

13 *The Standard*, 29 December 1879, discusses this issue.

14 *The Times*, 5 November 1841.

15 M. Grosley, *A Tour to London, or, New Observations on England and its Inhabitants*, 1772, pp 233–9.

16 Forbes Winslow, *The Anatomy of Suicide*, 1840, pp 265–80.

17 For two Dickens forays to the Paris Morgue, see 'Travelling Abroad' and 'Some Recollections of Mortality', both featured in *All the Year Round* and reprinted in *The Uncommercial Traveller*. See also Bianca Tredennick, 'Some Collections of Mortality: Dickens, the Paris Morgue and the Material Corpse', *Victorian Review*, vol.36, no.1, Spring 2010, pp 72–88. Gissing visited the Morgue in 1886: Paul Delany, *George Gissing, A Life*, 2008, pp 103–4.

18 Olive Anderson, *Suicide in Victorian and Edwardian England*, 1987, especially Chapter 4.

19 *The Times*, 27 October 1840.

20 Inquest on Alice Oswald: *Morning Post*, 10 September 1872; *Illustrated London News*, 14 September 1872. Further information: *The Day's Doings*, 21 September 1872. Unsympathetic reactions: *The Graphic*, 21 September 1872; *The Era*, 22 September 1872. Funeral: *Lloyd's Weekly Newspaper*, 22 September 1872. Copycat attempts at suicide: *The Globe*, 23 September 1872; and *Illustrated London News*, 28 September 1872. *Illustrated Police News*, 21 September 1872, published a typically tasteless drawing of Alice Oswald's leap from the bridge.

21 *Strand Magazine*, vol.1, no.2, 1891.

22 Arthur T. Pask, *The Eyes of the Thames*, 1889, pp 12–20.

23 *Morning Post*, 27 April 1874.

24 *Strand Magazine*, vol.1, no.2, 1891.

25 *Daily News*, 28 August 1905.

26 *Westminster Gazette*, 29 July 1893. The figures given are forty-seven bodies, of which five were women.

27 *The Picturegoer*, 22 August 1931, etc. The original film derived from a play of 1930 by Robert Sherwood produced in New York. It was based on Sherwood's encounter in 1918 with a girl, not on Waterloo Bridge but in Trafalgar Square: see John Mason Brown, *The Worlds of Robert E. Sherwood*, 1965, pp 248–50. The second *Waterloo Bridge* film dates from 1940 (starring Robert Taylor and Vivien Leigh), the third, retitled as *Gaby* and less faithful to the original, from 1956 (starring Leslie Caron and John Kerr).

28 *The Guardian*, 15 February 2024.

29 The introduction to the UK Drowning Prevention Strategy, by Jackie Doyle-Price, MP, states: 'In 2018, 30 people drowned in the river, accounting for 8% of drowning-related deaths nationally. Over the year, there were 688 recorded cases of people threatening to enter the Thames to take their life. 105 people actually entered the water, triggering interventions by the emergency services.'

9 FREE BUT FRAGILE

1 *South London Press*, 12 October 1878; also *Illustrated London News*, 12 October 1878.

2 *The Standard*, 8 October 1878.

3 *London Dispatch*, 30 June 1839.

4 *The Patriot*, 12 April 1841.

5 For the coal and wine duties, the fullest account is to be found on the website City Posts, under History of the Coal Duties, but even this is

incomplete. See also J.F.B. Firth, *The Coal and Wine Dues: The History of the London Coal Tax, and the Arguments for and against its Renewal*, 1887. Further information can be gleaned from David Owen, *The Government of Victorian London 1855–1889: The Metropolitan Board of Works, the Vestries, and the City Corporation*, 1982, *passim*; and Dale H. Porter, *The Thames Embankment: Environment, Technology, and Society in Victorian London*, 1998, pp 153–4.

6 David J. Crankshaw, 'Community, City and Nation', in Derek Keene, Arthur Burns and Andrew Saint, eds, *St Paul's, The Cathedral Church of London 604–2004*, 2004, p.68. 'Obscurity surrounds the process by which the coal duty thereafter became a long-term feature of the cathedral's annual income', adds Crankshaw.

7 On the Metropolitan Board of Works and the toll bridges, see Owen, *The Government of Victorian London*, pp 119–25.

8 A robust defence of the coal duties from the City Corporation's point of view can be found in *City Press*, 1 January 1859.

9 *Illustrated London News*, 15 February 1873.

10 *Daily Chronicle*, 5 April 1872.

11 *Courier and West End Advertiser*, 8 May 1878.

12 *Illustrated London News*, 1 June 1878. See also a long article in *Daily Telegraph*, 28 May 1878.

13 *Daily Telegraph*, 10 October 1878; *Architects' Journal*, 13 February 1924, p.299, confirms that ragstone was piled round the beleaguered piers.

14 *The Globe*, 3 December 1869.

15 Paving: *The Standard*, 28 June and 22 September 1880. Repairs by Bazalgette and Webster: *South London Press*, 28 May 1881; *The Standard*, 13 January 1882; *The Globe*, 10 October 1882. Involvement of Edward Bazalgette: Owen Fleming in *RIBA Journal*, vol.32, 1925, pp 287–9.

10 PICTORIAL

1 I follow here the chronology given in Richard Dorment and Margaret F. Macdonald, *James McNeill Whistler*, exh.cat., 1994, p.273.

2 Quoted from *Life Was Worth Living: The Reminiscences of W. Graham Robertson*, 1931, in Robin Spencer, ed., *Whistler: A Retrospect*, 1989, p.298.

3 Whistler recorded the old Westminster Bridge in an etching of 1859 published in the Thames Set, while his *Westminster Bridge (Building)* of 1861 shows a temporary bridge in front and glimpses of the new bridge behind.

4 *James McNeill Whistler: The Etchings, a Catalogue Raisonné*, published online by the Hunterian Museum, University of Glasgow. See also Margaret F. MacDonald, 'Whistler and the Thames', in Margaret F. MacDonald and Patricia de Montfort, *An American in London: Whistler and the Thames*, 2013, pp 13–30.

5 *Inspiring Impressionism: Daubigny, Monet, Van Gogh*, National Gallery of Scotland, 2015, for example, pp 57 and 82.

6 For Durand-Ruel's activities in London, see Anne Robbins, 'Durand-Ruel's Conquest of London', in Sylvie Patry, ed., *Inventing Impressionism: Paul Durand-Ruel and the Modern Art Market*, 2015, pp 170–93.

7 For Monet in London, the fullest account now is *Monet and London: Views of the Thames*, Courtauld Gallery exhibition and catalogue, 2024; for the 1887 letter about the *effets de brouillard*, see the opening essay, by Karen Serres, p.21; and for Monet's twice labelling the London weather as 'idiosyncratic', ibid., pp 36 and 38. Also useful are Richard Thomson, *Monet and Architecture*, National Gallery exhibition, 2018; Jennifer A. Thompson, 'Between the Balcony and the Studio: Monet's Struggle to Finish the Thames Series', in Nancy Norwood, ed., *Monet's Waterloo Bridge: Vision and Process*, University of Rochester, Memorial Art Gallery exhibition, 2018, pp 15–30; and George T.M. Shackleford and MaryAnne Stevens with Paul Hayes Tucker, *Monet in the Twentieth Century*, Royal Academy exhibition, 1998, pp 128–30.

8 *Cambridge Daily News*, 23 January 1899.

9 Shackleford and Stevens, *Monet in the Twentieth Century*, p.128.

10 Rémi Labrusse and Jacqueline Munck, 'André Derain in London (1906–07): Letters and a Sketchbook', *Burlington Magazine*, vol.146, April 2004, pp 243–60.

11 See the Wikipedia article on Emile Claus; also, www.sothebys.com/en/auctions/ecatalogue/2014/19th-century-european-

paintings-l14102/lot.44.html; https://victorianweb.org/painting/cityscapes/claus2.jpg.

12 But the quiet Constable was a Tory and a patriot, indeed something of a Little Englander; and his father-in-law, Charles Bicknell, was solicitor to the Prince Regent, whom he allegedly helped out of various scrapes.

13 The most rewarding analysis of the painting and its 'extremely involved' genesis, with sundry preliminary efforts, is Denys Sutton, 'Constable's "Whitehall Stairs" or "The Opening of Waterloo Bridge"', *The Connoisseur*, vol.136, 1955, pp 248–55. The 'abortion' remark is quoted on p.254.

14 For commentaries on the Constable, see the Tate website; also Malcolm Cormack, *Constable*, Oxford, 1986, pp 213–16; and Leslie Parris and Ian Fleming-Williams, *Constable*, 1991, pp 69–72. Farington, who saw an early sketch, wanted Constable to make more of the 'magnificence of the bridge & buildings', but he did not do so: *Farington Diaries*, vol.XV, col.5396 (11 August 1819).

15 Blore also drew for the Cookes a view of the iron bridge at Sunderland, never apparently published.

16 From the catalogue of *Un Univers Intime, Paintings from the Frits Lugt Collection*, exhibition at the Institut Néerlandais, Paris, 2012.

11 BATTLE OF THE BRIDGES

1 Royal Commission on London Traffic, Minutes of Evidence, 1905, qq. 6209–10, 6215–6, 17 July 1903.

2 For the eastern bridge as envisaged in 1898, see especially Owen Fleming, *RIBA Journal*, 7 March 1925, pp 287–9. Fleming was a key member of the LCC Architect's Department at that time.

3 Royal Commission on London Traffic, *Minutes of Evidence*, qq. 6217–9.

4 Georgia Politi, 'The Life and Works of Horace Jones PRIBA (1819–1887)', PhD, University of Cambridge, 2024, pp 213–14.

5 *Illustrated London News*, 30 November 1901, with drawings; *The Sphere*, 12 September 1903, with photographs; *The Globe*, 28 March 1904, for the opening. An 'Islington architect' wrote: 'it is morally certain that the elevation of Rennie's noble work is ruined': *Southwark and Bermondsey Recorder*, 17 June 1904.

6 *Southwark and Bermondsey Recorder*, 16 December 1905, 13 July 1907.

7 John Burns MP, Sir Aston Webb and Reginald Blomfield, *The Charing Cross Improvement Scheme*, 1916, p.13. A later date for this initiative, *c.*1896, is implied in the parliamentary speeches of Burns and Dickinson on the Charing Cross Bill that July: *Parliamentary Proceedings*, 3 July 1916.

8 *Railway News*, 30 July 1904.

9 *Morning Leader*, 20 June 1904; *Daily News*, 21 June and 13 July 1904; *St James's Gazette*, 20 June and 14 July 1904; *Daily Telegraph*, 19 December 1904.

10 *RIBA Journal*, vol.14, 1907, pp 8–9; Arthur Keen, *Charing Cross Bridge*, 1930, p.23 and illustration.

11 *Survey of London*, vol. 17, 1991, pp 7–10.

12 *The Times*, 12 November 1910. For the fuller version of Swinton's argument, see 'A "King Edward" Bridge', in *Nineteenth Century and After*, January 1911, pp 94–107, reprinted in Captain George S.C. Swinton, *London, Her Traffic – Her Improvement, and Charing Cross Bridge*, 1924, pp 52–70.

13 *The Globe*, 1 June 1914; *Railway News*, 5 December 1914; *The Times*, 1 and 5 June 1914.

14 *Pall Mall Gazette*, 15 February 1916; *The Globe*, 18 July 1916.

15 Alan A. Jackson, *London's Termini*, 1972, p.252. This book gives the best succinct account of 'The Battle of the Bridges', pp 253–9.

16 Parliamentary Proceedings, 3 July 1916; *RIBA Journal*, 20 July 1916, pp 293–4.

17 The original Burns, Webb and Blomfield articles appeared in *The Observer*, 8, 15 and 22 October 1916. The London Society pamphlet is entitled *The Charing Cross Improvement Scheme*. Blomfield claimed its authorship in Sir Reginald Blomfield, *Memoirs of an Architect*, 1932, p.232. This book's final chapter, pp 232–49, contains a clear account of the Waterloo–Charing Cross saga down to 1932, followed by the text of a speech Blomfield gave in 1932, pp 296–303.

18 'Castles in the Air at Charing Cross', *The Nineteenth Century and After*, November 1916, pp 964–80, reprinted in Swinton, *London, Her Traffic – Her Improvement*, pp 71–90.

19 Arthur Keen, in his *Charing Cross Bridge*, 1930, illustrates schemes by the following architects: T.E. Collcutt (1908); Paul Waterhouse (1913); D. Barclay Niven with T. Raffles Davison (1914); E.T. Hall (1916); S.D. Adshead (1917 and 1929); W.D. Caröe (1917); Ernest Herbert (1923); and John Murray (1929). To these may be added the Burns, Webb and Blomfield plan (1916), and schemes by Harold Falkner (1919), Adrian Barrington or Berrington (1923), Hamo Thornycroft (1923) and Reginald Blomfield (1925), as well as various engineers' plans.
20 *The Times*, 17 November 1916; see also the letter of endorsement from Sir Walter Essex, *The Times*, 21 November 1916.
21 Felix Barker and Ralph Hyde, *London As It Might Have Been*, 1982, p.50.
22 Jackson, *London's Termini*, p.255.
23 *Daily News*, 12 October 1923. For the exhibition in the spring, see *The Graphic*, 24 March 1923.
24 Blomfield, *Memoirs*, pp 234, 299; *Chelsea News*, 13 January 1933.
25 *Westminster Gazette*, 26 March 1924. *Illustrated London News*, 12 April 1924, has clear pictures showing where the problems lay.
26 *Westminster Gazette*, 9 April 1924.
27 Protest of the artists, *The Times*, 31 March 1924; letters from Bernard Shaw (cited by Christian Barman) and Reginald Blomfield, 1 April 1924; from Herbert Baker and D.S. MacColl, 3 April 1924. 'Canal bridges': *Daily Herald*, 2 June 1932. MacColl's contribution to the campaign is fully documented in Maureen Borland, *D.S. MacColl, Painter, Poet, Art Critic*, 1995.
28 Blomfield, *Memoirs*, p.234.
29 'Huge traffic blocks', 'City chaos': *Daily News*, 13 May 1924; schoolboys playing marbles: *Daily Mirror*, 16 May 1924.
30 Temporary bridge: *Daily Chronicle*, 2 May 1924; *The Sphere*, 20 June 1925.
31 Matthew Carmona and Andrew Renninger, 'The Royal Fine Art Commission and 75 Years of English Design Review: The First 60 Years, 1924–1984', *Planning Perspectives*, vol.33, no.1, 2017, pp 53–73.
32 *The Times*, 6 July 1925.
33 For the Lutyens scheme, see *Daily Chronicle*, 14 October and 9 November 1925; *Westminster Gazette*, 9 November 1925; and illustrations in *The Graphic*, 14 November 1925. See also Jane Ridley, *The Architect and his Wife: A Life of Edwin Lutyens*, 2002, p.348.
34 *The Times*, 10 November 1925.
35 Royal Commission on Cross-River Traffic in London, Report, 1926, Chapter III, paras 65–6. Morrison and the bridge: *Westminster Gazette*, 25 February 1925; *Daily Herald*, 11 November 1925. The proposed competition: *Westminster Gazette*, 24 May and 17 June 1926; Blomfield, *Memoirs*, p.234.
36 *The Times*, 30 April, 1 and 18 May, and 7 June 1926.
37 *The Times*, 7–10 June 1926.
38 Blomfield, *Memoirs*, p.234.
39 Parliamentary Proceedings (Lords), 3 March 1932 (Lord Lee of Fareham).
40 For the St Paul's Bridge, see Barker and Hyde, *London As It Might Have Been*, pp 50–52, illustrating a perspective of a scheme of 1914 by Albert Richardson. The idea went back as far as 1851 and was only finally killed in 1941, say Barker and Hyde. The cathedral authorities never favoured it.
41 But the Commission's official bridge scheme illustrated in *Illustrated London News*, 18 December 1926, is not the same as the later sketch for Charing Cross Bridge by Williams shown in *Daily Chronicle*, 15 December 1928.
42 Royal Commission on Cross-River Traffic in London, Report, 1926. Charing Cross Bridge, Chapter V, paras 121–32 and Appendix 8; Waterloo Bridge, Chapter III, paras 61–91.
43 Keen, *Charing Cross Bridge*, pp 54–5.
44 Blomfield, *Memoirs*, p.238.
45 *Daily Chronicle*, 15 February 1928.
46 Keen, *Charing Cross Bridge*, pp 51–65, analyses the 'official scheme' in full detail.
47 *Daily Chronicle*, 3 March and 4 April 1929. Blomfield, *Memoirs*, p.238, must be in error when he says the new LCC scheme was 'sprung on an unsuspecting public' in the autumn of 1929.
48 *Daily Herald*, 4 April 1930; *The Sphere*, 5 April 1930.
49 Parliamentary Proceedings, 19 February 1930; *Daily Mirror*, 20 February 1930; *Southwark and Bermondsey Recorder*, 20 February 1930; *Truth*, 26 February 1930. Also Ridley, *Architect and his Wife*, pp 367–9, not always accurate.

50 *The Times*, 28 March and 1 April 1930; Blomfield, *Memoirs*, p.240; Bernard Donoughue and G.W. Jones, *Herbert Morrison: Portrait of a Politician*, 1973, p.152. For the scramble, see letters in *The Times* from Frank Pick, 9 May 1930, and D.S. MacColl, 20 May 1930.
51 *Daily Herald*, 26 February 1931. Sir Giles Scott's papers in RIBA Archives, ScGG, 89/1, shed light on differences of opinion within the Advisory Committee.
52 Blomfield, *Memoirs*, pp 240–43.
53 *The Times*, 16 March 1931.
54 *News Chronicle*, 13 December 1930, 18 March and 9 July 1931; *Daily Herald*, 26 February and 30 July 1931. One of the runners-up was submitted by the curious combination of D. Barclay Niven, W.D. Caröe and E. Maxwell Fry (*News Chronicle*, 9 July 1931); Donoughue and Jones, *Herbert Morrison*, pp 151–3.
55 J.H. Forshaw and Patrick Abercrombie, *County of London Plan 1943*, 1944, pp 32–3.
56 *News Chronicle* and *Daily Herald*, 7 May 1946; *South Western Star*, 10 May 1946; *The Times*, 2 November 1946.
57 The Misha Black scheme is illustrated in Harriet Atkinson, *The Festival of Britain: A Land and its People*, 2012, p.9.
58 The formulation is Lord Charnwood's: Parliamentary Proceedings (Lords), 3 March 1932.
59 *Daily Herald*, 26 January and 30 March 1932.
60 *News Chronicle*, 11 March 1932.
61 *Daily Herald*, 17 February 1932.
62 *Daily Herald*, 7 April 1932; David Yeomans and David Cottam, *Owen Williams*, 2001, pp 49–51.
63 Parliamentary Proceedings (Lords), 3 March 1932.
64 *Daily Herald*, 2 June 1932; *Kensington News*, 17 June 1932.
65 Donoughue and Jones, *Herbert Morrison*, pp 203–4.
66 *Daily Herald*, 15 December 1932.
67 *Daily Herald*, 8 February and 19 June 1933; *Sunday Mirror*, 19 March 1933.
68 *Daily Mirror*, 4 October 1933.
69 *News Chronicle*, 3 and 21 October and 13 December 1933; *Daily Herald*, 24 January 1934; *Architect and Building News*, 27 October 1933, p.905.
70 Donoughue and Jones, *Herbert Morrison*, p.204.

12 A NEW BRIDGE

1 For Palmer's career, see the very full account by R.C.D. Baldwin in *Biographical Dictionary of Civil Engineers*, vol.3, pp 468–74.
2 See Malcolm Tucker's list of Thames crossings in Bridget Cherry and Nikolaus Pevsner, *London 2: South*, 1983, pp 707–16. Road crossings further upstream included Chiswick Bridge (1933), Twickenham Bridge (1928–33) and Hampton Court Bridge (1930–33), all arch bridges involving architect-engineer collaborations.
3 *Southwark and Bermondsey Record*, 4 April 1930; *The Times*, 9 February 1931.
4 *Chelsea News*, 10 November 1933; E.J. Buckton and H.J. Fereday, 'The Reconstruction of Chelsea Bridge', *Journal of the Institution of Civil Engineers*, vol.7, no.3, 1937–8, pp 383–5.
5 Walter C. Kidney, *Pittsburgh's Bridges: Architecture and Engineering*, 1999, pp 140–43.
6 *Biographical Dictionary of Civil Engineers*, vol.3, p.205 (Mike Chrimes); also H.J. Fereday, 'The Science and Art of Bridge-Building', *Journal of the Institution of Civil Engineers Australia*, vol.4, no.4, 1932, pp 129–30 (copy in Institution of Civil Engineers archives, London).
7 See letters from Buckton, under Palmer's name, to Scott, January 1931, in RIBA Archives, ScGG 89/1.
8 *The Times*, 15 February 1932.
9 *The Times*, 13 May 1930.
10 RIBA Archives, ScGG 87/1 & 2, 89/1; RIBA Drawings Collection, ScGG [74] 1–4.
11 *The Times*, 11 March 1932, in reply to a self-exculpatory letter from Scott published on 10 March. The two architects also exchanged letters, for which see RIBA Archives, ScGG 87/2.
12 RIBA Archives, ScGG 87/2.
13 RIBA Archives, 90/1 (Scott correspondence with Rendel, Palmer and Tritton).
14 E.J. Buckton, et al., 'The New Waterloo Bridge', *Journal of the Institution of Civil Engineers*, vol.20, no.7, 1943, pp 184–5 (discussion).
15 RIBA Drawings Collection, notably ScGG,Re,Pa&Tr[1](7)and (9) (RIBApix 97454 and 97455).
16 Mendham's scheme: RIBA Drawings Collection, PA678/9 (RIBApix 20893); also plans in

Architectural Archives, University of Pennsylvania. Oliver Hill's scheme: Institution of Civil Engineers archives, Waterloo Bridge scrapbook.

17 *The Builder*, 21 September 1934, p.478.

18 *Daily Herald*, 7 April 1932; *South London Observer*, 22 September 1934; David Yeomans and David Cottam, *Owen Williams*, 2001, pp 49–51.

19 RIBA Archives, ScGG 90/1, Buckton to Scott, 22 June 1934.

20 *The Times*, 12, 22 and 24 October 1934; *Architect and Building News*, 19 October 1934, pp 60–61.

21 E.J. Buckton et al., 'The New Waterloo Bridge', *Journal of the Institution of Civil Engineers*, vol.20, no.7, 1943, especially pp 153–4, and diagram on p.149.

22 Michael R. Lane, *The Rendel Connection*, 1989, p.116 (kindly communicated by Christine Wall).

23 C.H. Bressey, *British Bridges*, 1933, pp 464–5. The Waterloo Bridge scrapbook at the Institution of Civil Engineers contains a valuable unattributed article comparing the 1932 and 1934 designs, entitled 'Cantilever Type – 5-span in Reinforced concrete, Portland stone and Cornish granite'.

24 *The Builder*, 28 August 1942, p.170.

25 A.P. Herbert, *The Thames*, 1966, p.68.

26 *News Chronicle*, 13 October 1934.

27 RIBA Archives, ScGG 90/2, letters of March 1937.

28 RIBA Archives, ScGG 87/2.

29 *News Chronicle*, 18 June 1934.

30 E.J. Buckton and H.J. Fereday, 'The Demolition of Waterloo Bridge', *Journal of the Institution of Civil Engineers*, vol.3, no.8, 1936, pp 472–98, with discussion, pp 499–516; quotation, pp 496–7.

31 Christine Wall, 'William Arrol and Peter Lind: Demolition, Construction and Workmanship on London's Waterloo Bridges (1934–46)', in Ine Wouters et al., *Building Knowledge, Constructing Histories*, 2018, p.1350.

32 Bernard Donoughue and G.W. Jones, *Herbert Morrison: Portrait of a Politician*, 1973, p.205.

33 *Country Life*, 16 September 1939; information from Christine Wall.

34 From the excellent article about the bridge in *Newnes Practical Mechanics*, September 1942, pp 343–5.

35 *South London Observer*, 5 May 1939; *Illustrated London News*, 13 May 1939.

36 *Gloucester Citizen*, 14 October 1943.

37 *Hampstead News*, 13 December 1945.

38 RIBA Drawings Collection, notably ScGG, Re,Pa&Tr [1] 27–37.

39 *The Times*, 11 December 1945.

40 *Architectural Review*, August 1946, pp 45–7.

41 Ian Nairn, *Nairn's London*, 1966, p.118.

42 RIBA Archives, ScGG 87/1 & 2, 89/3.

43 Sarah Crellin, *The Sculpture of Charles Wheeler*, 2012, pp 85–6, 105 and 162.

44 Alun R. Graves, 'Barbara Hepworth's Designs for Sculpture on Waterloo Bridge', *Burlington Magazine*, vol.141, no.1161, December 1999, pp 753–6. For the competition, see also RIBA Archives, ScGG 92/1 & 2.

45 *Morning Post*, 20 October 1821.

46 *The Builder*, 14 August 1942, pp 130–31.

Index

Note: *italic* page numbers indicate figures; page numbers followed by n. and nn refer to notes.

PICTURE CREDITS

Frontispiece © Trustees of the British Museum, BM 1897,0113.242; **1** Taken from scrapbook owned by Richard Buxton; **3** Callum Moy, Essential London; **4** Historic England Archive, AL2400/048/01; **5** Central Press; **6** Associated Press; **7** © Trustees of the British Museum; **10** Guildhall Art Gallery/ London Picture Archive; **11** © Trustees of the British Museum, BM 1880,0911.583; **12** Lambeth Archives; **13** Hampshire Cultural Trust; **14** Historic Environment Scotland, EAW048078; **15** © Trustees of the British Museum, BM 1954,1103.7; **16** © Trustees of the British Museum, BM 1880,1113.1339; **17** *Illustrated London News*, 4 September 1847; **18** Wikimedia Commons/ Yale Center for British Art; **19** © Trustees of the British Museum, BM 1880,1113.1483; **20** IanVisits; **21** London Picture Archive, 31836; **22** National Galleries Scotland; **24** Sally Strachey Historic Conservation; **25** Topographical Collection/Alamy Stock Photo; **27** © Trustees of the British Museum, BM 1880,1113.1520; **28** Author's own; **29** Government Art Collection; **31** Wikimedia Commons/Yale Center for British Art; **32** Sir John Soane's Museum, SM 12/5/7; **33** Sir John Soane's Museum, SM/P.92; **34** © Victoria and Albert Museum, London, A 2010EH8952; **36** Royal Collection Trust, RCIN 702536; **37** West Cheshire Museums/Jessie Petheram; **38** Wikimedia Commons/Bonhams; **40** Roger Bowdler; **41** Antiqua Print Gallery/Alamy Stock Photo; **43** London Picture Archive; **44** Historic England Archive, HT02396, Henry Taunt (photo); **45** Library of Congress; **46** Jon Sparks/Alamy Stock Photo; **47** Mick Garratt/ http://www.fhithich.uk; **48** Wikimedia Commons/ Llywelyn2000; **49** Photo: Tate; **50** © Trustees of the British Museum, BM,R,9.39; **51** © Trustees of the British Museum, BM 1880,0911.592; **52** © Victoria & Albert Museum, London. Royal Photographic Society Collection, 1021RS0096; **53** Historic England Archive, DD97/00530; **54** London Picture Archives, 135304; **55** Lambeth Archives, 03108; **56** Royal Collection Trust, RCIN 702537; **60** © Trustees of the British Museum, BM 1880,1113.5399; **61** London Picture Archives, 91879; **62** Lambeth Archives, 05293; **63** © Trustees of the British Museum, BM 1897,0113.242; **65** Wikimedia Commons/Yale Center for British Art; **66** © Trustees of the British Museum, BM 1880,1113.1586; **67** Historic England Archive, CC97/01676; **69** Guildhall Art Gallery/London Picture Archives, 14415; **71** Lambeth Archives, 0155; **72** Historic England Archives, CC97/00110; **73** Lambeth Archives, 01549; **74** London Picture Archives, 263564; **75** Photo: Tate; **79** Wikimedia Commons/Watts Gallery; **80** Delaware Art Museum, Samuel and Mary R. Bancroft Memorial, 1935; **81** Photo: Tate; **82** Wikimedia Commons; **85** Historic England Archives, CC97/00510; **88** Museum of Fine Arts, Boston; **89** © Trustees of the British Museum, BM 1908,0616.47; **90** © The National Gallery, London. All rights reserved; **91** Ordrupgaard, Copenhagen; **92** National Gallery of Canada; **93** Carnegie Museum of Art; **94** Bridgeman Images/Musée de l'Annonciade, Saint-Tropez; **95** Private collection; **96** Photo © Cincinnati Art Museum/Gift of Mary Hanna/ Bridgeman Images; **97** London Museum; **98** Mutual Art; **99** Rijksmuseum, Amsterdam; **100** © Trustees of the British Museum, BM 1926,0628.3; **101** © Trustees of the British Museum, BM 1929,0220.1; **102** © Trustees of the British Museum, BM 1949,0411.1112; **103** The Picture Art Collection/Alamy Stock Photo; **105** Superstock/Alamy/National Museum of Wales; **106** Photo: Tate © Fondation Oskar Kokoschka; **107** The Metropolitan Museum of Art Collections, New York; **108** London Picture Archive, 236213; **109** London Picture Archive, 236186; **111** London Picture Archive, 142085; **114, 115, 116** Keen, *Charing Cross Bridge*, 1930; **117** London Picture Archive, 320808; **120** Maurice Edelman, *Herbert Morrison: Pictorial Biography*, 1948; **121** London Picture Archive, 234412; **122, 123, 124** RIBA collections; **126** Institution of Civil Engineers; **127** Chris Redgrave; **128** Author's own; **129** Institution of Civil Engineers; **130** London Picture Archive, 236162; **131** Royal Academy of Arts/The Artist's Estate, courtesy of Liss Llewellyn; **132** London Picture Archive, 92033; **133** Chris Wall/Daily Herald Archive; **134** Institution of Civil Engineers (Rendel, Palmer and Tritton papers); **135** RIBA collections; **136** London Picture Archive, 236112; **137** London Picture Archive, 236133; **138** London Picture Archive, 236035; **139** Sarah Crellin/The Fine Arts Society; **140, 141, 142, 143** Chris Redgrave

ARCHITECTURAL HISTORY OF THE BRITISH ISLES

Series Editor: Dr Timothy Brittain-Catlin, University of Cambridge

British architectural history has a very prominent reputation internationally and sets the standard for publishing and for the development of new ideas and narratives in the field. Covering all periods of architectural history, the series consists of accessible and authoritative studies of specific periods, styles, architects and types of building, and provides fresh insights into fascinating subjects with perpetual appeal. The series is not comprehensive in terms of its selection, but offers the best scholarship in this field, reflecting the richness and quality of British architecture.

London River and its Bridges, *c*.1939

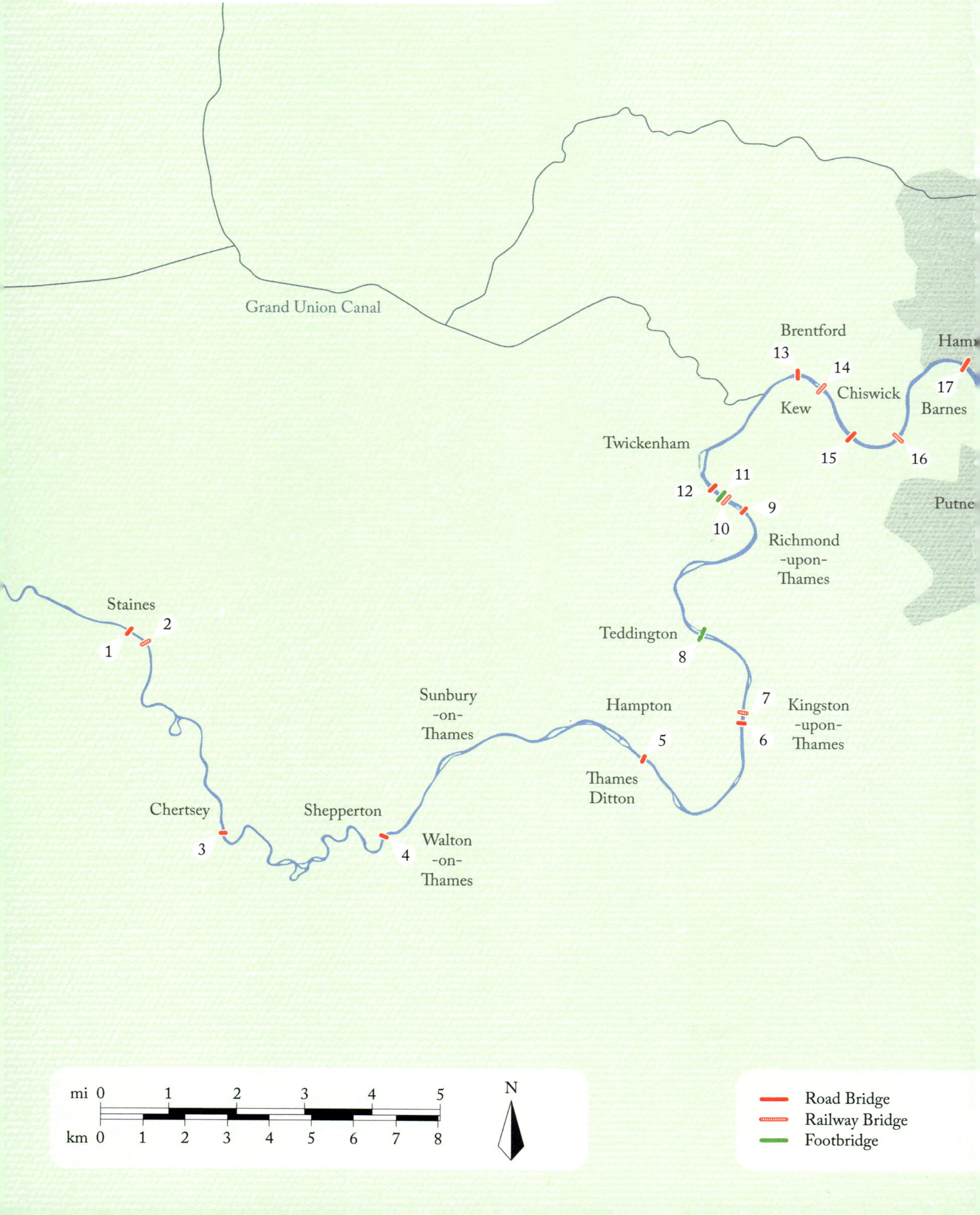